THE AMERICAN WAR ON ELECTION CORRUPTION

The Crusade to Restore Trust in Voting

SETH KESHEL

A POST HILL PRESS BOOK
ISBN: 979-8-89565-606-8
ISBN (eBook): 979-8-89565-607-5

Cover design by Jim Villaflores
Cover concept by Jeff Pedigo

This book, as well as any other Post Hill Press publications, may be purchased in bulk quantities at a special discounted rate. Contact orders@posthillpress.com for more information.

Post Hill Press
New York • Nashville
posthillpress.com

Published in the United States of America
1   2   3   4   5   6   7   8   9   10

To the Memory of Lt. Col. Donald J. Keshel,
United States Army (1943-2010)

TABLE OF CONTENTS

The Essential War for the American Future

By Newt Gingrich

As President Ronald Reagan once said, "Freedom is never more than one generation away from extinction." Whether on the battlefield or the public square, freedom must be constantly defended. Today, the most vital battle for the soul and structure of our Republic is the one Seth Keshel addresses in this essential book, *The American War on Election Corruption.*

If we are to maintain a free society, we must have confidence in our elections. Without fair and transparent processes—processes that respect the laws set up by the states—the basis of our self-governance collapses.

The crisis of confidence we currently face is a fundamental threat to the American experiment. We have reached a point where sophisticated, rigorous analysis is needed to cut through the noise and examine the specific anomalies and broken laws that plagued the 2020, 2022, and 2024 elections. We also need actionable solutions. Crucially, this analysis must be specific and grounded in fact, avoiding the pitfalls of conspiracy theories and fringe interests.

This is precisely why Captain Seth Keshel's book is indispensable.

I first became intrigued with Keshel's insights after learning of the extraordinary accuracy of his work in the last few

American elections. Keshel is, quite simply, the leading analyst of voter registration in America. His knowledge of voter registration patterns extends down to the precinct and county levels. He has a truly encyclopedic command of the data that most political professionals either overlook or simply do not possess.

Keshel approaches political forecasting not as a pollster relying on fleeting sentiment but as a strategic intelligence officer—because that's what he is. He firmly believes that voter registration patterns carry a deeper and far more reliable meaning than traditional polling. This belief is rooted in his background as a former Army captain and intelligence officer serving in Afghanistan. This background is not just a footnote; it is the source of his unique capacity to process and understand complex data systems.

Keshel has applied this level of rigor to his methodology. He has tracked voter registration by party across the country. He has deeply researched state election laws—and how fraudulent ballots in each state have been cast. He has blended this granular political analysis to create the only legitimate forecasting model of its kind.

Keshel's expertise is recognized at the highest levels. He has been commended by the president of the United States and has personally briefed White House staff on his findings.

The results of the 2024 presidential race confirmed the decisive power of Keshel's methodology. While many commentators and pollsters flailed, Keshel correctly called every one of the swing states. He also provided stunning detail, predicting that New Hampshire, due to the registration drift toward Republicans, would be incredibly close. Indeed, President Donald J. Trump almost carried the state, losing to Vice President Kamala Harris by a mere 2.8 percent of the vote.

His predictive analysis also suggested significant Republican gains in key states such as Pennsylvania, Michigan, Wisconsin, and Florida. He attributed these shifts to demographic changes and fundamental voter registration trends. Keshel's analysis suggested a strong performance for President Trump, and he was right.

These outcomes were not accidental; they were the consequence of a tectonic shift in the American electorate that Keshel was the first to decisively identify. However, in state after state, there are those who would seek to undermine our elections and corrupt our system.

Keshel's book is not merely a presentation of powerful data; it is an intelligence report on how we fight back. He highlights the critical impact of urban and suburban voting patterns, particularly in states like Texas and Nevada. He reminds us of the critical importance of voter turnout and how media narratives frequently attempt to shape—or distort—election outcomes.

The American War on Election Corruption provides the comprehensive, specific, and detailed framework necessary for every American concerned about the future of our representative government. Keshel's knowledge and forecasting skill, rooted in the rigor of military intelligence, offer us a clear-eyed view of what has gone right, what has gone wrong, where the broken laws and anomalies exist, and, most importantly, what we must do to restore and maintain integrity in our electoral systems.

Read this book and internalize these patterns. The fight for fair elections is the fight for the survival of the Republic—and Captain Seth Keshel has provided the essential battle plan.

The Week the Laughter Stopped

Americans were still languishing under draconian COVID-19 measures in 2021, the year the world I knew was turned upside down by a new national movement that came to consume my life while simultaneously making excellent use of thirty-six years of achievement, failure, and fate. Some states threw off the self-imposed chains early, while others, such as Hawaii, held on to them as long as humanly possible. Socially stunted children and depressed adults were of no concern to those who had burned everything down the year before, even after the political considerations associated with the outbreak of the virus had been relegated to the pages of history and a new administration sworn in.

That administration, led by President Joseph R. Biden, Jr., wasted absolutely no time running out of things to blame President Donald Trump's administration for and creating all-new crises of their own. In fiscal year 2021, which took place mostly under Biden's watch, at least 660,000 illegal aliens evaded US enforcement at the southwest border,[1] which upset all progress that had been made under Trump. The federal government wasted no time going after political opponents, pursuing countless people nominally involved or having committed only meaningless technical

---

1   "What Can the Data Tell Us About Unauthorized Immigration?," USAFacts, updated August 1, 2024, https://usafacts.org/articles/what-can-the-data-tell-us-about-unauthorized-immigration/.

infractions related to the events of January 6, 2021. Biden himself spent plenty of time deflecting from his inability to make the "return to normalcy" happen at a faster rate as Americans grew restless.

Then came the biggest blunder of them all—the Afghanistan withdrawal. Americans have long been sick of nation building and the endless military conflict that comes with those efforts and had no desire to stick around in countries like Iraq or Afghanistan; however, what we saw in the second half of August severely tarnished America's standing in the eyes of the world. After two decades of Americans having been told the war in Afghanistan was worth the blood and treasure, we crawled out on our hands and knees and in the most humiliating fashion imaginable. Seven months after assuming power, the Biden administration had imploded and lost all meaningful political capital.

Less than two years before, the first Trump administration was forging pathways to peace in areas long consumed by bloodshed and strife, recapturing control of the global economy with a populist approach, effectively using the military and getting it back to business and away from social experiments, and restoring the promise of a country that had stumbled its way into the twenty-first century. How in the hell did this nightmare come along in 2021?

One must return to the first week of November 2020 to reconcile it all.

Trump wasn't supposed to win in 2016; no matter where you looked, the consensus was that Hillary Clinton would become the first female president of the United States. *Newsweek* was so confident they fired off covers prematurely congratulating her for a win that would never happen. His win didn't surprise me at all because I had already studied the exact path he would take to crush Clinton's dreams. Millions of Americans, including many who voted for Trump in 2016, had low expectations for his first administration. Some chalked it up to their feelings about the man himself, and others figured he would be stymied by the power of the political establishment. Still, even skeptics couldn't help but enjoy the grandiose meltdowns of the American left, whose followers howled, shrieked, and nearly self-immolated online, in public places, and most certainly in private company as evidenced by the alarming uptick in mental health services consumption leading up to Trump's inauguration. Their tears served as a major unifying factor for the political right, which had spent most of the previous seventeen months since Trump announced his candidacy destroying one another and pounding their chests over whose conservative credentials were the mightiest.

For more than three years, all the way up until the worldwide outbreak of COVID-19, Trump kept the left uptight, irritated, and on the brink of a collective nervous breakdown. Executive orders, Supreme Court picks, a big tax bill, and constant hammering of professional propagandists kept leftists raging and providing new content fodder on such a regular basis it was impossible to consume it all, even in a day and age in which nearly everyone is struggling to put the screens down. The firehose was so steady it even carried Trump through some tough times, diverting the media cycle from issues like "Russiagate" and struggles with a Democrat-run House that took over, courtesy of the 2018 midterms.

Somewhere in Trump's first term, even before things got dark in early 2020, Republicans and rank-and-file Trump supporters took their eyes off the ball. Mimicking a classic military intelligence error, they underestimated their political enemies and the extent to which those enemies would go to unseat the first president in American history to have never held elected office or served in the military as a general officer. After all, Americans have been assured since the first day of social studies that cheating in elections is not only extremely rare, but nearly impossible to get away with. Ironically, that's not what history tells us.

We spent three solid years laughing at the left beginning on November 8, 2016 and, after a brief period of seriousness to discern the severity of COVID-19, returned to mocking them not only politically but for their fear-based approach to being anywhere near other human beings. This was never more obvious than when Biden would appear on the campaign trail and have a half dozen rally attendees arranged in a pattern of circles formed by tape on the ground to account for social distancing, which Dr. Anthony Fauci admits to having arbitrarily made up to placate Americans who needed Prozac more than anything else. We chuckled at the rally circles, doubled down when comparing Biden's rally attendance to the size of Trump's crowds, and grimaced in disbelief when he would get away with things like reminding black Americans that they "aren't black" if they didn't cower to social pressure and vote for him. The fog was so thick sometimes for Biden that many Americans thought Jill Biden was guilty of elder abuse. Surely, just surely, the American people saw this, right?

Summer gave way to election season, which began in September in some states, especially after many secretaries of state and governors made special provisions for mail-in ballots and adjusted timelines on the fly to maximize voter turnout. Up until the 2020 election, only four states (Oregon, Washington, Colorado, and Utah) had run all-mail presidential elections. In 2020, many states, such as Nevada, California, New Jersey, and Hawaii, authorized temporary all-mail elections, driving the mail-in share of ballots to 43 percent nationally, when it had been just 21 percent in

2016.[2] The crucial battleground state of Michigan, which had little experience handling mail-in ballots, soared from 25.7 percent mail-in ballots in 2016 to an eye-popping 49.1 percent in 2020.[3]

Pollster Richard Baris says it best when he refers to the 2020 election as a "quasi election." Sure, there were votes, and then there were the ballots. Those ballots came in Georgia, Pennsylvania, and Arizona for days on end. All three of those states, in addition to Wisconsin, Michigan, and Nevada, wound up in the Biden column. Trump carried just Florida and North Carolina among states thought to be battlegrounds. Once Pennsylvania, which had previously shown what looked to be an insurmountable Trump lead, was called for Biden on November 7, so went the 2020 election.

It was the week the laughter stopped.

While the American right howled in laughter and crafted meticulous memes vividly portraying the agony of left-wing voters for years, the left-wing politicos, operatives, think tanks, organizations, NGOs, government agencies, and complicit support networks worldwide had been plotting how to sabotage the 2020 election and ensure that the president who had seized political power from the permanently entrenched would be ousted come hell or high water. COVID-19 was the vehicle, and through death by a thousand cuts, a man who didn't wage a serious campaign received nearly 81.3 million votes[4] and shoved his way into the Oval Office.

---

2   Zachary Scherer, "What Methods Did People Use to Vote in the 2020 Election?," United States Census Bureau, April 29, 2021, https://www.census.gov/library/stories/2021/04/what-methods-did-people-use-to-vote-in-2020-election.html.

3   US Election Assistance Commission, *Election Administration and Voting Survey 2020 Comprehensive Report* (US Election Assistance Commission, 2021), XX, https://www.eac.gov/sites/default/files/document_library/files/2020_EAVS_Report_Final_508c.pdf.

4   Federal Election Commission, *Federal Elections 2020: Election Results for the U.S. President, the U.S. Senate and the U.S. House of Representatives* (Washington, DC: Federal Election Commission, October 2022), https://www.fec.gov/resources/cms-content/documents/federalelections2020.pdf.

When I joined the fight for election integrity in November 2020, with President Trump still in office and clinging to the soon-to-be-dashed hope that his case would be proven in courts with no appetite to listen, roughly 40 percent of Americans believed the election was "rigged,"[5] or in other words, illegal ballots had tipped the decisive margins for Biden. This isn't a far-fetched belief, given that just 42,918 votes in Arizona, Georgia, and Wisconsin separated Biden from Trump. Had those thirty-seven electoral votes gone to Trump, the Electoral College would have been deadlocked at 269 to 269, pushing the US House into action by state delegations.

Thanks to the efforts of those who never took their eyes off the goal of election integrity, a stunning 62 percent of Americans were concerned cheating would impact the 2024 election.[6] President Trump's microphone is the loudest, but he had help from many who couldn't look the other way on a quasi election that was conducted in a way that would cause Boss Tweed to hide his face in shame. I am one of those Americans, and I've had one of the biggest targets of all on my back. It's been incredibly hard to take a solid shot at me because of my command of data and, most recently, my accuracy in combining traditional political analytics with my own proprietary understanding of each state's capacity for ballots—not votes—on a county-by-county basis.

If you are afraid you'll be persuaded to abandon your faith that there exists a fair system of elections in a country made famous for its form of self-determination and representative government that became the envy of the world, you may want to

---

5   R&WS Research Team, "In December Poll, 40% of Americans Agreed with Statement 'The 2020 Presidential Election Was Rigged'," Redfield & Wilton Strategies, January 11, 2021, https://redfieldandwiltonstrategies.com/in-december-poll-40-of-americans-agreed-with-statement-the-2020-presidential-election-was-rigged/.

6   Rasmussen Reports, "62% Concerned About Election Cheating," Rasmussen Reports, July 24, 2024, https://www.rasmussenreports.com/public_content/politics/partner_surveys/62_concerned_about_election_cheating.

put this book down and grab that wadded-up copy of *The New York Times*, which almost certainly won't commit any more ink to covering what I have to say after they swung and missed in their 2024 attempt.[7]

If a constitutional republic is to survive in modern times, it will only do so when the citizenry trusts the most important processes. There is no more important process than elections. Through the electoral process, Americans select those who are expected to lead through difficult times, uphold law and order, and act in accordance with the lawful wishes of their constituents as merited and often as possible. Elections that subvert the will of the people are not elections at all and had President Biden wished to have practically no questions pertaining to his legitimacy surviving past his inauguration date, he would have invited every American to audit every ballot in every state just to prove his critics wrong. Instead, he went to Pennsylvania to dissuade any election audits the same week I became a national name at Mike Lindell's Cyber Symposium in Sioux Falls, South Dakota.

My story is complex because it has been my failures in life that have strengthened me the most, because I draw from those lessons when challenged and when I need encouragement to keep pursuing goals that matter. You'll come to have a graduate level of understanding into exactly why so many of your fellow human beings question the 2020 election, and you may join the many people I've persuaded in town halls, symposia, speaking events, or even plane trips over the past five years in realizing that there will be no America without an immediate overhaul of our electoral processes.

I'll show you how I used real data to throw off poll-obsessed media pundits in 2024 and how the future is far from settled

---

7   "Seth Keshel, 2024 Election Trump," *New York Times*, October 15, 2024, https://www.nytimes.com/2024/10/15/technology/seth-keshel-2024-election-trump.html.

despite a momentous electoral victory that was "too big to rig" for someone who will be remembered as one of the most consequential people in modern history. The next Republican presidential candidate will not have such a luxury at his disposal.

In 2023, while visiting my father's gravesite in Arlington National Cemetery, I came across the gravestone of former Navy Lieutenant Commander Jason Michael Price, who died too young at age forty-one in 2020. On his stone was the phrase, "Nothing great comes from comfort zones." No one said overhauling a process few Americans trust and upon which the premier power of the free world hangs in the balance would be easy. Beyond this introduction, you'll find a discussion of something too important to ignore, and upon which the freedom of future generations relies.

CHAPTER 1

Useless Knowledge

A strange thing happens when someone explodes overnight and amasses a large online following, as happened to me during the dog days of Biden's first tumultuous year at 1600 Pennsylvania Avenue. While many people are itching to see what the "next big thing" has to say, others are filled with resentment or suspicion for the poor soul who stumbled into notoriety. People tend to look at the phenom in such a way that suggests he must have always been successful, a natural in every undertaking. This was not the case with me. In fact, I spent most of the first half of my life trying to be who I was not and experiencing humbling setbacks every step of the way as I battled low self-esteem.

I entered this world as my father's fifth and final child, and my mother's only, born at the now-defunct Roosevelt Roads Naval Station on the east end of Puerto Rico. I wasn't on the island long, but it was long enough to enrage left-wing minds today by reminding them of my "Hispanic" origin. We were gone quickly to upstate New York by the time I was two, and then to Mississippi, where I grew up, after Dad retired from the Army.

Lieutenant Colonel Donald J. Keshel, even after death, remains the most influential figure over my development and core ethos. I grew up around a much tamer version of the old man than did my four half-siblings, who had dealt with significantly worse secondhand damage stemming from Dad's three combat tours in

2 1

Vietnam as an infantry officer. The steady diet of backhands and corporal punishment they received was generally downgraded to severe verbal lashings and a mercurial temperament for their distant half brother as I was growing up, essentially an only child.

I had a knack for academics early on, effortlessly bringing home report cards full of A+ marks. On the rare occasion I'd bring home an A-, that mark alone would be scrutinized by Dad as he pressured me to do better. As I grew older and schoolwork became more difficult, I would bring home the occasional B+. By the time I got my first C in honors trigonometry my junior year of high school, all hell broke loose. My father had high expectations for excellence that were sadly misplaced in my formative years when I needed to get over my fear of failure more than anything.

But grades weren't the area I was missing the mark in. I struggled with my weight and body image starting in middle school, and thanks to severe damage to my right ear, which never developed properly from birth, I didn't take naturally to athletics. Although I've since become confident and fit as a result of the discipline instilled in me during my military service, I have never been physically graceful or coordinated. Dad and I grew to love the game of baseball because of the historical significance of the game, the endless satisfaction of watching annual pursuits of time-honored records, and the intense statistical analysis that extended naturally from the national pastime.

I remember the faces and uniforms on the fronts of the many baseball cards I collected and, more relevant for today, the lines of statistics on the backs. I could quickly identify the peak years of a player, correctly discern years marred by injury, a gradual decline, and finally, the years in which the player's legs or pitching arm simply went out and ushered in the end of his career. I reaped constant criticism from baseball coaches for being so interested in stats, even during the games in which I was playing. I couldn't help but take note of the numbers materializing before my eyes, and even jinxed a perfect game once, sending my coach into a frenzy.

As for my on-field participation, you won't find much noteworthy detail to record. A good season for me in the years I played, from ages nine to fifteen, included at least one clean base hit, a handful of hard foul balls, and a few more groundouts than expected. I was terrible, and now that I no longer feel such immense shame about it, it has become humorous to recount. By the time I was playing eighth-grade, PONY league ball, I was over six feet tall and hovering around two hundred pounds. I was emerging from the round-faced, bespectacled image I had made for myself and starting to straighten up, but hand-eye coordination was severely lacking just as badly at fourteen as it had been when I was younger. There were times I would come up to bat for the first time, and a team that had never seen me play before would move all three outfielders back to the warning track. By the time I came up for my second at bat, they'd have everyone pulled in shallow.

Dad struggled to control his drinking and, between that and his own personal trauma, said a lot of hurtful things. One day after a game, when I was fourteen, Dad laid into me and told me how embarrassing it was to have a son so big that was such a poor player. What hurt me then is motivational fuel today, but as fate would have it, I would never play organized baseball again after that year. I tried out for my high school's baseball program that fall but given Hillcrest Christian School's constant presence in the state championship picture, I had no chance.

It wasn't just the hitting and defense that did me in; Coach Paul Wyczawski, our championship-caliber head coach who had a lengthy collegiate coaching career after my time at Hillcrest, had a standard I just couldn't make—the dreaded seven-minute mile. For weeks after tryouts, I hit the track and floundered, pushing nine minutes and finding myself early one evening in the coach's office.

"Coach Y," as he was known for short, said in his thick Minnesota accent, "Keshel, you can't hit, you can't run, and you can't really even field. To save you the pain of having to run another mile, I'm gonna cut ya loose." Knowing my love for the game and my penchant for statistics, he left open the door for me to work on the team as a student assistant, a role I would come to slide right over to as soon as football season ended every year. Being low on agility and big on size, I filled up space on Coach Dennis Thompson's offensive line and was only an average player who wished he would have been good at a different sport. I didn't work hard in the weight room, settled for getting by, and it showed. If I would have had the work ethic then that I have today, things would have been much different for me. That wasn't meant to be.

My baseball teammates soon came to know me as someone who didn't give out free base hits when it came time for judgment calls on scorekeeping and tried in vain to beat me in baseball trivia on bus rides. I remember specifically, when talking history with one of our coaches who taught that subject during classroom hours, a teammate overheard the conversation and told me I had nothing but "useless knowledge" that would never be of use once my time in baseball came to a close.

Over that four-year span in high school, I attended every Cougars game, tracked player stats, and interfaced with the numerous professional scouts and collegiate coaches who came to evaluate our impressively talented roster. They came to me for insight on player makeup, work habits, and things they may have missed while covering other portions of their territories. One of those coaches was Dan McDonnell, then an assistant coach at Ole Miss and now head coach at Louisville, where he has taken his team to the College World Series six times.

The Ole Miss Rebels baseball program, now a perennial power and 2022 national champion, was just three seasons into the Mike Bianco era after having been a Southeastern Conference also-ran for decades. The team had several players from Hillcrest on the roster, including future big leaguer Seth Smith and a three-time all-American named Stephen Head, who dominated as a two-way player on the mound and as a heavy-hitting first baseman. Thanks to Coach McDonnell's introduction that provided me with an open door to the program, I began tracking statistics during intrasquad games in the fall and winter ball portions of the preseason, reporting them to the coaching staff, and updating fans online in the early days of message boards. Once the 2004 season began, I was equipped with a radar gun and clipboard and given the duty of charting pitches to be analyzed by staff after games.

The 2004 team was loaded with talent and ranked as high as fourth nationally at the midway point in the season. A six-game losing skid hurt our momentum, but we were strong enough to host the first-ever Oxford Regional tournament after finishing the regular season and conference tournament with a record of 39 wins and 19 losses . We went into the regional on a four-game losing streak and immediately bombed out of the double elimination arrangement in two games in front of our home fans. Our season was over and, with the pressure on, our players had abandoned all discipline at the plate, swinging for the fences rather than looking to wear down the opposing pitchers and simply get men on base.

That disappointment followed the team into fall practice as the 2004–5 school year kicked off. Coach Stuart Lake, the Ole Miss hitting coach, recommended we devise a quality at-bats system to incentivize hitters to put more thought into their trips to the plate. It was a page straight out of *Moneyball*, Michael Lewis's highly successful book about how the low-budget Oakland Athletics cut corners and made ends meet to compete successfully with the rich juggernauts of Major League Baseball; Billy Beane's club took an unconventional approach to evaluating talent, stuck with it, and reaped the rewards. Such systems of evaluating talent and bargain hunting are now widespread at the game's highest levels.

This system came to be known as the "Keshel Cup," and it followed Coach Lake to two schools after he left Ole Miss—Charleston Southern and our old conference rival, the University of South Carolina, a premier college program. Our players loved the contest, frequently checked the dry-erase board for updates after intrasquad games, and most importantly, took the lessons learned into the 2005 season. I handled multiple other duties and, as I became more knowledgeable, was relied upon to provide insight on opposing players I would assess using various platforms and types of technology. Our team was incredible and, in that year and the one to follow, finished just one victory short of advancing to Omaha for the College World Series. It remains a feather in my cap to have had no meaningful playing career yet be relied upon by the coaching staff of a dominant Southeastern Conference program to provide reliable, accurate, and actionable information for high-stakes situations. I had helped lead Ole Miss baseball into a realm of advanced analytics a full decade before collegiate baseball became fully invested in that arena. This period would turn out to be indispensable training for the future, but I had no idea at the time. I had planned to stay around the game I loved for a lifetime.

In the summer of 2006, I had expected to be put to work as an associate scout for the Florida Marlins, which drafted one of our players, future National League Rookie of the Year and World Series champion Chris Coghlan, in the first round of the MLB Draft that year. Associate scouts are volunteers and outfitted with a radar gun, stopwatch, and clipboard, sent to the middle of nowhere to "bird-dog" for talent. If anyone checks all the boxes, the associate scout signals to the full-timers to put the player on the list for follow-up. Hall of Fame legends Greg Maddux and Nolan Ryan were found by associate scouts with an eye for generational talent.

That call never came. With this letdown, I began to realize that I was highly unlikely to find a meaningful career in the game I loved. I had experimented with Ole Miss Air Force ROTC in the spring but couldn't contract with them because of their strict physical standards and the persistent issues with my twice reconstructed right ear. The rejection from the Marlins then led me to consider my family's branch, the United States Army. With two conflicts raging, a constant need for company-grade officers, and my own disinterest in pushing paper after college, I went over to Barnard Hall one day, filled out paperwork with Major Andy Field, and waited for the verdict on my ear. A few weeks later, the news came back: *Waiver granted.*

I signed a cadet contract at once, which put me on an aggressive course to commissioning as a second lieutenant in just twenty-one months, pending successful completion of all course work and training requirements. One of the things I remember most about my sudden change of direction is how proud my father became of me. Two of my other siblings had served before me, and at the time I joined Army ROTC, my brother David, a chief warrant officer 5 and attack helicopter pilot by trade, still had another twelve years left in uniform.

The future revealed that my "useless knowledge" would deliver huge dividends.

CHAPTER 2

Applied Knowledge

I was a big fan of President Donald Trump as soon as he announced his candidacy in 2015, and primarily for the same reasons his other fans had his back. He said it like it was, proposed solutions over defense of ideology, and had clearly thought things out. If I had put one hundred dollars on him to win the GOP nomination in June 2015, it would have been worth thousands a year later. The greatest thing about Trump in those days is that he was busy crumpling up old, tired ideas and shoving them, along with their associated candidates, right off the end of the debate stage.

When Ted Cruz and John Kasich tried one last-ditch effort to stop Trump in the Indiana GOP primary, it backfired in such spectacular fashion that it instantly ended both of their campaigns. There were a few more primaries that had to play out, but the effective end point of the 2016 primary campaign was established in the Hoosier State. Polling for Trump in a hypothetical matchup against Hillary Clinton, who used party loopholes and infrastructure to snatch the Democratic nomination from Bernie Sanders, looked awful, but everyone figured it would normalize once the two-person campaign began in earnest. It never really did.

Polls, in my view, are like dark magic. They often say what the sponsor wants them to say, often account for 78 percent of the electorate but still issue definitive top lines, and still come with a margin of error that may miss hundreds of thousands of votes in margin but still be technically "correct" at the end of the campaign. A futile effort to "unskew" polls unfavorable to Mitt Romney at the tail end of the 2012 campaign still lingered, so people were hesitant to come out and say polls that were bad for Trump were skewed.

Media polling had Trump consistently being steamrolled in the popular vote and handily losing the states that have come to be known as the "big three" in the Trump era—Pennsylvania, Michigan, and Wisconsin—by double digits. The greatest disconnect immediately obvious to my thirty-one-year-old mind that summer was the fact that Trump was spending a substantial amount of time in the "Industrial Midwest" and the traditional swing states but relatively little in Texas, Arizona, Georgia, or any other Republican states that could potentially flip in the event of a double-digit national landslide on behalf of Clinton. Someone clearly had the scorecard filled out wrong, and a variety of clues made it obvious it was not Trump.

Some of the polling issues were caused by legitimate errors, such as the inability to poll remote regions of states critical for Trump's turnout, like northern Wisconsin, or detecting shy Trump voters who didn't even want to tell a stranger they were voting for him. This was an especially important piece of information in the "big three," in which the decisive voters were two-time Obama voters who changed coalitions to back the outsider candidate, Trump. Robert Cahaly of Trafalgar Group cracked the code near the end of the campaign by asking people who they thought their neighbor was voting for and wound up finding answers far more bullish for Trump than the direct question of who the voter was backing.

The rest of the polling issues were seemingly caused by a Clinton campaign that resembled Apollo Creed when he thought he was showing up for a fun exhibition bout against Rocky Balboa. The media corruption was palpable, and all excuses to explain it away are still incapable of passing muster nearly a decade later. A pair of late October polls and the media's admission of Ohio's clear alignment with Trump gave me everything I needed to know to accurately predict 2016.

A CNN poll[1] released in early September let it fly that Trump was leading in Ohio by five points. I will never be a polling enthusiast, but typically if a mainstream media poll shows a comfortable Republican lead, it is more likely that the candidate will win by even more when all ballots are counted than he will regress from that point. The CNN poll suggested Trump was looking at a dominant victory in Ohio in the high single digits.

The next tell for me that the race was tight and the media were covering for Clinton was a pair of mainstream media polls showing nonsensical polling data, especially when paired with what everyone was figuring out about Ohio and Clinton focusing her assets elsewhere. First, CNN launched a poll showing Clinton with a five-point lead[2] taken in the fourth week of October. They were immediately followed up by ABC, which showed Clinton with an astonishing twelve-point lead.[3] It is certainly ironic that in an age of infinite access to information, a majority of Americans couldn't figure out the ruse being foisted upon the nation. I knew it right away.

Just eight years before, Barack Obama had wiped the floor with John McCain, beating him by seven points, a margin of 9.6

---

1   Rebecca Savransky, "Poll: Trump Leads Clinton in Ohio, Florida," *The Hill*, September 14, 2016, https://thehill.com/blogs/ballot-box/presidential-races/295979-poll-trump-clinton-in-close-race-in-florida-ohio/.

2   CNN/ORC International Poll, October 20–23, 2016, https://i2.cdn.turner.com/cnn/2016/images/10/24/cnn.poll.pdf.

3   ABC News, "Stressed About the Election? If So, You've Got Company (POLL)," October 25, 2016, https://abcnews.go.com/Politics/stressed-election-youve-company-poll/story?id=43024209.

million, in the fabled popular vote. Seven points was also the difference between the CNN and ABC polls capturing responses for the Trump–Clinton race; in other words, CNN and ABC were missing nine to ten million votes in margin on the results of the election.

Either poll, if correct, spelled certain defeat for Trump; meanwhile, he was making plans to have his final rally in Michigan, which hadn't backed a Republican for president since 1988. Clinton followed behind him almost everywhere except for Wisconsin, knowing full well that she was in a world of hurt, per her internal numbers, and anything but a sure thing to take the ultimate prize.

Predicting the outcomes of presidential elections requires significant deductive reasoning skills. A major reason that polling national elections is such a useless exercise is because our presidential races consist of fifty-six separate races. They are the fifty statewide races, plus Washington, DC, and 5 split electoral votes belonging to Maine and Nebraska. With increased polarization and the center of electoral gravity shifting to the Midwest in 2016, this meant Trump could get destroyed in California by a record margin, tilting the national popular vote, but pull an inside straight with the right combination of states. I quickly discerned, as if playing poker, that Trump was betting on entering Election Day with 216 electoral votes in the bag, with all but one Romney state plus Ohio, Iowa, and the Second Congressional District of Maine backing him. I knew he had North Carolina, too, based on predictable voter registration by party statistics. His forecast most certainly had the Clinton campaign with 212 slam dunk electoral votes, primarily from hardline blue states but also including a few Bush states (Virginia, Colorado, and New Mexico) that had been slipping further away since they last went red in 2004.

Arizona and Georgia were still a cycle away from being close enough to steal, and Clinton's minimal efforts in both suggested the two camps knew they were going Republican again, even if by reduced margins.

That meant 110 electoral votes from eight states would decide the victor. Those eight states were Florida (29 electoral votes), Pennsylvania (20), Michigan (16), North Carolina (15), Minnesota (10), Wisconsin (10), Nevada (6), New Hampshire (4).

Given that Florida and North Carolina were and still are more Republican than the other six, it made sense that he had to carry both to have a chance at winning the entire thing. Florida required a flip from back-to-back pro-Obama outcomes. Trump, had he won both Florida and North Carolina and lost the rest, would have lost the Electoral College by a painful 278 to 260 margin. Realistically speaking, Trump needed one of these two pathways to get over 270:

- Florida + North Carolina + any of Pennsylvania, Michigan, Wisconsin, or Minnesota

- Florida + North Carolina + New Hampshire + Nevada

Minnesota sits left of Wisconsin and remains the most reliable Democratic presidential state, having not backed the GOP nominee since Richard Nixon won it in 1972. It would have only been won with a clean sweep of the "big three," and almost was. New Hampshire was always a stretch thanks to the affluent Republicans in traditionally GOP-friendly areas and its gradual departure from backing party nominees when it had once been one of the most reliable red states. I wasn't feeling bullish on Nevada because Arizona wasn't looking like it would come in as strong as it did for Romney, and the states are closely linked. The layperson should have been able to predict at least forty-eight of the fifty-six races correctly and seen that 110 electoral votes would decide it. I am certain both campaigns had the same map going into Election Day:

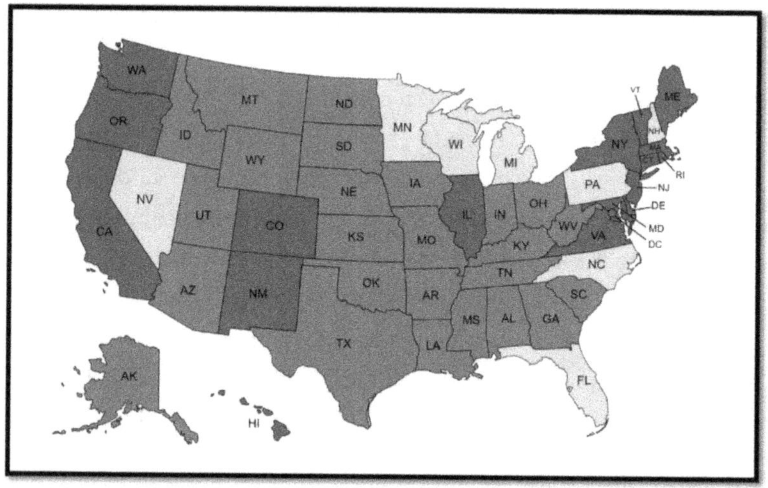

Map by Seth Keshel.

In an October 28 article for *American Thinker*,[4] I hit the nail on the head:

> Ohio is the key. Even the mainstream media seem to credit Trump with being up by at least four points there, while still expecting us to believe in a national race with the candidates separated by a dozen points. It is possible that Trump's economic populism could realign the Rust Belt for the GOP and weaken red bastions, but I'd prefer to go with history. Since 1964, Ohio has

---

4   "The Visual Guide to Disputing Media Polling," *American Thinker*, October 2016, archived at Internet Archive, October 29, 2016, https://web.archive.org/web/20161029112840/https://www.americanthinker.com/articles/2016/10/the_visual_guide_to_disputing_media_polling.html.

voted with the winner. Going back to 1896, you'll find an impressive bellwether record in the Buckeye State.

But wait, there's more. Since 1992, the year of the last map realignment, Pennsylvania has always been to the left of Ohio, and by an average of 4.9 points. In one of the rare GOP wins of the past 24 years, it was as close as 2.5 points. If Trump can win Ohio big enough, he will pull Pennsylvania, and potentially Michigan as well, especially if he benefits from higher black support and help from the legendary Reagan Democrats. Florida has voted right of Ohio in five of the last six elections, and North Carolina votes right of Florida.

Ohio, which I estimated to go to Trump in the high single digits, tipped me off to the true dispositions of Pennsylvania and Michigan. Iowa, with its similar pro-Trump movement, clued me in on Wisconsin and a tightening picture in Minnesota. Party registration figures made the outcomes apparent beforehand in both North Carolina and Florida. New Hampshire, with its libertarian streak and New England voter base, was one of the top "coin flips" in the race, and slightly more likely than not to stick with its usual presidential party, the Democrats.

Trump wound up winning Ohio by 8.1 percent, the largest margin in twenty-eight years, and thanks to the working-class realignment, Florida ended up voting left of Ohio. I knew Trump would carry Florida, despite the early urban vote dumps, thanks to a new skill I learned about from historian Larry Schweikart, who watched voter registration by party but didn't track it as religiously as I have come to do. Voter registration by party analysis is far more accurate for pegging the trajectory of presidential elections than polling is; these quadrennial elections are much more partisan, have the highest levels of turnout, and beg for people to stop gambling on polling markets and instead use hard facts.

The rule of thumb goes like this: Whoever makes the gains in voter registration between elections is likely to see the benefit in the margin. There are very few exceptions at the state level, and thirty states record voter registration by party. Several other states that do not can be predicted by using proxy states. In 2016, being much more of a novice than I am today, I accurately predicted Pennsylvania and Michigan to Trump using Ohio, and Wisconsin by using Iowa. Clinton's pillaging at the hands of minor party voters going for Gary Johnson or Jill Stein in Wisconsin saved me there on my prediction, and she almost lost Minnesota (1.5 percent) for the same reason. For Florida and North Carolina, I used voter registration by party to predict those forty-four collective electoral votes for Trump.

In the aftermath of the 2024 election, Florida is transitioning to be as red as Texas was in its GOP heyday. Republicans now enjoy a massive party registration advantage, and Trump won it by 13.1 percent in 2024. In 2016, elections there were a much different story. Beginning in the 1990s, statewide races, including presidential ones, had a great chance to come down to a nail-biter even if the choices on the ballot were an ice cream cone or a kick in the neck. Florida, like Ohio, was a key presidential bellwether. It had only failed to align with the presidential winner three times since 1924. It was a must-win for Trump in 2016, and all registration figures suggested he would have it:

FLORIDA - VOTER REGISTRATION INDEX TRACKER - CAPT. S. KESHEL					
ELECTION YEAR	2000	2004	2008	2012	2016
REGISTERED DEM	3,822,912	4,291,769	4,791,642	4,814,412	4,877,749
REGISTERED REP	3,448,799	3,917,788	4,100,209	4,261,823	4,550,311
REGISTERED TOT	8,805,972	10,381,246	11,386,103	12,007,581	12,863,773
REG ADVANTAGE	374,113	373,981	691,433	553,129	327,438
REG INDEX	D+4.2%	D+3.6%	D+6.1%	D+4.6%	D+2.5%
PRES MARGIN	Bush+0.0%	Bush+5.0%	Obama+2.8%	Obama +0.9%	Trump +1.2%

Chart by Seth Keshel.

Political observers will never forget the 2000 race in Florida between Vice President Al Gore and Texas Governor George W. Bush, with the latter carried by a margin of 537 votes out of nearly six million cast. Florida is a state that votes to the right of its party registration advantage, and when Bush won that race, Democrats held a registration advantage of 4.2 percent (expressed as "D+4.2%," meaning 4.2 percent more registered Democrats than Republicans statewide), or a lead of 374,113 registrations.[5] Between 2000 and 2004, party registration shifted six-tenths of a percentage point toward Republicans as Americans of all political stripes moved in droves to the Sunshine State, suggesting Bush's performance would improve. He won in his reelection campaign by 5.0 percent in a state that loves incumbent presidents and hasn't voted against one since Jimmy Carter in 1980.

Voter registration by party continues in the run-up to 2016 with accurate predictions:

---

5   Florida Department of State, Division of Elections, "Voter Registration Monthly Report, October 2000," Voter Registration Reports: Archived Monthly Reports, last updated December 9, 2025, https://dos.fl.gov/media/694063/voter-registration-report-archive-2000.zip.

- Voter registration swung over three hundred thousand registrations toward Democrats from 2004 to 2008, signaling major movement toward Obama and a flip.[6]

- Republicans made gains in the run-up to Obama's reelection campaign in 2012, suggesting a tighter race than 2008's 2.8 percent margin. Romney came within a point of flipping the state.[7]

In 2016, it was obvious that the 0.9 percent margin was about to be erased. With Trump as the apparent nominee who had already crushed Florida Senator Marco Rubio in his own home state primary, the GOP made up 225,691 net registrations on the Democrats after Obama had only won the state by 74,309 votes.[8] Even Clinton's election memoir, *What Happened*, expressed astonishment at Trump's turnout throughout the state. They thought she had the state in the bag. No one on her grossly overpaid staff of consultants had ever read a damn word about party registration analysis. Once Florida was called for Trump, the Javits Center, Clinton's election headquarters, fell into hushed

---

6   Florida Department of State, Division of Elections, "Voter Registration Monthly Report, October 2004," Voter Registration Reports: Archived Monthly Reports, last updated December 9, 2025, https://dos.fl.gov/media/694067/voter-registration-report-archive-2004.zip. (2016 - Dem minus Rep = 327,438. The 327,438 divided by total number of registered voters 12,863, 773 equals 2.5% favoring Dem) Florida Department of State, Division of Elections, "Voter Registration Monthly Report, October 2008," Voter Registration Reports: Archived Monthly Reports, last updated December 9, 2025, https://dos.fl.gov/media/694070/voter-registration-report-archive-2008.zip.

7   Florida Department of State, Division of Elections, "Voter Registration Monthly Report, October 2012," Voter Registration Reports: Archived Monthly Reports, last updated December 9, 2025, https://dos.fl.gov/media/694075/voter-registration-report-archive-2012.zip. The Democrat voter registration advantage was smaller in 2012 than it was in 2008, suggesting progress for Republicans and predicting Romney would fare better than McCain.

8   Florida Department of State, Division of Elections, "Voter Registration Monthly Report, October 2016," Voter Registration Reports: Archived Monthly Reports, last updated December 9, 2025, https://dos.fl.gov/media/697513/voter-registration-report-archive-2016.zip.

silence as the betting markets swung heavily for the guy none of the experts thought could win.

Unlike Florida, Romney had won North Carolina in 2012 as one of two states flipped away from Obama (with Indiana being the other). Romney's winning margin there was 2.0 percent, or 92,004 votes, with the state holding a Democratic registration advantage of 12.3 percent, or 818,443 registrations.[9] North Carolina is another state that always votes well to the right of its registration advantage, and from 2012 to 2016, it moved another three points to the right, favoring Republicans, by registration, suggesting a Trump margin larger than Romney's 2.0 percent:[10]

NORTH CAROLINA - VOTER REGISTRATION INDEX TRACKER - CAPT. S. KESHEL				
ELECTION YEAR	2004	2008	2012	2016
REGISTERED DEM	2,408,759	2,866,669	2,870,693	2,733,188
REGISTERED REP	1,750,359	2,002,416	2,052,250	2,086,942
REGISTERED TOT	5,079,830	6,264,733	6,649,188	6,918,150
REG ADVANTAGE	658,400	864,253	818,443	646,246
REG INDEX	D+13.0%	D+13.8%	D+12.3%	D+9.3%
PRES MARGIN	Bush+12.4%	Obama+0.3%	Romney+2.0%	Trump+3.7%

Chart by Seth Keshel.

Trump carried North Carolina by 3.7 percent, in line with party registration analysis.

In summary, the eight decisive states of 2016 were called correctly by a fusion process considering several disciplines, although much less precisely done than I did in 2024:

---

9   North Carolina State Board of Elections, "Voter Registration Statistics, Reporting Period: November 6, 2012, Statewide Total," accessed November 18, 2025, https:// vt.ncsbe.gov/RegStat/Results/?date=11%2F06%2F2012.

10   North Carolina State Board of Elections, "Voter Registration Statistics, Reporting Period: November 8, 2016, Statewide Total," accessed November 18, 2025, https:// vt.ncsbe.gov/RegStat/Results/?date=11%2F08%2F2016.

Florida—Obvious flip by party registration analysis.

North Carolina—Obvious hold by party registration analysis.

Pennsylvania—Predicted by the expected Ohio margin, with rightward movement expected thanks to the shift in party registration from D+13.3% to D+10.5%.

Michigan—No party registration, but predicted by the expected Ohio margin.

Wisconsin—No party registration, but predicted by the expected Iowa margin.

Minnesota—No party registration, but a close Trump loss predicted by the expected Iowa margin and expected flip of Wisconsin.

Nevada—Party registration shifted from D+7.2% to D+6.1%, suggesting a tighter outcome; I predicted a narrow Trump loss based on the expectation of a tighter-than-usual margin in Arizona.

New Hampshire—Party registration shifted toward Democrats, from R+2.6% to R+2.1%, but Trump nearly won the state (0.4 percent margin) thanks to Clinton's large third-party losses.

My lessons from the 2016 election, four years before a hobby would turn into a life-changing turn of events, were as follows:

- The media lie with impunity to shape electoral outcomes.

- Polling is a tool that is now used to manipulate minds by sponsors, the media, and campaigns.

- Fifty-six separate presidential races determine the victor, and approximately 80 percent of them in any given year are simple to predict by voter registration by party, proxies, and logical deduction.

- Forty-eight of fifty-six outcomes in the 2016 election were easily predictable not only by analysis, but by studying campaign behavior.

The "trivial knowledge" I had cultivated earlier in life turned out to be pretty handy, or at least I thought it was when I was making custom PowerPoint slides to share with my friends to commemorate how I told them so, and poke fun at how wrong they were. I attended President Trump's inauguration on January 20, 2017, having no idea whatsoever that before another four years would pass, I'd be fighting with all my might to get him back on the steps of the Capitol.

CHAPTER 3

A Quick Study

Army ROTC life came naturally to me. I was consistently regarded as one of the most motivated cadets in the Rebel Battalion because I had a chip on my shoulder and wanted to prove to the Army that they had made the right decision by giving me a waiver for my hearing loss, when the Air Force would not. I wear a hearing aid today in my right ear and am nearly deaf on that side without it. It has never drained properly and always required me to properly plug the ear while swimming, or risk a severe, weeks-long ear infection for rolling the dice. From a military perspective, my poor hearing made it unlikely I would be useful in a combat arms field, like my father's Infantry branch. I had no interest in being a six-foot-six instant target when putting my brainpower to work was a better use of my skill, anyway.

The days of low self-esteem were long gone. Far too often, I acted the other way around and had too much "can-do" attitude and belief that I could "wing it" and succeed without properly preparing. I had shot up in high school and leaned out, minus my senior year in which a new football coach did lunch box checks to make sure linemen were eating six meals a day, and I forced myself into excellent shape in my college years to meet the Army's physical fitness standards. I worked hard back then and did all I could to earn the best possible marks in ROTC so I could rank as high as possible and give myself as much say over my choice of branch or duty station as possible.

Dad had continued to ride me over grades after I left for college; they were good for the first three semesters, but my devotion to traveling with the Ole Miss baseball team in 2005 and a few tough classes left me with a 2.3 GPA for the spring semester of my sophomore year. After two decades, I still find no purpose for accounting, at least in my own life. That explanation didn't sit right at home, where Dad said, "What the hell did I work so hard for to send you to college?"

Being fully frustrated with school and hopeful a baseball career was in the works, I continued to underachieve and even managed to plunge my overall GPA under 3.0 after two more clunker semesters. After that, the old man gave up watching my grades and told me I'd have to learn my lesson the hard way—and that "*D* stands for dumbass." Army ROTC gave me renewed focus to try and finish strong in the classroom, even if the motives were selfish. Your GPA made up 40 percent of your overall cadet rating, and it didn't matter if you were majoring in an incredibly difficult field of study or something easy like criminal justice, the easy major that former Marine officer and my longtime friend Preston Walker picked. Preston was one of those guys who pushed me forward and helped me develop a "no-quit" attitude when I needed that degree of mental and physical toughness, as was my ROTC classmate Kyle McElhaney, who wound up flying Apaches after graduation. For hours, Kyle and I would flip over playing cards and perform push-ups and sit-ups in the numbers shown on the card faces. It wasn't long before I was a regular high performer on the physical fitness test, which goes a long way in bringing you hard-earned respect early in your career when there isn't much else to show on paper, or on your ribbon rack.

I fast-tracked through the ROTC curriculum, a good thing since I had already put myself on the five-year plan through Ole Miss, which is a common thing for students who come to love the place where they've "never lost a party." In my final fall semester, the senior cadets put forward their service branch choices. I ranked Military Intelligence (MI) first, but it was a long shot because my slacking off in the classroom for three semesters had put me at a tactical disadvantage on the Order of Merit List (OML), and somewhere in the middle of the pack. I was high enough on the OML to qualify for active duty service, which I wanted, but all signs suggested I'd have to make my way to the MI branch through a construct called a "branch detail."

A branch detail is like a rental arrangement between two service branches within the Army. Some branches, like MI, the Signal Corps, and the Adjutant General's Corps, don't need many lieutenants or captains, but more majors. Conversely, combat arms branches like Infantry, Field Artillery, and Armor need more lieutenants to supervise all the soldiers making up the ranks. An officer on a branch detail goes to his combat arms branch until he makes captain and goes to a stop along the Army's education path called Captains Career Course and switches over to his basic branch. When I attended the MI Captains Career Course, we had plenty of combat arms officers who joined us, and they brought a level of tactical knowledge and skill the homegrown MI officers didn't have. To our advantage, we had several years of experience in MI tradecraft, presenting intelligence, defending analytical assessments, and MI-specific training they didn't have. Successful teams at the Captains Career Course had a good mix of the two camps. Branch reveal day finally came during the Fall 2007 semester, my last fall at Ole Miss.

THE AMERICAN WAR ON ELECTION CORRUPTION

Keshel—Military Intelligence, Branch Detail Field
Artillery; Duty Station Fort Polk, Louisiana

The Tenth Mountain Division has a brigade combat team at
Fort Polk, a muggy swampland that consistently ranks among
the least desirable duty stations anywhere in the Army. That's
saying something, because the Army also gives a service member
high odds of finding a posting at Fort Riley, Kansas, Fort Sill,
Oklahoma, or Fort Drum, New York. I was slated for Fort Polk
after a training tour at Fort Sill to become a Field Artillery officer
on loan from the MI branch. I didn't have the OML ranking to
vault over the other cadets and take a slot for MI right out of
school; I would have to wait. There were two schools of thought
when it came to becoming a lieutenant who is verging on deaf-
ness in one ear and preparing to enter the Field Artillery branch.
I was either so deaf the big guns wouldn't do any more damage,
or I was going to have what remained of my hearing blown out
of my skull. On the positive side, I had the brainpower for the
complicated formulas and gunnery equations that are associated
with the artillery profession, and I wasn't going to be expected to
be a ground-pounding infantryman. That would have been worse,
and I know firsthand because we had a cadet who commissioned
a year before me that wanted to be an Adjutant General's Corps
officer and got to take the scenic branch detail route through
Infantry first.

Once our assignments were revealed, the suspense was over
and everything else seemed anticlimactic. Everyone still had to
punch the clock and graduate, show up early in the morning
to pound out miles, and train junior cadets, but with the nation
entering George W. Bush's eighth year in office and conflicts raging hot on two fronts, our minds were elsewhere. It seemed as
if our commissioning date, May 9, 2008, would never come. My

spiffy dress blues from Marlow White in Leavenworth, Kansas, approved by the eagle-eyed Lieutenant Colonel Jim Shaver, our professor of military science, needed only the two shoulder boards with gold bars fastened to make things official.

My parents were set to do the honors of "pinning" on the insignia. Once the big day finally rolled around, my parents showed up in Oxford early to rehearse their roles in the ceremony. Over and over again, Dad got his shoulder board fastened with no issue, while my mother fumbled with hers. This led to some interesting commentary from the old man about how she'd better not mess it up when it came time to do it for real. Later that afternoon, I took the stage and, in a great twist of irony, it was my mother who put hers on with no issue, and Dad unable to fasten his. I did all I could to conceal my amusement and maintain military bearing as Dad grumbled out colorful phrases beneath his breath. I was getting commissioned in the Army and receiving my business management diploma that weekend; Dad had long since secured his "master's of the profane arts."

After they departed the stage, I turned and faced my brother David, who gave me my first salute. He served another decade in the Army after that and is still one of the most highly respected aviators in the history of the branch, well known for his combat skill and valorous actions in the early days of the Iraq War. His oldest son Donald II, my nephew, still serves in the Army today. My commissioning ceremony remains a point of pride in my life and symbolizes the proud continuation of the Keshel family tradition. A month of easy living commenced, ending upon my arrival in Lawton, Oklahoma, on the evening of June 7, my first day on active duty.

I had orders to spend the next seven months at Fort Sill to complete a now-defunct course called Basic Officer Leader

Course, phase II, which consisted of lieutenants from all Army service branches, and then the Field Artillery–specific course, which required more focus to master a tradecraft that became significantly more complex the higher an officer rose in the ranks. As is the standard for my life, God had vastly different plans for putting me where he wanted me. This became clear before I had even finished my first week of training.

All lieutenants in my class filed through a hearing and vision screening center as part of standard in-processing; no big deal for everyone but me. I hadn't yet had LASIK to fix my nearsightedness, but with my contact lenses, I had no issues with the vision screening; however, the familiar and unnerving hearing screening posed an entirely new set of challenges, as I struggled to pick up faint beeps and screeches for what seemed like an eternity. I was asked to wait behind and eventually summoned by the technician evaluating my report. That was the day I learned about medical profiles.

Soldiers receive a temporary or permanent medical profile of six numbers, with each number ranging from 1 to 4, and covering six areas under the acronym of PULHES:

> P: Physical condition
>
> U: Upper extremities
>
> L: Lower extremities
>
> H: Hearing
>
> E: Eyes
>
> S: Psychiatric/Stability

A soldier with a sprained ankle may receive a temporary profile for *L* with a rating of 3, and for the time specified, could be restricted from certain activities, like carrying a heavy load.

Conditions thought to be permanent, if rated 3 or 4, require the Medical Evaluation Board to determine if the Army will retain or dismiss the service member, or switch him to a different functional area. My profile came down as "permanent H-3." The medical recommendation for someone like me, with no prior service experience and barely on active duty at all, was to dismiss me from the Army. The Field Artillery branch, before my first week in the Army was over, was already off the table. The fight for my career had begun; I had never expected this to be an issue since I had been granted a waiver for my hearing loss two years before, but the big Army and Cadet Command quite clearly had different standards for service that were never effectively communicated.

I spent the next six weeks juggling field exercises, the classroom, and running around Fort Sill seeking knowledge and allies I thought would help me in my pending board review, scheduled for July 30, just a few days after I was set to complete the Basic Officer Leader Course II. The board would consist of a full colonel, three lieutenant colonels, and a major, the medical officer, who would all be taking testimony, evaluating my case, and casting votes to determine my fate. I had only one person who came to bat for me—my dad. We had met earlier in the month in Arlington, Texas, to watch a ballgame together and discuss what needed to be done to get me through this board; true to his word, he drove the six hundred miles to Lawton, had breakfast with me, and then faced the board after I had already appeared in front of them to make my case to be switched to the MI branch.

After a period of silence that felt like hours, I was summoned to appear before the board once again. The colonel presiding said, "You must have a guardian angel. Against my own recommendation, this board has decided to retain you by a vote of three to two and transfer you to the Military Intelligence branch. You better have a good career—now get out of here." I later found out that the deciding vote was cast by a Lieutenant Colonel Watson, who had been plagued by his own hearing issues throughout his career. When God shows up in my life, He shows up big.

Dad congratulated me and, in a flash, was gone. It was as if he'd shown up to do a routine mission in keeping his son in the Army to develop the skills I would need to tackle bigger missions in life, and nothing more. Looking back to that Medical Evaluation Board, I feel confident I would have never had so much impact in the fight for freedom, liberty, and fair elections had I not developed the personal resilience and analytical capacities I did while in uniform. Handling important intelligence under severe stress with high stakes sharpened my already respected analytical abilities and conditioned me to withstand serious scrutiny, animosity, and outright hatred from those who wanted nothing more than for me to sit down and shut up.

I wasn't fully out of the woods yet after the board hearing and had to pull some strings that were substantially above my pay grade. My first order of business was to head over to the Field Artillery schoolhouse and inform the training company commander, Captain Tim Hansen, of the board's decision. He cancelled my previously ordered training course and made me his unofficial executive officer, or "XO" in Army-speak. I handled miscellaneous items for him for two months, filled in for him at events he was too busy to attend, and had enough time in the margins to punch my ticket west. After some haggling and production of completed paperwork, I was formally accepted by the MI branch, under the condition that I would accept an assignment to their training units at Fort Huachuca, Arizona, after I completed my MI-specific training there. It wasn't a deployable unit in the big Army, but I was ready to go after having been in limbo for so long. I reluctantly agreed and awaited orders to be on my way.

I packed up my truck and turned in the keys to my ratty, furnished apartment next to a run-down casino one day in early October, eventually arriving in the Old West town of Sierra Vista, Arizona, just down the road from the storybook town considered "too tough to die," Tombstone. For months, I had what is called "snowbird" duty, which is something prospective student officers may find themselves on while waiting for classes to start. For most, this was usually no more than a few weeks. Since my transition to the MI Corps was sudden, and there had been no class reservation for me, I spent more than two months waiting to sit in a class with room for one more. Snowbird duty is easy living—a full paycheck, no mandatory early physical fitness formations, and only the occasional work detail—yet I didn't want it. I was ready to prove myself.

As I made my way through the MI curriculum, serving as class physical fitness officer, I noticed the unit patches adorning the left sleeves of my classmates. Those who weren't immediately returning home for National Guard or Reserve duty were going to hard-charging units stationed all over the world and inevitably headed for combat tours. I have a much different opinion about deployments now that I've done one, but as a bachelor, I was itching to get "downrange" and show I had what it took—that I wasn't a charity case allowed to serve only because of my family's service history. The problem for me was that I had already agreed to move a few buildings over and manage enlisted trainees at a time in which someone had to really try to *not* get a combat patch. In sticking with this original assignment, I would position myself to make the rank of captain by 2011, with no combat unit service in which I would actively practice the intelligence craft. That had to change.

David, my pilot brother, was stationed in Korea then. I had caught wind that his former commander, Colonel Daniel Williams, was destined to take command of the Fourth Combat Aviation Brigade in Fort Hood, Texas, after his tour of duty in Washington, DC, working for the secretary of defense. Looking back, I made a major error in judgment by not running my request through my brother, but I got the wild hair to call Colonel Williams one day and make my request to be assigned to his unit. My MI branch manager was unrelenting and unwilling to move me to any other assignment than the one she had me pegged for, and she used my hearing problem as just rationale. Colonel Williams was welcoming and bent heaven and earth for me because of his relationship with David. My branch manager was livid when she found out what I had done. She wasn't alone.

One late weekend night, I got a call from Korea. It was my brother, and he wasn't happy and most certainly wasn't buying my half-assed attempts to laugh off what I knew was coming:

"You're a ****ing second lieutenant in the United States Army, and you've got the balls to call the secretary of defense's office to bother a full bird colonel? What in the hell is wrong with you?"

This reaming went on and on, until I finally said, "Dave, are you done?"

"Yea, I'm done!" he replied, only to be caught by me on the back end:

"Don't you mean, 'Yea I'm done...sir?!'"

US forces have served in Korea for seven decades to prevent the peninsula from exploding into a mushroom cloud of obliteration. David's response to my barb, exercising the technicality of a higher rank over the most senior warrant officer grade possible, was thoroughly nuclear.

I completed my initial MI training and arrived at Fort Hood in April. The brigade was just returning from deployment to Iraq, and I was too late to get a "cup of coffee" on a deployment. I had no idea at the time that the Fourth Combat Aviation Brigade under the incoming commander, Colonel Williams, would have the shortest dwell time in the history of Army aviation and find itself scattered across "The Graveyard of Empires" a year later. With my forthcoming assignment to the First Attack Reconnaissance Battalion, my consequence-free training days were officially over.

Captain JaMarco Bowen and First Lieutenant Geoff Wightman were over the S2 (intelligence) section and took quickly to off-loading extra duties to me. Captain Bowen was expecting orders to leave and Wightman, a West Pointer, was going to be taking over as primary S2 upon Bowen's departure. Both of these officers took great care in giving me challenges in which I would either sink or swim, primarily the challenge of the weekly pilot briefings. My role was to inform them of relevant global intelligence or information in an unclassified setting that would prepare them for any missions on the horizon.

Before we even knew an Afghanistan mission was imminent, I had already begun including weekly blocks on coalition efforts and enemy activity unfolding there. Most of our pilots had never served there, and the challenges of conducting aviation operations in that country were vastly different and often more severe there than in Iraq. I got over any nerves quickly, ensured by the weekly exposure to field-grade officers and senior warrant officers. One day, I repeated a line I had heard while completing my entry-level MI training at Fort Huachuca. I told the meeting attendees that anyone could give them steak (information), but I intended to put the sizzle on the steak (interpretation and analysis). The nickname "Sizzle" stuck, and I continued to build rapport with those I expected to one day serve in combat with.

My fleeting time learning as one of the only officers in the brigade with no combat experience was filled with memorable perspective. In the fall, I came out on the promotion list to first lieutenant, along with just about every other second lieutenant that had commissioned in early 2008. That promotion is nearly automatic, and in order not to make it, you must be either extremely out of shape and unable to pass the physical fitness test or in trouble with the law. Dad wanted to attend the ceremony on November 30, which was inevitably going to be something informal at the end of the duty day since it's not exactly a promotion to general. I shrugged it off and told him he didn't need to bother to make the eight-hour drive, but he insisted.

Promotion day arrived, and my parents were there for the ceremony. They were joined by my brother David, who was on temporary duty at Fort Hood. Colonel Williams pinned the new insignia, a subdued black bar on the combat uniform, and did the honors for two other lieutenants moving up with me. Dad congratulated me after the ceremony, and I started back in on the false humility routine, referring once again to the promotion as automatic and unimportant. What he said next has never left my mind as a reminder to celebrate the small victories in life:

"Son, I served with a lot of second lieutenants in Vietnam who didn't live long enough to make first lieutenant."

To this day, I never shrug off "automatic" promotions, accomplishments, or progress. His words shook me and alerted me to how naive I still was. I had undergone a lot of personal and professional growth, but I still had no concept of what Dad's time in combat must have been like, and how it must have impacted him physically and mentally. At a unit dining event in December, Colonel Williams shook my hand in the receiving line and said clearly, "Poppy fields in June, brother, poppy fields in June."

That could mean only one thing—Afghanistan. And six months from then.

Much would change in my twenty-five-year-old world from that point forward. I got married for the first time in February 2010. Shortly after, I learned Dad had pancreatic cancer, which was a death sentence given his age and poor health. In addition to figuring out how to maintain a relationship long distance and getting my mind right to handle a year of stress and rigor handling intelligence matters in combat, I had to get ready to say goodbye to the man I had truly come to know once I decided to enter military service.

In those final days together, we bonded tremendously. He shared with me many lessons learned from his service in Vietnam, including his wartime motto, "Push it away." He said I'd have to do that whenever troubles came up in order to focus on the mission at hand. Infantry officers can't get distracted, or they'll place their men in direct danger and make decisions that jeopardize the mission and give tactical advantages to the enemies. If intelligence officers make combat mistakes, they misinform everyone in the unit and create a strategic disadvantage that never goes away until understood and subsequently corrected.

One of the most memorable moments of my life occurred on the back porch at my parents' home in Mississippi, which they bought while I had been in college. I was there on block leave and spent about a week visiting at the end of May 2010. I had been back once before since Dad received his diagnosis for a long weekend, but this trip was different. I knew it would be the last time I'd ever see him on earth. I had been a Christian since I was seventeen and was the first in my family to be vocal about my faith. This put me at odds with some of my other family members, and Dad and I danced around the topic if it came up.

Dad faced death bravely. He rarely complained about it and had sworn off any aggressive treatments to treat his illness, which is called the "silent killer" because it shows no symptoms before emerging, often as a stage 4 cancer. There was no avoiding the topic of death at the table, where he sat puffing a cigarette and finishing off a drink. He began talking to me about what to do when he died, and the conversation suddenly shifted to what he would say when he came face-to-face with God. By the end of our conversation, Dad decided to put his faith in Christ. This transformed him in such a way that he continued to write about his newfound faith and inform me, while I was overseas, about what he had been reading in the Bible.

As June drew near, the day finally came for me to say goodbye. I loaded up my truck to journey westward and approached Dad's spot at the head of the kitchen table. In a show of respect, I popped to the position of attention and saluted Dad. He had been moving slowly and losing weight at an alarming pace, but in this moment, he sprang up out of that chair like he was my age and returned my salute. After a tearful goodbye, I backed out of the driveway for the last time and watched his reflection disappear from my rearview mirror.

I was stepping into the unknown. Thanks to some last-minute changes within the brigade, I was being thrown to the wolves and would fill in as the primary S2 (intelligence officer) while the usual one was tending to a family matter and would miss the first three months of the deployment. My unit would occupy a former Soviet airfield in far western Afghanistan, near the Iranian border and in an area where Americans had only recently begun to conduct operations in and out of. The intelligence picture was sparse and had to be created from scratch, first by the intelligence section we relieved and then cultivated and developed further by Task Force Comanche.

With little tactical intelligence to draw from, the pages of history offered coalition forces in Afghanistan the best guidance. The British and Soviets had failed to tame Afghanistan and for some reason, the United States government thought it would successfully use, as a warrant officer from my unit said, "A battle-ax to perform open heart surgery." It was another way to say that we would be using a force meant to kill and destroy to shape "hearts and minds," presumably to one day hand over peacekeeping duties to local security forces. Dad loved to read history and read it until he was bedridden. Over the next decade, Americans would come to fully appreciate why Afghanistan was called "The Graveyard of Empires," and I would have my own late-night revelations about what my future entailed.

History is always the greatest guide.

CHAPTER 4

A History of Election Fraud

In his 2021 farewell letter to America,[1] World War II hero, former presidential candidate, and Kansas Senator Bob Dole left behind a hilarious barb targeting the sacred Democratic city institution of election fraud:

"I also confess that I am a bit curious to learn if I am correct in thinking that Heaven will look a lot like Kansas, and to see, like others who have gone before me, if I will be able to vote in Chicago."

Dole's dig at the Windy City could have likewise been applied with the same impact to Philadelphia, Detroit, Atlanta, or any number of dysfunctional metropolitan areas in which the ruling officials have come to understand that poverty is a far more effective means of controlling the population and its requisite dependency than teaching self-reliance and personal responsibility. In the 2020 presidential election, Joe Biden carried eighteen states[2] by which his winning margin was guaranteed by his margin in just one county. For example, in Maine, Biden's winning margin in Cumberland County, one of eight counties he won, was 69,175 ballots. Trump carried eight counties statewide, for a combined

---

1   Bob Dole, "A Farewell Letter from Senator Bob Dole," KRSL.com, December 13, 2021, https://krsl.com/local/farewell-letter-senator-bob-dole.

2   Seth Keshel, "Democrats Control 18 States With Just a Single County in Each - Inside the Impact of Urban Election Rigging," captaink.us, June 16, 2022, https://www.captaink.us/p/democrats-control-18-states-with?utm_source=publication-search.

margin of 32,052, not even enough to erode half of the margin of Maine's premier Democratic workhorse county. Among the seventeen other states like this that Biden won, the geographically small urban areas overrode several states that were overwhelmingly Republican by land size, such as Minnesota or Nevada.

In states with enough outlying Republican margin to override urban Democratic margins, such as Arizona, so much of the ballot count was centralized that it makes targeting for ballot fraud a simple planning exercise. In that state, Maricopa and Pima Counties contributed 76.5 percent of the 3,397,388 presidential ballots certified in Biden's victory, only the second Democratic presidential win in Arizona since 1948. Sparsely populated red states like Wyoming or South Dakota lacked the urban density for the collection of fraudulent ballots to tip the balance in states dominated by rural voting tendencies. Other red states, like Florida or Texas, had conservative-leaning suburban areas to blot out Democrat-run urban cores, in addition to dominant GOP margins in rural areas.

The great irony—given that America was founded at a time of peak government distrust and now has a way of life, extended over centuries, that is propped up by *inalienable* rights the government itself cannot strip—is that American government officials, agencies, and think tanks all go to great lengths to assure Americans just how rare election fraud is. I suppose, in this sense, there are no official reports of termites under homes if no one bothers to check. The Constitution enshrines our rights and provides checks and balances because the framers knew that man's inclination is to seek power, and once in power, hold to it by any means necessary.

In "Federalist No. 51" (1788), summarized by the National Constitution Center as "Human beings are imperfect and ambitious, so we need a government structure that guards against abuses of power,"[3] future President James Madison wrote:

> Ambition must be made to counteract ambition. The interest of the man must be connected with the constitutional rights of the place. It may be a reflection on human nature, that such devices should be necessary to control the abuses of government. But what is government itself, but the greatest of all reflections on human nature? If men were angels, no government would be necessary. If angels were to govern men, neither external nor internal controls on government would be necessary. In framing a government which is to be administered by men over men, the great difficulty lies in this: you must first enable the government to control the governed; and in the next place oblige it to control itself.

Modern Americans have witnessed the nature of man on full display not only in third world countries where there is no concept of a bill of rights but in recent years here in their home country. Americans have been misled about military conflicts that have cost significant blood and treasure, lied to about a virus that, years later, cannot be definitively proven to have natural origins, and found themselves attacked by arms of the US government over ideological purposes. Why in the hell would Americans not naturally suspect that the means of obtaining high offices would not be gamed in such a way that it would ensure the most corrupt among us a permanent place at the political table?

---

3   National Constitution Center, "6.5 Primary Source: James Madison, Federalist No. 51 (1788)," Constitution 101 Resources, accessed November 1, 2025, https://constitutioncenter.org/education/classroom-resource-library/classroom/6.5-primary-source-james-madison-federalist-no-51-1788.

In my eyes, since we have for some reason allowed government to run elections, the burden of proof should be on *them*, not us, to prove the elections are fraud free and worthy of the public trust. Most of the criticisms of the 2020 US presidential election have been ignored in America but widely criticized when they manifest in other nations. The *Journal of Democracy*[4] echoed concerns that the 2024 Pakistani National Assembly elections, which had delays lasting longer than forty-eight hours to announce full results, were rigged by writing, "The delayed results seemed to lend credence to widespread concerns that the contest was fixed." The BBC, writing in 2016 about election corruption in African nations,[5] noted several specific items as telltale markers of fraud:

- Mathematically impossible voter turnout

- Irrationally high turnout in some areas, which dwarf aggregates elsewhere

- High percentage of disqualified ballots

- Totals of votes that do not reconcile with number of issued ballots

- Results that don't match polling station totals (in other words, made-up votes)

- Delays in announcing results

The last bullet point is damning in the context of recent American elections. A glut of mail-in ballots is typically the excuse for the delays, but why would Americans tolerate a system that leaves behind so much suspicion when generations as young as

---

4   Ayesha Jalal, "Inside Pakistan's Deeply Flawed Election," *Journal of Democracy*, February 2024, https://www.journalofdemocracy.org/online-exclusive/inside-pakistans-deeply-flawed-election/.

5   Elizabeth Blunt, "Vote Rigging: How to Spot the Tell-Tale Signs," BBC News, September 2, 2016, https://www.bbc.com/news/world-africa-37243190.

millennials remember talking about election results the next day in social studies class? Western observers and think tanks take such great care to identify obvious signs of electoral malfeasance occurring on the other side of the globe, but when it happens in elections that will determine the most powerful offices in the world, it is ignored. Arizona, which relies heavily on mail-in ballots, has roughly one-third the population of Florida but takes two weeks to finish counting ballots. Florida leaves no doubt by the end of election night who has won which races and has nearly all its ballots counted by midnight. The delays are clearly by design, as were the stoppages of vote counting in Pennsylvania, Michigan, Wisconsin, and a handful of other states as incumbent President Donald Trump built massive leads on November 3, 2020.

Still, Americans are told election fraud is extremely rare and that sufficient mechanisms exist to ensure fraudulent ballots are neither cast nor counted.

Election fraud deniers want Americans to forget a prominent scheme with mail-in ballots, allowed due to the Civil War, that attempted a steal of the 1864 presidential election from Abraham Lincoln in favor of one of his former generals, George McClellan. Roughly 150,000 Union soldiers cast votes from the field,[6] using unit tally sheets overseen by commanders, or in the case of New York's troops, by individual mail-in ballots that would be completed, notarized, and put in the mail. Democratic operatives Moses J. Ferry and Edward Donahue, Jr., were caught forging ballots and applying fake signatures made to represent those belonging to non-voting, wounded, dead, or fictitious soldiers for New York's presidential race, which was thought to be critical for determining the victor.

---

6   Meilan Solly, "The Debate Over Mail-In Voting Dates Back to the Civil War," *Smithsonian*, October 20, 2020, https://www.smithsonianmag.com/smart-news/debate-over-mail-voting-dates-back-civil-war-180976091/.

Lincoln had doubted his own reelection chances just months before Election Day, but sudden battlefield success put him on course for a national landslide. Still, New York was close, decided by less than a single percentage point, suggesting significant insight existed as to which states would be decisive in light of ongoing political events, just like in modern elections. Ferry and Donahue were sniffed out by a Lincoln supporter named Orville Wood, who caught wind of the plot by posing as a McClellan backer and establishing rapport with the rival camp. Notice the target was New York's loose absentee balloting system and not a state's consolidated unit tally sheet under strict chain of custody measures.

Another dark figure from those days is William "Boss" Tweed, a shameless fraudster from New York City who controlled Tammany Hall, the Democrats' political muscle that helped the party exercise control over local and state politics for two decades between the 1850s and 1870s. The Bill of Rights Institute issued a damning description of Tweed's exploits related to the electoral process:[7]

> The Tweed Ring also manipulated elections in a variety of ways. It hired people to vote multiple times and had sheriffs and temporary deputies protect them while doing so. It stuffed ballot boxes with fake votes and bribed or arrested election inspectors who questioned its methods. As Tweed later said, The ballots made no result; the counters made the result. Sometimes the ring simply ignored the ballots and falsified election results. Tammany candidates often received more votes than there were eligible voters in a district.

---

7   Bill of Rights Institute, "William 'Boss' Tweed and Political Machines," accessed [November 4, 2025, https://www.billofrightsinstitute.org/essays/william-boss-tweed-and-political-machines.

> In addition, the ring used intimidation and street
> violence by hiring thugs or crooked cops to sway
> voters' minds and received payoffs from criminal
> activities it allowed to flourish.

When Tweed's people weren't busy actively defrauding elections, they were skimming money from public projects, bribing judges, and giving handouts to immigrants to lighten the ballot fraud quota for any upcoming elections. Tweed wasn't even shy about it, like today's election fraudsters are, and what is truly interesting is that his root methods for manipulating election results don't vary much from today's, technology aside. Stuffing ballot boxes with fake votes is no different than allowing mail-in ballots to be assigned to fraudulent or invalid registrations, collected over an extensive early voting period, and then subsequently deposited in a drop box to be counted by an elections department with no concern for signature verification or any other means of guaranteeing elections are run with integrity.

Dole meant to be funny as he bid farewell to the nation he served for so many years, but he was sadly accurate in his condemnation of Chicago and, by extension, the standard American metropolis overseen by lawless officials. We may wait for years for a serious effort to investigate a major stolen election, such as one for president, Senate, or the US House, but even under Biden's hapless administration, the feds were busy chasing down election fraud and, for those willing to do some digging, leaving behind the recipe for exactly how it is done.

After the 2022 election cycle, the US Attorney's Office of New Jersey rolled up a New Jersey Democratic operative named

Craig Callaway,[8] former president of the Atlantic City Council, for "depriving, defrauding, and attempting to deprive and defraud the residents of the state of New Jersey of a fair and impartially conducted election process by the fraudulent procurement, casting, and tabulation of ballots." According to the investigation, Callaway recruited and paid citizens to pose as authorized messengers for voters who did not vote on their own accord to obtain absentee ballots and hand them over to Callaway and his cohorts. Callaway got slapped with a two-year prison sentence in July 2025.

It isn't always a case of trying to edge out Republicans, either; Democrats in Connecticut engaged in a widespread scheme surrounding mail-in ballots to keep incumbent Bridgeport Mayor Joe Ganim in office and had no issues engaging in election fraud against their fellow party members in the 2023 primary.[9] Five were charged, and the evidence was thick enough even a blue-state judge couldn't ignore it. The first primary was tossed out after Ganim had won reelection in November, requiring him to get through a reordered primary and another election to remain mayor. Ganim is in his eighth term as mayor, and his associates have also taken heat for their actions in the 2019 election cycle. Is it any wonder Democrats control nearly every large city?

The political establishment and their media cheerleaders absolutely loved the documentary *Kill Chain: The Cyber War on America's Elections*, a dystopian narrative centered around the American left's fear that Trump would steal the 2020 election

---

8   US Attorney's Office, District of New Jersey, "Political Organizer and Former President of City Council of Atlantic City Charged with Submitting Fraudulent Mail-In Ballots," February 1, 2024, https://www.justice.gov/usao-nj/pr/political-organizer-and-former-president-city-council-atlantic-city-charged-submitting.

9   Division of Criminal Justice, "Five Charged Following Investigation into Handling of Absentee Ballots in 2023 Elections," State of Connecticut Judicial Branch, February 21, 2025, https://portal.ct.gov/dcj/press-releases/division-of-criminal-justice/02212025bridgeportarrests?language=en_US.

and entrench himself permanently in power. It released several months before the election and featured Democratic senators like Mark Warner (Virginia), Ron Wyden (Oregon), and Amy Klobuchar (Minnesota), who suddenly had nothing else to say on the subject of unsecured elections once it turned out Trump wasn't the one doing the stealing. The same people who promoted and cameoed in *Kill Chain* would go on to spend the next four years labeling the majority of Americans who came to distrust the 2020 election results as "dangerous to democracy."

If one digs deeply enough into the never-ending news cycle, they'll find treasure even in the mainstream media's archives. Dr. John Lott, president of the Crime Prevention Research Center, wrote a column[10] published by *Newsweek* in August 2020 using detailed research to demonstrate exactly why President Trump was up in arms over the sudden changes to state election laws and procedures that would flood the election with countless millions more mail-in ballots than ever handled before.

Lott's research noted that the vast majority of European nations either strictly forbid mail-in balloting or have extremely strict controls over the process. Mexico, Israel, Russia, and many other nations focal in today's world, recognize the threat posed by mail-in balloting and make it practically impossible to do anything but vote in person. Dr. Lott was one of many of sound mind and educated opinion called "delusional." He said it best in his column by writing, "If concern about voter fraud with mail-in ballots is delusional, it is a delusion that is shared by most of the world."

This worldwide phenomenon has persisted to this very day, as the January 3, 2026, capture of Venezuelan dictator and pres-

---

10   John R. Lott Jr., "Voting Fraud Is a Real Concern. Just Look Around the World | Opinion," *Newsweek*, August 4, 2020, https://www.newsweek.com/voting-fraud-real-concern-just-look-around-world-opinion-1522535.

ident Nicolas Maduro by US forces reminds us. Maduro held on to power in 2024 in an election so rotten, that most of the world decried its outcome. The Friedrich Naumann Foundation for Freedom detailed the heist:[11]

> The presidential election in Venezuela took place on 28 July 2024. It ended with proven fraud: Chavista incumbent Nicolás Maduro allegedly won with 51.95 per cent of the votes cast compared to 43.18 per cent for the opposition candidate, Edmundo González. In a brilliantly prepared process, supported by volunteers in 58,000 volunteer groups, the clever opposition obtained copies of around 85 per cent of the election files (Spanish: 'actas de escrutinio'), the results from over 30,000 polling stations in the country, digitised them on election night and calculated the true result as an estimate from this huge sample: around 67 per cent for González and just 30 per cent for Maduro, proving clear electoral fraud by the Maduro regime!

The world is quick to point out dictators maintaining power in Venezuela or sub-Saharan African nations, but slow to extend the same skepticism to elections in Western nations, especially the United States. The rest of the world runs from mail-in balloting while Democratic run states move at breakneck speed to expand the practice to the greatest extent imaginable. While glaring instances of electoral manipulation are widely acknowledged in distant history—from those noted in this chapter to others,

---

11   Karl-Heinz Paqué, "An Electoral Fraudster as President of Venezuela?," Friedrich Naumann Foundation for Freedom, accessed January 19, 2026, https://www.freiheit. org/venezuela-electoral-fraudster-president-venezuela.

including the 1876 Rutherford B. Hayes–Samuel Tilden election, Lyndon Johnson's exploits in Texas, and claims surrounding the electoral votes of Illinois and Texas that pushed John F. Kennedy over Richard Nixon in 1960—today's academic hall monitors have no choice but to distance themselves from modern examples today's voters lived through.

Long-suffering Washingtonians watched Christine Gregoire topple Republican Dino Rossi in the state's 2004 gubernatorial race *after* Rossi won not only the initial count, but the recount. After lengthy deliberations, miraculously found absentee ballots in King County put Gregoire on top by 133 votes. That state has remained without a Republican governor for four decades.

Then there is the case of Al Franken, the Democrat who managed to fumble his US Senate seat to Republican Norm Coleman in Minnesota while running alongside Barack Obama in his 2008 national landslide. That loss was apparent until Marc Elias, the Democrats' ace when it came to the legal theft of elections, dove in. In *Rigged,* Mollie Hemingway wrote of Elias:[12]

> He further cemented his legend when he ran Al Franken's 2008 recount and legal challenges, which overturned the result of the election and led to a radical transformation of the country. The day after the election, Franken had lost the race to Republican senator Norm Coleman, but by only 727 votes. In swooped Elias and his team of attorneys and experts, who systematically set out over the course of six months to turn the 727-vote loss into a 312-vote victory. The ultimate decision in Franken's favor gave Democrats a

---

12   Mollie Hemingway, *Rigged: How the Media, Big Tech, and the Democrats Seized Our Elections* (Regnery Publishing, 2021), 15.

supermajority in the Senate, which they used to
enact the sweeping health care legislation known
as Obamacare.

Hemingway, along with many others, noted Broward County's efforts to keep Bill Nelson in the Senate against Florida Governor Rick Scott, who narrowly upended Nelson in 2018. In the same election, Ron DeSantis narrowly defeated Andrew Gillum, paving the way for Florida to become a solid red state. His ascent to the governorship was nearly derailed by Broward's Supervisor of Elections Brenda Snipes and would have been had Republican leaders not circled the wagons on election night once the cheating became obvious.

Future historians will judge these listings and make an attempt to disparage the selections for the sake of partisanship. In the interest of fairness, I must also point out that mail-in balloting is the cheat method of choice when Republicans play the game, too. North Carolina Republican Mark Harris had his 2018 congressional victory squashed[13] when news broke that his operatives rigged his election with mail-in ballot fraud. The race was overturned by the State Board of Elections, which ordered a new race.

Anyone who brings up the most obvious conspiracy of all in modern discourse is immediately shouted down, called an "election denier," and deemed a "threat to democracy." Unfortunately for those quick to judge, history has our backs. Election fraud is the norm, as are all efforts by men in power to stay in power.

---

13   Khorri Atkinson, "North Carolina Board Calls for New Election in Disputed House Race," Axios, February 21, 2019, https://www.axios.com/2019/02/21/north-carolina-election-board-fraud-9th-district.

CHAPTER 5

Letters of a Lifetime

After spending a few days zipping across the world on a plane and processing through Manas Air Base in Kyrgyzstan, I finally landed at Kandahar Airfield, Afghanistan—better known as KAF. The sprawling base was constantly under attack, usually by indirect fire, but sometimes by suicide attacks targeting the perimeter of the base. It stunk like hell, thanks to the lingering scent of a waste reservoir colloquially called the "KAF Poo Pond," which stewed in the triple-digit heat and served as a target for the Taliban fighters with their Chinese-made rockets. Kandahar Province is the symbolic homeland of the Taliban and a place they were not willing to simply walk away from.

Those early days were slow and spent adjusting to being ten time zones away from my starting point. I had flown over with Staff Sergeant Brent Head, the senior noncommissioned officer in the S2 section, which I was leading in absence of its usual captain. Sergeant Head was an infantryman earlier in his career and, after taking the beating associated with that line of work for long enough, moved over to the Military Intelligence field. He was a seasoned combat veteran with a knack for molding soldiers and, I would soon find out, an understanding of what it took to turn green officers into capable ones in a short time frame. We were awaiting a Black Hawk flight out to Shindand Air Base, a short distance from the Iranian border in Regional Command-

West (RC-West), where we would kick off our one-year tour with a short relief in place of Task Force Ready, a Germany-based aviation unit on its way back home. While we were waiting one day for a call that could come at any moment, on the same day President Barack Obama sacked Stanley McChrystal from the effort in Afghanistan over a controversial *Rolling Stone* article, a rocket attack struck KAF, and all the base's alert systems began blaring, followed by the English-accented "Rocket attack, rocket attack" proclamation, given that we were on a British-run airfield. Being the rule-abiding lieutenant I was, I executed the standard operating procedure for an indirect fire attack exactly as I had been instructed. I dove under the bunks, then immediately began to move toward a bunker. As I grabbed my rifle and helmet and began to run out of the tent, I caught Sergeant Head's eye. If looks could have killed, I would have dropped dead right then and there. He had never moved from his bed or even bothered to put the magazine he was reading down. It may have been my first such attack, but it wasn't Sergeant Head's. I would never flinch at a rocket attack again, and there were plenty of opportunities. If it doesn't hit you before you even heard the rocket attack, then you never really had anything to worry about in the first place.

I'd love to look back and write about the early days of my Afghanistan deployment and remember myself as a natural in combat operations but that wasn't the case. I was competent enough to take immediate ownership of our intelligence summary, which we inherited from Task Force Ready and continued to adapt over time, making it the most widely disseminated intelligence summary in RC-West and a source of valuable information for coalition forces in the region. I was also capable of withstanding scrutiny from senior officers and defending my intelligence assessments early in the tour, but emotionally, I was struggling with the understanding I was going to soon lose Dad. Mail call was undoubtedly the highlight of my first two months in country, and Dad did his part to leave me with handwritten memories I draw from today, long after his death. We would talk every couple of days from the phone tent, but true to form, Dad put his best words in ink.

In a letter dated June 28, 2010, Dad reminded me about the importance of maintaining a positive, can-do attitude in the face of adversity, which has stuck with me on the front lines of the battle for national election integrity. In that letter, he wrote:

> Your attitude is everything. Additionally, your attitude is your altitude. Those with a poor attitude suck energy from a group, those with a positive attitude inject energy into a group. Maintaining a good attitude is hard yet rewarding. You feel good about yourself when you look in the mirror to shave, you reward those who love you by removing fear and uncertainty from their lives. Because a good attitude reinforces the belief in those who love you that you are in fact everything they think you to be and in fact possess all the qualities they have and still attribute to you. It is a gift to those you love and removes uncertainty from their lives.
>
> A poor attitude is quickly noted by others. Superiors weigh you by it, peers judge you by it, subordinates respond to it for they are particularly afraid and need guidance that is positive. The enemy takes advantage of it if able. Attitude maintenance is a difficult thing, yet essential to both our physical and mental well being and in

this manner, our performance. There remain 24 hours in each day and they are constant as are the moon's pull upon the ocean tides. Your attitude impacts those you love by encouraging and reinforcing that which they believe or conversely, if it is poor, calling into question the validity of that which they believe. Remember always son, love knows no time zones.

Across these time zones Dad sends you his love and his hope that your heart and mind be refreshed in our love and our prayers.

I had no idea I would share those words with thousands over a decade later, let alone in a published book, but they are vividly stamped into my mind and serve as a reminder that others are watching me. Mail took more than two weeks to make it between the United States and our scattered operating bases in Afghanistan, but I made sure to write in addition to emails and calls. Since then, I've always had an affinity for the written word and prefer to write handwritten "thank you" notes or greetings over typewritten ones. When I would complain about our living conditions, which were very primitive compared to other unit dwellings in country, Dad reminded me of his conditions he experienced in combat, which made things fall into perspective once again. I *could* handle sleeping during parts of the day with insufficient cooling. After all, those who had gone before me had it much worse.

Sergeant Head and I worked around the clock, splitting graveyard and days shifts as we got the intelligence operation off the ground. A few weeks after we arrived, we finally received reinforcements to help distribute the workload and create intelligence products while briefings, staff meetings, sleeping, and eating had to get done. Days felt tremendously long, as I had been warned by others who had served in our post-9/11 conflicts, but at the same time, weeks would disappear into one another. Wake up, eat, work out, take up shift, clock out, eat, sleep. Repeat.

Within the Army, as with the other service branches, there exists a competitive rivalry in which soldiers of various specialties, particularly those of the combat arms, mercilessly demean those assigned to noncombat specialties as soft, unmotivated, or perpetual residents of the forward operating bases, otherwise known as "fobbits." We, of course, returned the jabs in terms of intelligence, brainpower, ability to write complete sentences, and our lack of interest in eating crayons or playing in the dirt, while also bragging about having marketable skills once we hung up our uniforms. I never directly engaged the enemy, nor was I directly engaged by the enemy, so I don't have a Combat Action Badge or any valor designators on my ribbon rack; still, a year compiling intelligence in a largely uncharted and unscouted region the size of the US state of Georgia within a warlord-run nation creates a tension that is hard to break loose from. Intelligence officers can't afford to be wrong, especially in a constantly changing environment in which the enemy has predictable tactics and weaponry one week and then may completely adapt on all fronts the next. Intelligence drives operations, and the intelligence officer has the unique role in which he *must* critique the plans of the commander and operations staff if it is going to wind up leading friendly forces into a death trap.

I took plenty of verbal beatings early on that helped me get my mind right and "push it away." Near the end of August, the unit began to plan for my departure on emergency leave as Dad neared the end. Late in the evening of September 7, 2010, my brother David's birthday, I called home at the end of a shift to check on Dad. My mother answered the phone and said, "He just passed." Early the next morning, I was on a helicopter back to KAF, then on to Kuwait, and then, after spending just one night there, on a commercial flight back to Texas. Dad wanted to be interred in Arlington National Cemetery, but thanks to a significant backlog of veterans receiving burials with full honors, his ceremony would have to wait until January, when I wouldn't be able to make it thanks to my deployment demands. His nonmilitary service was held just down the street from where I grew up, at Griffith Memorial Church in Jackson, Mississippi. My brothers Jon and David were both there, as was my best friend growing up, Jimmy Davis. Jimmy, who wound up marrying David's daughter (my niece), practically grew up at my house and once joked he would write a book called *Growing Up Keshel*. He'd had his ups and downs with my Dad, but on this afternoon, he wept as if he had lost his own.

Our longtime barber, Tim Biard, who knew my Dad in a way few others did, delivered one eulogy, and I delivered a second wearing my dress greens with a newly stitched combat patch. Dad had asked me to wear exactly that as I made my remarks. In a way, feeling confident of his eternal destiny and hurting with him over the debilitating cancer, I felt relieved that he had peace. The human side of me missed him and knew I'd have to take "push it away" to heart if I wanted to maintain my sanity for the next nine months of my tour overseas. Ten days hurried by, and in a blink, I found myself back in Kuwait. This time, it took several days to get out of there. I finally caught a seat on a C-17 to KAF, and after a day there, made it back to Shindand in the middle of the night.

A lot had changed in the two weeks I had been gone. The nights were much cooler, a welcome relief, but Captain Bryan Kolano had finally arrived in country after being permitted to tend to the birth of his first child over the summer. Our S2 section finally had two officers and a full complement of noncommissioned officers, which would make us much more efficient. We now had two experienced officers capable of leading the section. I had progressed substantially in just a couple of months, thanks largely to having to sink or swim and from having had others around me working to sharpen my skills and making me learn from mistakes.

With Dad's passing behind me, I felt like I was able to immerse myself in getting the mission done. I had understandably spent a lot of time bracing for the final goodbye and having to temporarily leave the mission behind, but once I returned, I felt a stirring to do him proud and quit feeling sorry for myself. My focus improved, my responsibilities increased, and so did my capabilities as an intelligence officer. With the repetitive nature of staff work, it is easy to repackage the same assessment, stopping to polish them up only briefly. Digging a bit deeper into daily activities, intelligence assessments, and mission requirements made it possible to create actionable intelligence briefings that properly prepared our pilots for their missions.

A major confirmation for me that I was maturing as an intelligence officer with a nose for forecasting occurred during a series of deliberate operations in Badghis Province. Our aviation task force consisted of three helicopter platforms—AH-64D Apache attack helicopters, UH-60 Black Hawks, and CH-47 Chinooks—and was regularly called upon to provide support to Special Operations forces in RC-West and our international allies. My intelligence section provided critical support for these operations, analyzing lunar data, terrain, civil considerations, enemy equipment and weapons capabilities, and the dissemination of any late-breaking reporting deemed valid enough to impact the mission. The Black Hawks and Chinooks then inserted ground forces under the watchful eye of the Apache air weapons teams, armed to the teeth with 30 mm guns, rockets, and most impressively, Hellfire missiles that could be outfitted with a wide variety of warheads—including those designed to strike inside caves and cook everything inside of them.

Early in the deployment, before I left for home on emergency leave, an insertion into this region had gone sideways, resulting in significant damage to aircraft and a number of casualties to the ground troops. The intensified coalition presence in RC-West had kicked up a pissed-off anthill of insurgents that had been relatively dormant over the years for lack of kinetic operations. During President Obama's 2010 troop surge, that would change not only in RC-West but also in RC-North along the borders of Uzbekistan and Tajikistan, primarily in Kunduz Province, where our widely dispersed brigade, known as Task Force Iron Eagle, also provided air support. Shortly after I returned to Afghanistan, we got word we were going back into the same village. The *Intelligence Preparation of the Battlefield* played an important role in determining whether our second visit would succeed or fail.

Black Hawks and Chinooks are lift and cargo aircraft, respectively. Black Hawks provide routine personnel transportation between bases during day-to-day operations and rapidly insert troops during deliberate operations, sometimes called "air assault" missions. Chinooks often carry out the same mission and can carry substantially more troops or be outfitted to insert heavy equipment. Neither platform is relied upon to bring firepower against the enemy, although they carry crew chiefs to provide defensive cover fire with door guns. The Apaches, better described as "flying death machines," have sophisticated weaponry, optics, and technology valued in the tens of millions of dollars designed specifically to eradicate enemy personnel, heavy equipment, or defensive positions. Saddam Hussein's army couldn't handle them, and I knew it firsthand from having watched my brother David's gun tapes from the 2003 invasion as he wiped out tanks and armored personnel carriers as if they were pixels on a video game. Somehow, the primitive and severely outgunned insurgent fighters of Afghanistan had figured out exactly how to stymie Apaches, and it was our job to help regain the edge that should have been guaranteed by having such superior weaponry.

Intelligence work has changed drastically since the end of World War II and the advent of the ability to transmit information in real time over any distance. In John Keegan's *Intelligence in War*, the point was made that for coalition forces to be successful in the so-called War on Terror, a reversion to primitive intelligence operations is necessary thanks to the difficulty in combating enemies wearing no uniform and employing tactics designed to fool modern intelligence gathering methods and combat procedures.[1] Insurgents throughout both Afghanistan and Iraq had learned that Apaches used infrared radar to detect the heat signatures of combatants, which provided a massive fighting advantage at night the enemy could not approach. By covering themselves under burlap sacks or hiding under tree canopies along rivers, they learned they could frustrate the efforts of the Apache air weapons teams to locate and subsequently vaporize them.

I reviewed what we knew of the first insertion and plotted everything I could on a map. I had always favored primitive means of intelligence analysis, much like how I prefer basic data and analytical methods in my work on elections over the "advanced analytics" and polling that the so-called experts, who always get it wrong, swear by. Likewise, I felt that modern Army

---

1   John Keegan, *Intelligence in War: Knowledge of the Enemy from Napoleon to Al-Qaeda*, (Alfred A. Knopf, 2003), 317.

intelligence training focused too much on advanced systems, which could fail for a variety of reasons, rather than training the minds of its officers to think like the enemy and rely on methods of analyzing data and information in ways that could be easily replicated in any theater of operations. There has never been a power outage impacting a map or pattern analysis wheel, whereas our messaging systems in Afghanistan regularly failed and went out countrywide, often grinding operations to a halt.

My recreated map of the operations area painted a clear picture. The enemy had engaged our ground forces with both small arms and machine-gun fire and rocket-propelled grenades from the river running alongside the village. We requested imagery support from higher headquarters to get a better view of the infiltration area and compared it with other databases showing us different aspects of the terrain, and this helped focus our enemy assessment on what was both *most likely* and *most dangerous*: The enemy, if not caught totally off guard, was likely to engage coalition forces the same way they did when they had success in the first operation—from the cover of the tree canopies to elude detection by the Apaches while inflicting casualties and potentially disabling one or more aircraft, which would be a massive public relations win for the Taliban.

This time, equipped with precise coordinates provided by the Task Force Comanche S2 section, our Apache crews quickly identified enemy fighters looking to take advantage of key terrain, as predicted. Those insurgents never stood a chance and, this time, were cut down en masse with no casualties to ground troops. Rather than dwelling on negative outcomes from the first insertion, the operations and intelligence sections took key lessons into the next operation and delivered a devastating blow to enemy fighters in the region. The lesson for me was that precision and specificity are much better qualities in forecasting and planning than swinging wildly and hoping you get it right.

The growth of my analytical skillset wasn't limited to tactical considerations. My nightly activities included reading open-source items to inform my understanding of the overall political situation in Afghanistan, which impacted overall coalition strategy and trickled down into RC-West. Afghanistan's parliamentary elections took place around the time Captain Kolano and I traded places, and the stench of corruption lingered long until after I had returned to the country from bidding farewell to Dad. While Western mainstream news media won't report on their own fraudulently run elections, they were as happy then as they are today to sound the alarm on elections in places like Afghanistan. This is from *The New York Times*, September 24, 2010,[2] which claimed results would be untrustworthy in a third of Afghanistan's precincts:

> The complaints to provincial election commissions have so far included video clips showing ballot stuffing; the strong-arming of election officials by candidates' agents; and even the handcuffing and detention of election workers.
>
> In some places, election officials themselves are alleged to have carried out the fraud; in others, government employees did, witnesses said. One video showed election officials and a candidate's representatives haggling over the price of votes.

---

2   Alissa J. Rubin and Carlotta Gall, "Widespread Fraud Seen in Latest Afghan Elections," *New York Times*, September 24, 2010, https://www.nytimes.com/2010/09/25/world/asia/25afghan.html. Sharifullah Sahak and an Afghan employee of The New York Times also contributed.

As time ticked by, investigations revealed a picture so grim, it had to make Westerners wonder what the hell all the bloodshed and investment was for. By October, *The Guardian* reported nearly a quarter of the country's 5.6 million ballots had been disqualified.[3] Vote-buying schemes were rampant through the country, and in Taliban-controlled areas, turnout reached ludicrous levels. Thousands of ballots at a time were discovered in fields, guaranteeing that all efforts to bring stability and security to the "Graveyard of Empires" were offered in vain.

There we were—nine years into the combat effort in Afghanistan post-9/11, and the country couldn't even run an election without almost a quarter of its ballots being tossed. This would be like if more than thirty-six million ballots were disqualified in the 2020 US election, which was still over a decade away as I read reports in disgust and began to question if I had the will to continue serving in a war that seemed increasingly pointless. One thing I had no doubt over was that depriving a nation of a free and fair vote will never be acceptable, tolerable, or allowed to stand.

---

3 Associated Press, "Quarter of Afghan Election Ballots Thrown Out for Fraud," *Guardian*, October 20, 2010, https://www.theguardian.com/world/2010/oct/20/afghanistan-election-fraud.

CHAPTER 6

Changing Seasons

If you expected to read a story about a military career straight out of *Band of Brothers*, you picked up the wrong book. Regardless of any degree of talent or skill, or life experience I've gained since serving, I was a standard staff officer. Had I stayed in uniform long enough, I may have commanded a company and would have likely been promoted twice by now as I neared retirement eligibility, but a long military career wasn't in the cards for me. The deployment to Afghanistan was the high point of my career and fundamental to my development into what Democracy Docket describes as a "prominent election conspiracy theorist."[1]

Something had gone awry one night as I worked a dusk-to-dawn shift around the halfway point of the deployment. When time allowed, I read during graveyard hours, mixing professionally broadening subjects with favorites such as historical fiction, sports, or military strategy. My brain had been filled with military schoolhouse doctrine singing the praises of counterinsurgency operations, which hindsight shows us failed miserably in our post-9/11 conflicts, and had begun to question the efficiency of our operations in Afghanistan thanks to my newly acquired knowledge from having seen it with my own two eyes. Was firing

---

1   Matt Cohen, "A Prominent Election Conspiracy Theorist is Setting His Sights on Michigan For 2026," Democracy Docket, July 24, 2025, https://www. democracydocket.com/news-alerts/a-prominent-election-conspiracy-theorist-is-setting-his-sights-on-michigan-for-2026/.

$70,000 of Hellfire missiles at $50 of spare parts assemblies that were used to make repeaters really a pathway to victory in the "Graveyard of Empires"?

Counterinsurgency in Modern Warfare, by Daniel Marston and Carter Malkasian, altered my career plans by providing critical knowledge about the true fates of historical counterinsurgency operations, and the often futile efforts made by powers over the centuries to assert control.[2] Afghanistan is the size of Texas and a neighbor to six other nations that senior enemy commanders used as safe havens while we were busy mowing down their bottom-rung fighters with the most advanced weaponry in the history of warfare. Through classified channels, I could access a frequently updated document called the "patch chart," which showed prospective brigade combat team deployments extending all the way out to 2018, nearly eight years later. There I was, twenty-six years old, reading about the failures of counterinsurgency throughout history and staring at a future that promised continued journeys to fight in an unwinnable conflict until at least my mid-thirties.

I returned home from that deployment hoping things would change in the world and that public fatigue over the fruitless missions would set in and send the military back to regular duties, such as training with allies and being used as a defensive force rather than an expeditionary one. I moved to Arizona with my now-ex-wife for continued military education, and while there, my first child, a daughter, was born. Eden arrived just as I was receiving orders to report to Fort Wainwright, Alaska, to serve as the primary S2 of the First Stryker Brigade Combat Team's cavalry squadron. That brigade, in similar fashion to my first unit, was just returning from a deployment to Afghanistan and was

---

2   Daniel Marston and Carter Malkasian, eds., *Counterinsurgency in Modern Warfare* (Osprey Publishing, 2008).

expected to transition to a mission focused on the security of the Pacific Command area of operations in line with what I was hoping for as the future of the post-9/11 Army. Regional commanders and the Pentagon were growing increasingly concerned about Chinese aggression in the South China Sea and beyond, which remains a persistent threat and fear looming over many nations suddenly on less-than-ideal terms with a persistently ambitious China.

Months into my tour of duty, on an icy, below-zero December unit exercise at Joint Base Elmendorf-Richardson, I read another book that further entrenched me into my increasingly contrarian viewpoints, putting me at odds with our nation's hawkish foreign policy goals. Dr. Ron Paul's *Liberty Defined* likened the modern United States to the Roman Empire, which pursued expansionism while ignoring extensive domestic decay, unraveling, and social upheaval for centuries prior to collapsing.[3] I became increasingly cynical about investing more time and energy in Afghanistan and—just like when I watched our own government stand beside the results of that country's blatantly corrupt 2010 elections—again pondered what the future looked like out of uniform.

After nearly a year in Alaska and seeking to provide stability for my family, I grew frustrated with the constant back-and-forth over forthcoming missions and rumored deployments to Afghanistan and set out to pursue the tedious process of becoming a civilian. I put my paperwork in to leave the Army, drew the wrath of senior officers in my brigade, and by December 2013, was off active duty. While fond memories and "what ifs" sometimes set in, I have no doubt my useful service to the United States Army had elapsed by the time my mind became convinced that there was no way for us to win the war in Afghanistan. Joe

---

3   Ron Paul, *Liberty Defined: 50 Essential Issues That Affect Our Freedom* (Grand Central Publishing, 2012), 63.

Biden's disastrous withdrawal would hammer home that hypothesis with a resounding thud almost eight years later. I'm proud I served and carried on the family legacy and—despite my disagreements with our reckless and inefficient use of the most powerful fighting force in the world—am thankful for the leadership opportunities afforded me and the crucible to test my brainpower under stressful circumstances no civilian job can recreate. I would not have the confidence and ability to separate fact from fiction, or important from trivial, that I have today without those formative years in service.

The next seven years were full of broken bridges and lost trails that all blended together to sharpen my skill set for what would come in November 2020. I started out with a Houston-based oil and gas company with a penchant for hiring veterans, only to find myself on the wrong end of commodity prices and a layoff that happened just five days before my son, Eli, was born in 2015. Having never been unemployed, I then panicked and took the first job I could get my hands on, which I quit in seven weeks. After an unconventional job search at the end of 2015, I wound up working in an analyst position at the Texas Medical Center, where I was employed when I made my accurate prediction of Trump's 2016 victory. My third child, Willow, came into my life a month after Trump shocked the world.

Thanks to a failed merger, my number was eventually called when I had my second layoff in two years. Rather than panicking this time around, I took my time looking for a job commensurate with my skills, experience, and education, which was about to include an MBA degree from Liberty University. Spring turned to summer, and summer turned to fall, while I remained on the sidelines. As I dwelled in unemployment and personal turmoil, I came to grips with the sad reality that I had never truly been grateful for the employment-related blessings God had sent my way over this first decade of my post-college career, which included nearly six years in the military and approaching four in the private sector at that point. I had sadly forgotten Dad's admonition to practice proper attitude maintenance and ensure I was instilling confidence in those who relied upon me, such as my three young children all under six years old. After realizing I needed to take control of my thoughts, emotions, and actions, I experienced one of the most fortunate breaks of my life...

Delivering Mexican food for seven dollars per hour.

On paper, this turned out to be the worst job I ever had financially; however, in practice, the job was priceless and taught me everything I needed to relearn to be successful in what the future would hold. All I had to do was be on time, in the right place, and in the right uniform, which is one of the first things a soldier learns to do in service and something that gives him a high likelihood of developing into a reliable future leader. No one needed me to turn water into wine or continuously prove my mettle as a veteran or former military officer. This job, I believe, was divinely provided to break me of my pride.

With a difficult life lesson out of the way, I transitioned into a salesman at the beginning of 2018, having been placed by a military headhunter with a local technology company selling traffic control equipment. I excelled at using my energy to find new business all over the country and came to cover more territory than anyone else in the company. Just like today, I was known for high-personal energy, an ability to instantly connect with audiences, interjecting humor into otherwise mundane discussions about statistics or technical data, and commanding the room with military precision. By mid-2019, I was traveling coast-to-coast, closing huge deals, and planting the company flag into new ground on a weekly basis; I was ready to take over the world. But during one March 2020 trip to Wisconsin, that world came to a screeching halt. COVID-19 had arrived in grave fashion, hailed by the media with flashing red graphics, endless talk of despair, and most damaging, a near-total shutdown of our country's economy. The plot to remove the president was at full throttle, and with very little left to do in a job I once saw as a permanent pathway to success, I pondered how I should push back against all of the lies, fake polling, and rule-changing happening at breakneck speed.

I have little doubt my time in the traffic control industry, with its high travel demands and sink-or-swim level of personal responsibility, prepared me to handle the workload I never knew would exist in those days leading up to November 3, 2020. Soon, I would advance down the most uncertain trail of them all.

CHAPTER 7

Three November

If you search my name today on a mainstream search engine, you'll find hate articles and critiques labeling me as an "election denier" or other descriptive terms stipulated by so-called experts who have one thing in common—being frequently wrong. Allies often think I received some sort of political education while a member of the Military Intelligence Corps, when my service there simply honed the talents I already owned as a God-given endowment. Stories have circulated about what I must have been doing during Donald Trump's first term while waiting around for "the steal." I was a politically engaged private citizen doing my best to impact local change, meeting with my local representatives and volunteering in grassroots efforts, with bragging rights among friends and family members for pegging the correct outcome of an election "the experts" said Hillary Clinton was 98 percent likely to win. I had been throwing around the idea of running for the Texas House of Representatives if Phil King, the longtime office holder in my new district, declined to run for reelection at any point.

Dad would have chided me for my poor attitude maintenance in 2020, the year global control freaks destroyed the Western world for political gain, but most likely would have understood my anger. Having relocated to just west of Fort Worth in 2019, I smelled a scam from the moment COVID-19 hit the states and knew it would be leveraged against the Trump administration in an all-hands-on-deck effort to make their time in Washington, DC, a one-term arrangement.

My personal involvement in the 2020 election, aside from my harboring hope that President Trump would be reelected, begin restoring the US economy, and resume his popular 2016 campaign agenda, began in the summer when all the ridiculously bad polling indicating a Joe Biden landslide started hitting the news. Concerned friends and family came to me for reassurance and then asked if I thought I could repeat my on-the-money 2016 performance. Thanks to the fraudulent media polling, online betting markets offered lucrative odds if you were willing to put your money on Trump, like 3 to 1 in Pennsylvania or 2 to 1 in Florida, depending on the day and which polls were being pushed the hardest. I wagered thousands of dollars using the same methods to inform my predictions that I had employed in 2016, with no idea of just how poorly things would turn out with the impending quasi election, and how badly it would make me lose my ass financially.

Without the last-minute and mostly illegal changes to 2020 election procedures—like all the one-time allowances for no excuse, mail-in ballots, extended early voting, or outright cheating—the 2020 election looked like a more likely win *on paper* for Trump than the 2016 election did. None of the mainline red states appeared to be in play, despite what polling said, as Americans watched a Biden–Harris campaign bus get chased off the highways in Texas.[1] Biden had been clobbered in early Democratic primaries, only to run off with the nomination after the Democrats forced every candidate but Bernie Sanders to drop

---

[1] Kate McGee, Jeremy Schwartz, and Abby Livingston, "Biden Camp Cancels Multiple Texas Events After a 'Trump Train' Surrounded a Campaign Bus," The Texas Tribune, October 31, 2020, https://www.texastribune.org/2020/10/31/biden-trump-texas-bus/.

out of the nominating contest to force a head-to-head Super Tuesday matchup, which Biden eked out, generating enough momentum to make his nomination inevitable. Once he had become the apparent nominee, no one wanted to see his campaign events, which the media quickly wrote off as "responsible citizenship"—crediting the no-shows with a refusal to spread COVID-19 to the vulnerable, a stark contrast from the unruly Trump supporters who supposedly wanted to bring about the mass extinction of senior citizens. You couldn't get a haircut, but junk science suggested Walmart was safe and that the virus passed overhead if seated at a restaurant as opposed to standing around in the waiting area.

I've taken plenty of heat for downplaying many 2020 election claims related to anecdotal accounts, such as the volume of yard signs favoring Trump, door-knocker testimonies, and even crowd size, but no one can deny that the difference in enthusiasm behind both campaigns was obvious to any fair-minded individual. The polling in September and October was reminiscent of that circulating in 2016, such as NBC with a Biden fourteen-point lead,[2] twice the margin Barack Obama beat John McCain by and suggesting a margin of victory of over twenty-one million votes, which bordered on criminality.

The media were also busy setting the stage for what would transpire once election season finally came to a halt. Hawkfish, a political data firm that former New York City mayor Michael Bloomberg founded, developed a theory that became widely circulated in the press:[3] A "red mirage" would emerge as ballots

---

2   NBC News and The Wall Street Journal, "200781 NBC/WSJ October Post-Debate Poll 1b," October 2020, https://www.documentcloud.org/documents/7221894-200781-NBCWSJ-October-Post-Debate-Poll-1b.html.

3   Christopher Zara, "What Is a 'Red Mirage'? Michael Bloomberg's Hawkfish Warns of a Nightmarish Election Crisis," Fast Company, September 1, 2020, https://www.fastcompany.com/90546007/what-is-a-red-mirage-michael-bloombergs-hawkfish-warns-of-a-nightmarish-election-crisis.

were tabulated on election night, suggesting a dominant Trump reelection victory, but as mail-in ballots continued to be counted, a "blue shift" would take over, nudging the battlegrounds in favor of Biden. Talking heads had no reservations putting trust in polling no matter how badly that had blown up on them in 2016, and elected officials did their part, too. On November 2, Pennsylvania Attorney General Josh Shapiro, now the state's governor, tweeted,[4] "If all the votes are added up in PA, Trump is going to lose." Looking back, in the context of his complaint about Trump's legal teams challenging the mail-in ballots, Shapiro should have used the term "ballots" instead of "votes" to describe what would be "added up."

Shapiro had been banking on a seven-week delay between the mailing of ballots and Election Day, the latter point being the one Steve Bannon would reference over the following years as "Three November." Not every state went crazy with changes like the battleground states did, but there were adjustments made all over the map. Texas Governor Greg Abbott used his emergency powers to authorize a third week of early voting, but true to tradition and disinterested in fighting for space in the early voting lines, I strolled out to cast my vote first thing in the morning that Three November in Parker County, enjoying the mild temperature underneath a perfect blue sky. With that duty in the rearview mirror, the waiting began.

With thousands wagered, I had predicted Trump would again win the battleground states of Florida, North Carolina, Pennsylvania, Michigan, Wisconsin, and Arizona, flip Nevada, and punch his ticket for a second term. Notably, I was not tracking Georgia as a competitive state, as Trump had won it in 2016

---

4   Josh Shapiro (@JoshShapiroPA), "If all the votes are added up in PA, Trump is going to lose," X, October 31, 2020, https://x.com/JoshShapiroPA/status/1322640510637477889.

with a 5.1 percent margin of victory, while neither candidate spent much time or many resources there. Additionally, while polling is mostly useless to me, *The Atlanta Journal-Constitution*–sponsored poll by Landmark Communications measured a seven-point Trump lead at the beginning of September,[5] suggesting the campaigns would be digging in on other states thought to be in play. That pollster had Trump leading Clinton in every poll in 2016, and Trump wound up winning by a higher margin than the last poll had predicted.[6] Georgia, based on polling and the relative lack of interest from campaigns to schedule visits, seemed like a lock for Trump in the mid-to-high single digits. As it turned out, Georgia would find itself at the center of the 2020 controversy within the next forty-eight hours.

My predictions that Trump would carry those battleground states were staked to the same traditional indicators that had helped nail my calls in 2016, especially in the states registering by party—Florida, North Carolina, Pennsylvania, Arizona, and Nevada. While the mainstream media fantasized about a Biden victory in Florida, I knew it was unlikely for many reasons, including the fact that Florida loves incumbent presidents, backed George H. W. Bush in 1992 in a doomed reelection campaign, and hadn't voted against one since 1980 when it spurned Jimmy Carter for Ronald Reagan. Additionally, President Trump moved to Florida in his first term, giving him a home field advantage that placed undeniable headwind against any likelihood of Biden winning the Sunshine State and dooming Trump's prospects

---

5 Greg Bluestein, "WSB Poll: Trump Builds Lead Over Biden in Georgia after RNC," *Atlanta Journal-Constitution*, September 2, 2020, https://www.ajc.com/politics/politics-blog/wsb-poll-trump-builds-lead-over-biden-in-georgia-after-rnc/B7XVX4WYHJG4BIQMVTM2AJEEQM/.

6 Landmark Communications, "Landmark/Rosetta Stone Releases Final Sunday Poll of Georgia Voters for President, Senate," November 7, 2016, https://landmarkcommunications.net/landmarkrosetta-stone-releases-final-sunday-poll-of-georgia-voters-for-president-senate/.

before the election even moved to the Central time zone. And then there was the party registration indicator, which told me all I needed to know.[7]

FLORIDA - VOTER REGISTRATION INDEX TRACKER - CAPT. S. KESHEL						
ELECTION YEAR	2000	2004	2008	2012	2016	2020
REGISTERED DEM	3,822,912	4,291,769	4,791,642	4,814,412	4,877,749	5,303,254
REGISTERED REP	3,448,799	3,917,788	4,100,209	4,261,823	4,550,311	5,169,012
REGISTERED TOT	8,805,972	10,381,246	11,386,103	12,007,581	12,863,773	14,441,869
REG ADVANTAGE	374,113	373,981	691,433	553,129	327,438	134,242
REG INDEX	D+4.2%	D+3.6%	D+6.1%	D+4.6%	D+2.5%	D+0.9%
PRES MARGIN	Bush+0.0%	Bush+5.0%	Obama+2.8%	Obama +0.9%	Trump +1.2%	Trump +3.4%

Chart by Seth Keshel.

Florida, with a perfect track record on party registration shift analysis going back to the twentieth century, showed remarkable Republican gains in Trump's first term, pushing the overall Democratic registration advantage under a single percentage point and trimming the lead by 193,196, four years after Trump had won the state by just 1.2 percent. All indications from the

---

7   Florida Department of State, Division of Elections, "Voter Registration Monthly Report, October 2016," Voter Registration Reports: Archived Monthly Reports, last updated December 9, 2025, https://dos.fl.gov/media/694063/voter-registration-report-archive-2000.zip.

Florida Department of State, Division of Elections, "Voter Registration Monthly Report, October 2004," Voter Registration Reports: Archived Monthly Reports, last updated December 9, 2025, https://dos.fl.gov/media/694067/voter-registration-report-archive-2004.zip.

Florida Department of State, Division of Elections, "Voter Registration Monthly Report, October 2008," Voter Registration Reports: Archived Monthly Reports, last updated December 9, 2025, https://dos.fl.gov/media/694070/voter-registration-report-archive-2008.zip.

Florida Department of State, Division of Elections, "Voter Registration Monthly Report, October 2012," Voter Registration Reports: Archived Monthly Reports, last updated December 9, 2025, https://dos.fl.gov/media/694075/voter-registration-report-archive-2012.zip.

Florida Department of State, Division of Elections, "Voter Registration Monthly Report, October 2016," Voter Registration Reports: Archived Monthly Reports, last updated December 9, 2025, https://dos.fl.gov/media/697513/voter-registration-report-archive-2016.zip.

most reliable projection tool were that Trump would expand his margin of victory in his new home state, and with Ron DeSantis and Rick Scott having resisted the 2018 midterm headwinds to win the governorship and flip a US Senate seat, respectively, Florida wasn't looking so much like a toss-up anymore.

Also in good news for Trump was the fact that North Carolina had followed Florida in a GOP party registration surge since he had taken office. Republicans had cut 4 percent off the long-standing Democratic voter registration advantage, netting a gain of 254,832 registrations[8] in a state Trump had already won once by 3.7 percent. North Carolina's voter registration figures suggested a comfortable win that would allow for resources to be concentrated once again in the tipping-point states in the "Industrial Midwest," and to a lesser degree, Wisconsin.

NORTH CAROLINA - VOTER REGISTRATION INDEX TRACKER - CAPT. S. KESHEL					
ELECTION YEAR	2004	2008	2012	2016	2020
REGISTERED DEM	2,408,759	2,866,669	2,870,693	2,733,188	2,623,000
REGISTERED REP	1,750,359	2,002,416	2,052,250	2,086,942	2,231,586
REGISTERED TOT	5,079,830	6,264,733	6,649,188	6,918,150	7,361,219
REG ADVANTAGE	658,400	864,253	818,443	646,246	391,414
REG INDEX	D+13.0%	D+13.8%	D+12.3%	D+9.3%	D+5.3%
PRES MARGIN	Bush+12.4%	Obama+0.3%	Romney+2.0%	Trump +3.7%	?

Chart by Seth Keshel.

The normally reliable Ann Selzer, who figures significantly into the collective lack of trust in American elections for her role in the 2024 race, let one big cat out of the bag with a late October poll where Trump led by seven points in Iowa.[9] It tipped

---

8   North Carolina State Board of Elections, "Voter Registration Statistics, Reporting Period: November 3, 2020," accessed November 20, 2025, https://vt.ncsbe.gov/RegStat/Results/?date=11%2F03%2F2020.

9   Katie Akin, "From 'Terrible' to Golden, Ann Selzer and the Iowa Poll Were Proved Right, Again," *Des Moines Register*, November 4, 2020, https://www.desmoinesregister.com/story/news/politics/2020/11/04/iowa-poll-closely-matches-election-results-how-did-ann-selzer-do-it/6159615002/.

off those with legitimate election knowledge that Biden was not winning any of the battleground states, like Wisconsin, by a large margin, if he was winning them at all. Ohio, which had flipped along with Iowa in 2016, was clearly Trump's if Iowa was showing such a strong margin. By logical deduction and basic analysis of historical presidential election state alignments, Trump's campaign should have expected to have Florida, Iowa, Ohio, Georgia, and North Carolina in the bag; Texas, despite fear mongering and fraudulent media polling, wouldn't be going to Biden if North Carolina and Florida were going to Trump. That electoral hand positioned Trump with 248 electoral votes pending the outcomes of the following races:

- Pennsylvania (20 electoral votes)
- Michigan (16 electoral votes)
- Arizona (10 electoral votes)
- Minnesota (10 electoral votes)
- Wisconsin (10 electoral votes)
- Nevada (6 electoral votes)
- New Hampshire (4 electoral votes)
- Nebraska's Second Congressional District (1 electoral vote)

The quickest, easiest, and most likely pathway to victory with Trump sitting on 248 electoral votes would have been to win Pennsylvania and hold Arizona. Florida's Republican tailwind, after Trump had won it and the "big three" of Pennsylvania, Michigan, and Wisconsin four years earlier, suggested Pennsylvania and Michigan, at minimum, were Trump's. That outcome, regardless of what happened in Arizona or any of the other emerging battlegrounds, would guarantee Trump's reelection. History suggested that would happen, since Florida had served as a perfect leading indicator of Pennsylvania and Michigan's presidential leans in an unbroken streak dating back to 1952, when neither Biden nor Trump were even ten years old. If Florida moved right from the previous presidential election, Pennsylvania and Michigan followed every time. If Florida moved left, the industrial pair did the exact same. I always prioritize history over propagandized polling, and a full spectrum analysis of the 2020 campaign had me even more confident of Trump's reelection than I had been of his 2016 victory.

While the key party registration indicator bolstered the list of Trump red states and suggested an edge in the Industrial Midwest, plus Nevada, his strength in Iowa lent positive indications for Wisconsin and even hope for Minnesota, in which he heavily campaigned. The party registration indicator went against Trump in New Hampshire and Arizona, suggesting he would be unable to carry the former despite a photo finish in 2016. Arizona, as it turned out, would turn into ground zero for the coming election integrity movement.

The Grand Canyon State was the most reliably Republican presidential state in the second half of the twentieth century. It, along with its largest county, Maricopa County, had backed Democrat Harry Truman narrowly in the 1948 election before flipping Republican for Dwight D. Eisenhower in 1952. It didn't back another Democrat for president until Bill Clinton in his 1996 reelection campaign, who won by a slim margin aided by a third-party spoiler. Arizona was the only state to not back any Democratic presidential nominee between 1960 and 1980, siding with native son Barry Goldwater in 1964, and even staying Republican in Bush 41's disastrous reelection campaign of 1992. After the 1996 Dole slipup, made possible only by third-party defections, it returned to its GOP presidential loyalty for another five straight elections, backing Trump by just over 3.5 percent in 2016, with a large third-party vote share sandbagging his margin of victory.

The two elections in Arizona in which Barack Obama had run, against John McCain and Mitt Romney in 2008 and 2012, respectively, had over 98 percent of the vote allotted between the two major party candidates. In 2016, Trump had won Arizona by the narrowest GOP margin since 1992, with him and Hillary Clinton combining for just 93.8 percent of the total vote. Over 159,000 votes went to candidates other than the two nominated by America's two leading parties. With Trump posting a nearly identical vote tally to Mitt Romney's, and Clinton's gain (a 135,935 gain over Obama's 2012 total) marking the third-highest single election jump in party history in the state, it is clear that most of the minor candidate votes in 2016 belonged to disaffected Republicans who would likely come back to the fold in 2020. Logic suggested Trump would consolidate that in 2020, requiring a gain larger than anything the Democrats had ever had in one cycle to beat him in what had been the nation's most reliably Republican state for nearly seven decades. Texas, now viewed as the king of Republican states, backed four Democrats from 1952 through 2024, although its GOP presidential streak remains intact since 1980.

Arizona Republicans had registered 269,164 net new voters since Trump's 2016 win,[10] a party record for a four-year stretch between elections. Curiously, Democrats had vaulted past that mark in the same span, adding a net of 287,001 to their 2016 count. The total voter roll ballooned by 692,686, a number exceeding the growth between the two previous election cycles

---

10   Arizona Secretary of State, "State of Arizona Registration Report: 2016 General Election Voter Registration - November 8, 2016," Voter Registration Counts, 2016 Election Cycle (2015 & 2016), accessed November 24, 2025, https://apps.azsos. gov/election/voterreg/2016-11-08.pdf.

Arizona Secretary of State, "State of Arizona Registration Report: 2020 General Election Voter Registration – November 3, 2020," Voter Registration Counts, 2020 Election Cycle (2019 & 2020), accessed November 24, 2025, https://apps.azsos. gov/election/VoterReg/2020/state_voter_registration_2020_general.pdf.

combined. In recent years, it has become obvious that voter registration corruption is the primary vector for manipulating elections. In 2020, that was not a well-known factor. With Trump pending a large consolidation of lost 2016 voters who backed minor party candidates, the state's history of backing Republican candidates, and the GOP having registered a record number of new voters, Arizona looked like a Trump hold in the making, even if the strength of the GOP party registration advantage had dipped slightly left.

ARIZONA - VOTER REGISTRATION INDEX TRACKER - CAPT. S. KESHEL					
ELECTION YEAR	**2004**	**2008**	**2012**	**2016**	**2020**
REGISTERED DEM	914,264	1,022,252	952,931	1,091,323	1,378,324
REGISTERED REP	1,055,252	1,118,587	1,120,992	1,239,614	1,508,778
REGISTERED TOT	2,643,331	2,987,451	3,124,712	3,588,466	4,281,152
REG ADVANTAGE	140,988	96,335	168,061	148,291	130,454
REG INDEX	R+5.3%	R+3.2%	R+5.4%	R+4.1%	R+3.0%
PRES MARGIN	Bush +10.5%	McCain +8.5%	Romney +9.1%	Trump +3.5%	?

Chart by Seth Keshel.

Trump's hold of the rock-solid red states—Texas, former battlegrounds Iowa and Ohio, plus Georgia, North Carolina, and Florida, all explained in detail within this chapter—gave him a starting point of 248 electoral votes, just 22 shy of the needed majority. By party registration analysis and correlation to Florida since 1952, Pennsylvania and Michigan were Trump's, and Arizona looked to have the juice and consolidation of the soft Republican base to go red for the seventeenth time in eighteen tries. That alone would give Trump 295 electoral votes, 11 shy of his 2016 total pending the outcomes of Nebraska's Second Congressional District and Wisconsin to match, and Minnesota, Nevada, and New Hampshire to exceed.

New Hampshire, despite Trump's campaign overtures there, didn't look like it was going to make its first appearance in the red column since 2000. Minnesota, despite its standing as the most loyal blue state dating back to its unbroken Democrat streak's origins in 1976, looked ready to tip over, and Trump's constant presence in the Iron Range suggested he felt that Pennsylvania, Michigan, and Wisconsin were under control, as he didn't *need* Minnesota to win. He was going for a kill shot.

One of the most forgotten moments from Election Day—long lost in the aftermath of the election night fallout and the chaotic period between November 7, 2020, the day Biden was declared the winner, and his certification on January 6, 2021—is the strange and telling plea of Minnesota Attorney General Keith Ellison. He took to Twitter late in the afternoon to urge voters to show up in person with a friend to vote because they apparently didn't think they had enough votes to hold down the most reliable Democratic state stretching back more than four decades. The irony is that Democrats spent all of 2020 building a mail-in balloting army that would begin gathering ballots as soon as they were sent out, which meant September in the case of Minnesota. Ellison, despite his state having one of the longest voting periods in the nation that year, didn't think Biden and the rest of the Democratic ticket, including Tina Smith running against Jason Lewis for US Senate, had the gas to get across the finish line:

"If you've voted, great! Can you please call a friend? Spend a little time getting friends, fams, and folks out to the polls. We don't have all the votes we need quite yet. So, help a friend (even a brand-new friend) vote. Right now would be awesome."[11]

---

11   Keith Ellison (@keithellison), "If you've voted, great! Can you please call a friend? Spend a little time getting friends, fams, and folks out to the polls. We don't have all of the votes we need quite yet. So, help a friend (even a brand new friend) vote. Right now would be awesome," X, November 3, 2020, https://x.com/keithellison/status/1323746158557253632.

Ellison's statement would have been along the same lines of Texas's Attorney General Ken Paxton going online on Election Day and sounding the alarm that Texas Republicans must get out to vote immediately or risk losing a presidential election for the first time since 1980, or any statewide office since 1994. The alarm would have been viewed with skepticism once none of the races finished within five points, just as I viewed Ellison's statement once Biden beat Trump in Minnesota by a margin nearly as high as Obama's over Romney in 2012. This was four years before Trump's working-class message penetrated the Upper Midwest, turned Iowa into a cakewalk, and flipped neighboring Wisconsin for the first time in thirty-two years. Minnesota had gone to Clinton by just 1.5 percent, sandbagged by a few points by the same large minor-party candidate vote share that had harmed Trump in Arizona.

Even with Minnesota wiped off the board early on Three November, everything else still looked peachy for Trump. North Carolina was tighter than expected, but Georgia was a romp on Election Night and Texas was red (but not red enough). When Miami-Dade County dropped its results showing a narrow Biden victory, everyone knew Trump had Florida. The twenty-nine electoral votes from Trump's new home state were huge, but the winning margin of 3.4 percent was more than two points right of Trump's 2016 margin, suggesting Pennsylvania and Michigan would follow to the right, when they had already been Trump states four years before.

On cue, Pennsylvania, Michigan, and Wisconsin showed massive Trump leads, right in line with Hawkfish's "red mirage" scenario so expertly planted months before in the minds of the public. While Hawkfish spent years taking victory laps for supposedly preempting the narrative of the ensuing "big lie" (Trump's efforts to overturn the 2020 election, which were absolutely necessary), the real-time numbers in all three states, especially Pennsylvania, coincided with exactly what I expected to see. Pennsylvania's party registration indicator was so heavily in favor of Trump and the Republican Party that it, along with a decade of Democratic decline, signaled a race likely to find the Keystone State redder than many long-standing red states. In Trump's term, Republicans had outgained Democrats for net new registrations by a rate of 21 to 1.[12]

If a consistent Florida-aligned shift wasn't enough to convince someone to wager on Trump in Pennsylvania, the party registration data would. Of all the states I've studied, Pennsylvania's is by far the most dramatic and convincing that things weren't on the up-and-up in 2020. Its overwhelming Republican shift in the age of Trump made Florida's look like child's play and showed the shifting of change from one pocket to the other.

ELECTION YEAR	2004	2008	2012	2016	2020
PENNSYLVANIA - VOTER REGISTRATION INDEX TRACKER - CAPT. S. KESHEL					
REGISTERED DEM	3,985,486	4,479,513	4,266,317	4,217,456	4,228,888
REGISTERED REP	3,405,278	3,243,046	3,131,144	3,301,182	3,543,070
REGISTERED TOT	8,366,663	8,755,588	8,508,015	8,722,977	9,090,962
REG ADVANTAGE	580,208	1,236,467	1,135,173	916,274	685,818
REG INDEX	D+6.9%	D+14.1%	D+13.3%	D+10.5%	D+7.5%
PRES MARGIN	Kerry +2.5%	Obama +10.3%	Obama +5.4%	Trump +0.7%	?

Chart by Seth Keshel.

12   Pennsylvania Department of State, Division of Voter Registration, "Commonwealth of Pennsylvania 2016 Voter Registration Statistics - Official November 8, 2016," Voting & Election Statistics Archive, accessed November 21, 2025, https://www.pa.gov/content/dam/copapwp-pagov/en/dos/resources/voting-and-elections/voting-and-election-statistics/voter-registration-statistics/2016%20Election%20VR%20Stats.pdf.

Pennsylvania Department of State, Division of Voter Registration, "Commonwealth of Pennsylvania 2020 Voter Registration Statistics - Official November 3, 2020 Election," Voting & Election Statistics Archive, accessed November 21, 2025, https://www.pa.gov/content/dam/copapwp-pagov/en/dos/resources/voting-and-elections/voting-and-election-statistics/voter-registration-statistics/2020%20Election%20VR%20Stats%20%20FINAL%20REVIEWED.pdf.

Trump had been the key for revitalizing the Pennsylvania GOP, and his rise as party standard-bearer brought in 170,038 net new Republican registrations for 2016, as Democrats continued to lose membership. The net shift in registrations toward the GOP from 2012 to 2016, 218,899, spelled doom for the Clinton campaign, which relied on polling data and ignored traditional metrics that are almost always right. Trump ended up with the first Republican presidential win of the commonwealth since 1988, effectively closing the curtain on what many thought was an inevitable coronation.

In 2020, the shift was even steeper, a net gain of 230,456 in the voter roll and 241,888 net new Republicans lined up to reelect Trump. If there was supposed to be a Republican crisis in Pennsylvania due to COVID-19, voter registration figures suggested the exact opposite. They pointed to Democratic extinction, and as Trump ran up the score in the "big three," the betting markets followed his momentum and showed the incumbent as the heavy favorite. As millions of Americans thought the political hurdles imposed by COVID-19 had been overcome, the unthinkable happened:

Fox News called Arizona at 11:20 p.m. Eastern Standard Time with just a sliver of the state's votes counted.[13] This premature call, which would represent just the second Democratic presidential win in seven decades if it held up, killed Trump's momentum, and within hours, Georgia, Michigan, Pennsylvania, and Wisconsin stopped relaying counts to the public. With just a single call, the joy of Three November turned to peril, uncertainty, and a sinking feeling as soon as everyone woke up on November 4.

---

13   J. M. Rieger, "Trump Allies Push Back on Fox News's Arizona Call," *Washington Post*, November 4, 2020, 1 min., 2 sec., https://www.washingtonpost.com/video/politics/trump-allies-push-back-on-fox-newss-arizona-call/2020/11/04/26f513a0-117d-492c-859d-43152f7ec394_video.html.

CHAPTER 8

Aftermath

Attitude maintenance wasn't happening for me on November 4. I hadn't slept, was terrified for the future of the country, and knew I was witnessing a bloodless coup unfold before my eyes. Michigan and Wisconsin, gone. Still, I had enough presence of mind to realize Georgia was now instrumental in the plan to kick Trump out of the White House. Once North Carolina, which hadn't finished to the right of Georgia since 2000, went for Trump, it became necessary for those behind the curtain of this coup to swap out the plan to rip off North Carolina's fifteen electoral votes with one to snatch Georgia's sixteen instead. The crisis situation in Georgia was made possible by the adoption of automatic voter registration in 2016, which flooded voter rolls in metro Atlanta, and also by its sudden mail-in ballot expansion, resulting in 1,316,943 mail-in ballots being counted,[1] up from 207,716[2] (an increase of 634 percent) in Trump's 2016 victory in the Peach State.

Just as Keith Ellison had slipped up in admitting the reality of a close race in Minnesota, Georgia Secretary of State Brad

---

1   Georgia Secretary of State. "Total Votes Excel," November 3, 2020-General Election, Results Reports, Excel spreadsheet, last updated January 3, 2025, https://results.sos. ga.gov/cdn/results/09378a07-e6cf-4f66-be7c-ca4aa534f99a/Total%20Votes%20 Results_96d898ad-4389-48a1-be92-abcabc52d940.xlsx.

2   Georgia Secretary of State. "Total Votes Excel," November 8, 2016 – General Election, Results Reports, Excel spreadsheet, last updated January 3, 2025, https:// results.sos.ga.gov/cdn/results/09378a07-e6cf-4f66-be7c-ca4aa534f99a/Total%20 Votes%20Results_399b6a55-3715-41fb-9821-091a0e3542bf.xlsx.

Raffensperger, who trashed me in his own book about the 2020 race, made perhaps the biggest slip of that entire chapter of American history when he went on *The Today Show* and told the hosts that Georgia had 4.7 million votes cast,[3] a record beating the previous high mark set in 2016. On screen during the interview it was shown that Trump led Biden by 2.2 percent, or 103,705 votes, a margin cut significantly from the time at which most Americans went to bed thinking Trump had reelection in the bag. Raffensperger's words projected a sense of finality in the vote count:

"Well, we have about two percent left to go. We had great success yesterday. We had four-point-seven million voters that voted—a record breaker for us, beats the four point one in 2016.... We have about two percent left to go, and you can see where we are right now with the results that have been reported. I don't think it will change any of the outcomes..."

In the wee morning hours of November 6, Biden overtook Trump and never relinquished the lead. From the time of Raffensperger's statement to *The Today Show*, the total vote count grew by 6.4 percent, or 300,000 ballots, as the state certified almost five million votes to the exact number. Raffensperger clearly didn't think the outcomes would change because adding another 2 percent to the pile of 4.7 million votes would put Raffensperger's estimate for the final ballot count at roughly just shy of 4.8 million. Biden could have won every outstanding vote, if that were the final count, from the morning of November 4 and still lost to Trump by the slimmest of margins. In the aftermath of the Georgia electoral fiasco, Americans were shamed for questioning the administration of races like this, in which the

---

3   GA Ballots, "Raffensperger says Georgia had a Record 4.7 Million Votes Cast; Final Count Was Nearly 5 Million," posted July 4, 2023, YouTube video, 1 min., 24 sec., https://www.youtube.com/watch?v=P3NeqIQ-K30.

secretary of state somehow misplaced over 200,000 ballots from the outstanding count in a state Biden only "won" by 11,779 votes. At some point between not expecting outcomes to change and shaming fellow Republicans for calling out the electoral malfeasance in Georgia, Raffensperger seems to have been instructed to dance to a different tune and get in line with Georgia replacing North Carolina's missed electoral gains for the Biden campaign. Again, bagging Georgia would have meant Trump needed just Pennsylvania and Arizona (or Nevada) to win.

At 11:33 a.m. on November 4, even after a major stoppage in Pennsylvania's vote counting, Trump still held what appeared to be an insurmountable lead there.[4]

With an estimated 79 percent of the vote tabulated, Trump had already shot past his own winning vote total from 2016, as well as Obama's from 2012. He was up by 9.1 percent, or 512,636 votes, but the fact that Michigan and Wisconsin had been called in the wee hours of the morning cast a pall over everyone's expectations for Pennsylvania to have anything resembling a predictable ending in line with Trump's apparent landslide margin, which immediately began to slip. The count continued until Biden found a lead just outside mandatory recount territory at 80,555, with both the statewide and national race called by the press on November 7. Newt Gingrich, who authored the foreword to this book, put it simply, "I think that it is a corrupt, stolen election."[5]

My mind had long been prepared to see the discrepancies in open-source data. To the average American, lured to sleep by

---

4   "Votes Reported in Pennsylvania," in Trip Gabriel and Nick Corasaniti, "The View in Pennsylvania: Democrats are Confident, Even as the Trump Team Considers Legal Challenges," *New York Times*, November 4, 2020, image, https://www.nytimes.com/2020/11/04/us/politics/pa-election-results.html.

5   KSDK News, "Newt Gingrich Says He Thinks 'This Is a Corrupt and Stolen Election,'" posted November 8, 2020, YouTube video, 13 sec., https://www.youtube.com/watch?v=kF-2b8vBRrA.

media propaganda and informed by polling sponsored by the same people, the result would have bordered on believable if not for the sudden stoppage of count reporting in battleground states Trump was uniformly winning. I was so certain—based on the enormity of the steal, the brazen attempts to boot observers in places like Detroit's TCF Center, late-night vote spikes at impossibly high rates favoring Biden, and what was shaping up to be a razor-thin margin of victory once the dust settled—that no stone would be left unturned by Trump's legal team and armies of grassroots patriots to reverse the fraudulent outcomes and ensure Trump would be the man inaugurated on January 20, 2021.

I began making phone calls. Everyone was quick to blame Philadelphia, Milwaukee, and Detroit for the outcomes in their states, but my scans of the vast countrysides of these battlegrounds revealed to me that the ballot harvesting operation had reached beyond every factory, hill, stream, forest, and creek in Trump Country. I reached a staffer here and there at the county-party level, got in touch with a few state party chairs, but also found many unconscionably went on vacation while the biggest steal in history was still underway. My optimism over the coming counterattack quickly turned to pessimism, especially after I began to sense the feeling of inevitability after the election was called for Biden. News networks, on the other hand, were full of angry conservative voices calling the election what it was, including Sidney Powell. I had already begun compiling spreadsheets, making slides, and sharing information over what little social media I used in those days, like a personal Facebook account known only to friends or colleagues amassed over the past two decades. In watching Powell, I decided to take a leap of faith.

Lieutenant General (US Army, Retired) Michael Flynn turned out to be the person who dragged me, a far junior intelligence veteran, into the battle for election integrity. I had first messaged General Flynn on LinkedIn in June 2016, thanking him for his role in drawing needed attention to the Hillary Clinton email scandal, which foisted a major counterintelligence threat upon the country. In his brief response, sent ten days later, he wrote, "I'd ask you to encourage people to vote for Trump. Our country needs fresh leadership." I wouldn't hear from him again for more than four years. In that period, he had become Trump's national security advisor but was quickly sent packing after being caught up in the Russiagate nonsense that plagued much of Trump's first term. He spent the next several years in hot legal water fighting for his personal liberty, with Powell as his key defense. On November 5, 2020, the day I resolved myself to dig in and fight against election corruption, I messaged General Flynn on the same thread that had been opened years before:

> 7:34 PM Seth Keshel, MBA: We can't accept this—when are we going to take a stand? This is stolen.

> 7:58 PM Mike Flynn: Now

Over the next two days, I sent the general dozens of slides encompassing my analysis and lending credence to my conclusions. He asked me to email him everything I had and requested I turn all my findings into declarations of facts that could be submitted alongside the forthcoming cases challenging the election results in various states. I was connected to Powell and her team who were busy scrambling for actionable items against an incredibly tight deadline to file suits, prevent or reverse certifications, and send manipulated results back the other way—something that had never been done at the scale needed to tip things in favor of Trump.

One of the most memorable things General Flynn wrote came via email in those early days of November: "We will not cede one inch of the terrain we currently hold."[6] By mid-November, I had met Flynn, Powell, Patrick Byrne, and a host of others who would become important figures in the national battle for election integrity that I had no idea waited around the corner in 2021. Such a movement was not of concern; the only concern anyone had was ensuring Donald J. Trump remained president of the United States. We had until January 6, 2021, to make that happen, but every day that passed cemented the national expectation that Biden, not Trump, would hold our highest office.

I spent countless hours hunting sworn statements and evidence that justified what the numbers told me, and in the process, met James Tesauro and James Charles Phillips, two of my best friends, who got behind their steering wheels to dig around in swing states and produce valuable information. Networks of freedom fighters from all states, not just battlegrounds, submitted loads of information damning to any notion American elections are trustworthy. Certifications were rammed through and court cases were dismissed for all types of reasons, including finding the president of the United States himself to have no legal standing, casting a dim light over the proceedings. That didn't stop anyone from pushing forward on social media, which resulted in mass expulsions, or from trying to get as many prominent US representatives and senators on board with objecting to the certification of the election results.

To the American left, January 6, 2021, represents the height of insurrection and right-wing political violence. They don't pay attention to the obvious evidence of entrapment, and most certainly don't care that so many Americans were deprived of the

---

6   Michael Flynn, email message to author, November 10, 2020.

right to a fair and speedy trial and indefinitely locked away until Trump pardoned them in 2025. To many on the right, January 6 remains a somber day in which Congress ignored the objections that far too few elected officials lodged and made expedient use of the disruption to quickly certify Biden as the winner under cover of darkness. The dismissive attitudes of those who shrugged off the very first investigations into the 2020 election added major fuel to the fire of the coming election integrity movement, just as the injustice toward January 6 detainees, many of whom should have been slapped with nothing more than misdemeanor charges, if any charges at all, launched the parallel January 6 justice movement. Some election integrity stalwarts, such as David Clements, would straddle both movements and provided critical visibility to millions in the coming years.

On January 7, I opened Twitter to check on thousands of unread notifications only to find that President Trump announced he would conduct an "orderly transition" on January 20. The battle to keep President Trump in office had failed, and there were many reasons why.

First, timelines for filing lawsuits over election results are extremely tight, and with such tight timelines, it is difficult to find enough evidence to meet the legal burden. In some states, such as Arizona, proof of as many fraudulent ballots as the margin separating candidates is required. Biden's margin in Arizona's quasi election was 10,457. If lawsuits alleged the discovery of 10,456 fakes, it wasn't enough.

Second, election fraud is very hard to prove all the way down to the ballot. My analysis identifies broken trends, indicators, bellwethers, and predictors and makes key observations with voter registration by party. It suggests, as a physician may note that an average-sized man claiming to weigh four hundred pounds is lying about his weight, where history and political trends high-light certain states or counties as having surprisingly high ballot counts that stand out from their historical norms. I have always believed mail-in ballot fraud stemming from corrupted voter rolls, and aided by ballot harvesting, is the primary means of padding vote totals. States with mail-in balloting have signature verification standards and procedures. But then again, Americans must then find the mental capacity to trust that the unaccountable and irresponsible government processes are ensuring that every signature matches up and that no political agendas to flout this process exist.

Third, judicial corruption and the unwillingness of many high courts to insert themselves into divisive issues, especially those that can be argued to take place at the state level, thwarted the best shots we had. Texas Attorney General Ken Paxton filed a brilliant suit, *Texas v. Pennsylvania,*[7] which alleged that the mis-handling of elections by defendant states Pennsylvania, Georgia, Michigan, and Wisconsin disenfranchised Texas's thirty-eight electors, which voted for Trump. Seventeen other states signed on to the lawsuit, which was never taken up by the US Supreme Court. If the states, and even the president himself, don't have standing to challenge corrupt elections, then who does? Courts have tipped the scales before, like when the Supreme Court gave George W. Bush the win over Al Gore in Florida's infamous 2000 election, which helped usher in electronic voting systems. But in 2020, it seemed to be a full-court press to ensure that the arguments asserting the corruption of the quasi election never received a full and public hearing.

---

7   Valeria Negron, "Supreme Court Rejects Texas Bid to Invalidate Election Results in Four States Trump Lost," JURIST, December 11, 2020, https://www.jurist.org/news/2020/12/supreme-court-rejects-texas-attempt-to-invalidate-election-results-in-four-states-lost-by-trump/.

Blamed for inciting January 6 protests and Capitol incursions, the people most involved in pushing back against electoral corruption in the interlude between "Three November" and January 20, 2021, expected to be investigated, if not fully rounded up like January 6 participants, shortly after Biden took office. I received a letter from lawyers representing Dominion Voting Systems directing me to *cease and desist* from posting about them and discussing any potentially impactful findings that suggest electronic manipulation of elections. Even then, I didn't focus much on machines, especially not from any specific vendor. Powell spent plenty of time going after Dominion and dealt with them legally for years; I suppose the letter I received was sent by virtue of my association with Powell and not with any real justification or history of having singled out Dominion by name, but the rush to silence me made me question electronic manipulation even more.

With the battle at a halt, I went back to selling technology, but without the same zeal I once had. My nights on the road were spent analyzing the impossible, wrestling with my own thoughts and motives, and trying to decide if I wanted to move on with life when all I saw on the news was an administration abusing its power, targeting its political opponents, and locking Americans away indefinitely. Between that cease-and-desist letter and the first prisoners crying out for release, I realized the war hadn't ended on Three November or the following days. It had only just begun, and there had to be justice. Looking toward the future, I thought to myself, "To hell with 270 electoral votes—time to overturn the entire rotten system."

CHAPTER 9

Highly Respected

The only thing that kept me employed in my day job in those early days of 2021 was the lack of public agencies open for meetings with salesmen. Revenue numbers tanked, as many public agencies lacked funding for maintenance budgets and routine expenditures. The company I had worked for since 2018 had merged with a large corporation and blended product lines with a former competitor, forcing me to learn new products and travel to new states. As I treaded water and tried to find open doors with customers, I continued to ponder where exactly I was supposed to impact the battle for America's future with something that could only be described as a niche skill set.

There had been a few interviews here and there, but none with widespread reach, and eventually a few local meetings in Texas. By June, I had several interviews that went viral, especially on Telegram, the messaging platform people flocked to when Twitter was busy banning everyone with a dissident opinion. I made my first post on my very own Telegram channel on June 26 after being pushed to set up a platform there; soon, many tens of thousands searching for answers would come watch what I had to say.

I used that platform to dish out election statistics that often predated the lifetimes of anyone watching my channel. With a very basic system of evaluating vote trends by county, I issued crude evaluations of each state, listing which ones, down to individual counties, I believed were most disparate in the 2020 election and which ones were least likely to contain electoral manipulation. Massive news outlets began to run with my assessments, and on July 17, the biggest show of them all called my number. While on a trip to Washington state, I paced the streets of Winlock speaking to Peter Navarro, who was filling in for Steve Bannon on his podcast *War Room*. For the first time, that national audience, many of whom had never heard of me despite my massive surge on Telegram, heard what I had to say. They continued to have me and David Clements on in tandem throughout the year as the push for election audits went nationwide.

My new national voice quickly translated into requests for speaking events, especially as I trickled out 2020 analyses. In April 2021, the Arizona Senate approved a first-of-its-kind full forensic audit of the previous November's Maricopa County election, which saw President Donald Trump become the first Republican presidential nominee to lose the county since 1948. Even Bob Dole had won the county in his fluke upset statewide loss in 1996, but this time, Trump's gains from 2016 both statewide and in Maricopa County were single-cycle Republican records in a state that always voted Republican. The speculation over the audit's findings fueled nationwide interest in full transparency, especially in the key battleground states that vaulted Biden into office. On July 21, in Flora, Mississippi, I spoke at my first public speaking event—one county from where I grew up. While Mississippi was and is not anything resembling a competitive state politically, kicking off a significant speaking tour in familiar territory made sense. I met former Marine Corps sniper Thomas "Sonny" Morgan at that event, beginning a friendship that included many thousands of miles on the road in the years to come. Two days later, James Charles Phillips and I were in Grand Rapids, Michigan, for another appearance featuring many high-profile speakers. By July 29, when I spoke in front of a huge audience in North Richland Hills, Texas, I had succeeded in attracting the haters. Bud Kennedy of the *Fort Worth Star-Telegram* was one of my earliest:[1]

"Parker County resident Seth Keshel, the Trump backers' legal adviser who concocted charts of 'statistical tendencies'…has made his goals clear at recent local and national rallies…. See, it's not really about 2020. It's about ginning up votes for 2022 and 2024."

By this point, I had already set my sights on solidly red and blue states that wouldn't have changed winners in fair 2020 elections but would have produced drastically different outcomes. Kennedy was particularly defensive over Tarrant County's 2020 presidential outcome which, like Maricopa County, saw the first Democratic presidential win in many decades (since 1964), despite Trump's gain over his winning 2016 totals representing the all-time new record for net new votes gained in a single cycle for any Republican. From 2008 through 2016, a span of three presidential elections, Democrats Barack Obama and Hillary Clinton had between 3.3 and 3.9 million votes statewide in Texas, never punching through the 4 million threshold. In 2020, Biden cleared not only the 4 million mark but made it all the way over 5 million to a total that was more than a half million *greater* than Trump's winning 2016 mark. Had Trump not poured in a record Republican gain statewide, one even steeper than native son George W. Bush's 2004 increase, he was at risk of losing the state. No, Bud, the numbers did not and still don't add up, even

---

1 Bud Kennedy, "Why 'Audit' Tarrant County Now? Because This Isn't Really about the 2020 Election," *Fort Worth Star-Telegram*, updated September 27, 2021, Opinion, https://www.star-telegram.com/opinion/bud-kennedy/article254363258.html.

after Kamala Harris lost back over four hundred thousand of Biden's voters and Attorney General Ken Paxton has continued to prove cheating in elections.

Hawaii, on the other side of the political spectrum, gave another stunning example of an election gone wrong. Trump's gain in Hawaii, an increase in votes of 52.8 percent, was his steepest gain as a percentage, excluding Utah's quirky specifics tied to a Mormon independent candidate; still, despite such a massive gain in one of the country's smallest states, Trump lost Hawaii by substantially more votes than he did to Clinton. Joe Biden, a political retread with two failed presidential campaigns behind him in his younger years, blew past the Hawaiian Obama's record vote totals as if they had been set in Hawaii's infancy. It just so happens that the Aloha State had switched to universal mail-in voting, in which every registration present on the voter roll receives a ballot. In 2016, according to Hawaii's election records, 234,336 ballots were designated "absentee."[2] Hawaii's legislature pushed through universal mail-in voting in 2019, recognizing it as a key factor in keeping permanent control of statewide politics with Democrats. The immediate result was an explosion in ballots significant enough to neutralize Trump's highest percentage gain and vault Biden to the electoral standing Obama could have never dreamed of having in his home state.

James Charles and I were in Atlanta having lunch and prepping for an event in Cherokee County on the sweltering afternoon of August 3, 2021. While still learning the ropes of Telegram, I had just days earlier posted a *New York Times* cover spoof I thought was real and received a ton of angry messages from subscribers to stop sharing fake news. On this day, however, I received dozens

---

2   State of Hawaii, Office of Elections, "General Election 2016 – State of Hawaii - Statewide November 8, 2016," Results, General Election, https://files.hawaii.gov/elections/files/results/2016/general/histatewide.pdf.

of text messages simultaneously with a press release bearing my name and immediately shrugged it off as a fake. It read:

Statement by Donald J. Trump, 45th President of the United States of America

Highly respected Army intelligence captain, Seth Keshel, has just released his Report on National Fraud Numbers with respect to the 2020 Presidential Election. I don't personally know Captain Keshel, but these numbers are overwhelming, election-changing, and according to Keshel, could be even bigger in that they do not account for cyber-flipping of votes. They show I won the election—by A LOT! Now watch the Democrats coalesce, defame, threaten, investigate, jail people, and do whatever they have to do to keep the truth from surfacing, and let the Biden Administration continue to get away with destroying our Country. The irregularities and outright fraud of this election are an open wound to the United States of America. Something must be done—immediately!

I felt it had to be bait to make me post something out of sheer excitement, calling my credibility into question. My first text was to Liz Harrington, who had come alongside President Trump as a key mouthpiece after the 2020 race. I had been discussing my findings as I investigated at the county level, finding the most ideal counties for election audits. She had taken the liberty to share my findings with President Trump, and that statement was 100 percent authentic.[3] As Amy Kremer, chair of Women for America First, introduced me that evening in Woodstock, Georgia, it came with the recognition that my research and analysis had just been commended by the president of the United States. From that point forward, I would take the stage perceived as someone who spoke with an air of authority, an ally of the greater movement to save the United States, and a veteran who returned to service without a uniform, rather than the latest viral online influencer waiting to sputter out and be forgotten.

I also knew my time as a relatively unknown traveling salesman was coming to a close. With President Trump pushing me out there in the middle of an information war, I could no longer hide. My weekly business trips became punctuated by moonlighting as a public speaker. I would do my best to blend in and sell equipment by day as I was recognized in airports, trade shows, and customer meetings, then get freshened up for an evening in front of increasingly large audiences looking for truth in a world filled with lies and misinformation. Ironically, I was the one accused of spreading disinformation, and this only made people want to hear what I had to say even more.

On August 21, while taking a break from the road, President Trump took the stage in Cullman, Alabama, and put me on blast once again,[4] this time in front of millions of live viewers and tens of thousands in attendance:

> A recent trend analysis of all 50 states based
> on population growth, voter history, and voter
> registration data by one of the most respected

---

3   Donald J. Trump, "Statement by Donald J. Trump, 45th President of the United States of America," August 3, 2021, https://web.archive.org/web/20210804164415/https://www.donaldjtrump.com/news/news-jjpbtgs9bn0.

4   Roll Call Factbase Videos, "Speech: Donald Trump Holds a Political Rally in Cullman, Alabama - August 21, 2021," posted May 13, 2025, YouTube video, 1:30:53, https://www.youtube.com/watch?v=0zMhI5b2g5w.

people in that industry, somebody so respected— military person—Captain Seth Keshel, found over eight million excess Biden votes. In other words, he had eight million more votes than he's supposed to have. And his estimate is conservative; he considered it very conservative, and I believe he said he didn't even go to the machines. This is without even looking at the machines. Remember, I'm not the one trying to undermine American democracy. I am the one trying to save American democracy.

I thought I had been busy up to that point, but the demand for my time and unique skillset was only beginning. The rush to silence my voice was in full swing, and the expectations of most following the election integrity battle were straightforward— make the case to the public, the legislatures, and the courts, then count on unprecedented action to reinstate the rightful president. Time would prove us naive, but I knew it was out of my control, and my only mission was to *prove the steal*. After that night in Alabama, there was no going back for me.

Ten Points They Can't Answer For

In the summer of 2021, more than a dozen years after I'd been nicknamed "Sizzle" in my first military unit for promising to put the "sizzle" on the "steak" (the actionable analysis on the subject matter), the same dynamic emerged. Just as there were intelligence officers who repeated headlines and memorized important-sounding terminology to regurgitate in front of their commanders, there was also no shortage of large social media accounts looking for clicks and engagement that were willing to share out any junk that aligned with their beliefs, or the perceived beliefs of those who subscribed to their channels.

The social media economy is simple. Ad revenues for Twitter, later known as X, didn't exist in 2021, but amassing more followers has always led to more shares, interviews, speaking engagements, and sponsorships. Few have the responsibility to handle this sort of platform responsibly once observing firsthand how much clout it affords. I enjoyed the large social media following and made myself far too accessible to far too many people, eventually leading to disrupted relationships, unnecessary rivalries created by split factions, and widespread confusion among the subscriber base over who to follow for accurate information. I learned quickly not to engage in back-and-forths over trivial nonsense because the people I wanted to influence most were those busy doing the heavy lifting at the county level, which meant meeting with local officials, volunteering as poll watchers or election judges, registering voters, requesting public information, and doing anything possible to bring transparency where it was lacking.

From the beginning, I valued accuracy over talking trash online and precision over being the guy to jump on a half-baked story before anyone else did. With the media constantly breathing down my neck, one critical mistake could derail everything I had worked on and relegate me to being viewed as the latest conspiracy theorist who capitalized on a topic of great interest to a public looking for answers. Trust is very hard to reestablish once lost, and I went to great lengths to show my work and collaborate with local sources when I had important information to publish.

I don't take logical leaps. My analysis takes to heart the words of Colonel Benjamin Martin, played by Mel Gibson, in *The Patriot*. Martin told his sons, who were preparing to fire at redcoats, "Aim small, miss small." While I was always more than happy to visit deep blue states like California, Washington, or Illinois, I knew my mission was simple. Only 42,918 ballots separated Biden and Trump in Arizona, Georgia, and Wisconsin; Trump victories in those states would have deadlocked the Electoral College at 269 electoral votes each. Yard signs and anecdotes from Los Angeles didn't matter nearly as much to me as precise electoral analysis at the county level in the slate of battleground states deviating remarkably from established norms that had made the 2016 election so easy for me to predict.

The election integrity movement was after something that had never been done before, and perhaps never will be done. While elections have indeed been overturned for proof of having been fraudulently decided, including races for the US House,

US Senate, and gubernatorial races, no presidential race had ever been overturned or even seriously challenged. The 1876 race between Democrat Samuel Tilden and Republican Rutherford B. Hayes saw two sides nearly come to blows over the electoral votes of Florida, Louisiana, and South Carolina, with both sides committing widespread fraud. Republicans were tossing Democratic ballots, and Democrats were using intimidation to suppress would-be Republican voters. Hayes wound up inaugurated in 1877 after being awarded the twenty electoral votes that had been disputed.

Then there was the 1960 race between John F. Kennedy and Richard Nixon, in which the latter's campaign alleged election fraud in Chicago and throughout Texas. Had they been successful in reversing the outcomes, Nixon would have overtaken Kennedy by the slimmest of margins and become president eight years earlier than he actually did. George W. Bush had been handed a 537-vote margin in Florida in 2000 courtesy of the US Supreme Court, but allegations of widespread fraud were absent. Even though the numbers from 2020 appeared so obvious to me, overcoming the impenetrably high legal bar of invalidating the results of an election held almost a year earlier was the most daunting of all tasks. But that didn't mean we wouldn't give it our best shot.

Little more than a week after Donald Trump's press release, and ten days before he put me on blast in Cullman, I made my big splash from the stage in Sioux Falls, South Dakota, at Mike Lindell's Cyber Symposium. Even from those early days, I didn't fashion myself as any sort of expert on electronic voting systems, nor did I have anything to do with the internal happenings of Lindell's team, which has splintered into factions as the years have passed by. The event was wonky and conducted mostly by those who disclosed highly technical research. I sat on a panel with

David Clements, known widely as "The Professor," Dr. Douglas Frank, and Draza Smith that saw the four of us exchange points on the 2020 election. Clements and I, both similar in age and uniquely personable, were viewed as peers and had created a plethora of digital content outlining the unique election integrity situation in many different states, including his native New Mexico. He was one of the stars of Lindell's event.

Mike had flown me in fully aware that I was not there to discuss anything "cyber," but to provide a zoomed-out context of the entire election infrastructure using historical fact and precedent as my guide. Late in the afternoon on August 11, with a worldwide audience watching and shows like *War Room* live-streaming the action, I took the stage in a blue blazer and my signature brown leather cowboy boots,[1] fully aware that what I had to say was going to be widely publicized and highly scrutinized and would further complicate my employment prospects. I was not yet charging anyone for my speaking events beyond what it had cost to get me in and out and had foolishly hoped the battle for setting the 2020 election straight for the history books would be brief, accelerated by the completion of the Maricopa County audit, which was just around the corner.

I'm not a big speech planner. I pace the stage and engage directly with audience members, crack edgy jokes, and remember the data I put on my slides by heart. I am well known for not carrying notes of any kind because it was drilled into me as a young intelligence officer that no one wants to sit there just to watch you read. That capacity for "useless knowledge" I was always mocked for while growing up was about to come in handy,

---

1   KanekoaTheGreat, "Mike Lindell Cyber Symposium - Seth Keshel 'Behind the Election Integrity Curtain,'" presentation at Mike Lindell's Cyber Symposium, video, August 11, 2021, posted August 11, 2021, 35 min., 47 sec., Rumble, https://rumble. com/vl12q1-mike-lindell-cyber-symposium-behind-the-election-integrity-curtain-seth-kes.html.

because the purpose of my presentation wasn't to convince the spectators—which included influencers, media, legislators, and other political officials who mostly agreed with me—but rather to convince the rank-and-file Republican who had been conditioned for months to move on from Trump that there was serious validity to the claims levied.

I settled on a fast-moving, engaging presentation featuring what I call "The Ten Irrefutable Points of the 2020 Election." I had helped get them published in short form in The Western Journal shortly before the symposium, and felt comfortable enough with the material to let it fly on the big stage with hardly a stumble. With my combination of physical stature, composure, and subject matter, I had no trouble keeping the attention of the audience as I provided an overview of the 2020 election's main discrepancies in a format any average Joe could understand. Simplifying complex topics is another skill military officers usually have in abundance, as it is common knowledge that all military writing should be drafted at an eighth-grade level of reading comprehension to ensure everyone in a military unit can read and understand it when it comes before them.

IRREFUTABLE POINT ONE— BELLWETHER COUNTIES

I leaned right into the first point, "bellwether counties," and pointed to a map of nineteen counties that had backed every presidential winner since 1980. Bellwethers, or leading indicators of final election outcomes, come and go, but these nineteen were the most relevant and consistent of an arrangement of counties that hadn't missed since 1976 or before—like in the case of Valencia County, New Mexico, which had been perfect since Eisenhower nabbed it in 1952. All nineteen had backed Trump in 2016, and curiously, eighteen of the nineteen backed him in 2020. The only exception was Clallam County, Washington, which sits at the northern end of the Olympic Peninsula and undoubtedly tilted left due to Washington's universal mail-in voting law and the increased focus of ballot harvesters working to inflate Biden's popular vote total. States often have their own notable bellwether counties, such as Pennsylvania's Luzerne County, which aligned with every presidential candidate carrying the Keystone State from 1936 through 2016, only to back Trump and fail as a predictor in 2020. These counties are mostly small and represent the working-class demographic that vaulted Trump to the presidency four years before they nearly all failed as predictive entities simultaneously. It seems they didn't get the message to abandon the incumbent in 2020, but since bellwethers only represent correlation, I would have to continue providing "sizzle."

IRREFUTABLE POINT TWO—
BELLWETHER STATES

Before I did that, I introduced the second point, "bellwether states," which graduated the first point into a higher and more comprehensive tier of analysis. Most are familiar with the quadrennial rollout of Florida or Ohio being critical to the contenders' chances, with Ohio having missed only twice between 1896 and 2016 (in 1944 and 1960) in aligning with the ultimate winner, and Florida being perfect all but once since 1964. Combining Florida, Ohio, North Carolina, and Iowa, however, gave a candidate an unbeatable hand. Since 1896, all four had gone to the same candidate thirteen times (including Trump in 2016), and all thirteen times they aligned with the same candidate, they always chose the winner. That is, except for in what Americans were told was the most secure election in the history of the Republic, when

Trump won all four again but somehow lost to a candidate who didn't campaign with any degree of sincerity.

IRREFUTABLE POINT THREE—SHARE OF PRIMARY VOTE

"Share of primary vote" was the third point and tucked into the presentation specifically to address "Never Trump" Republicans who insisted Republicans weren't fully behind Trump and that a different candidate, perhaps the chameleon Joe Walsh, would have prevailed if nominated against Biden. Presidential primary elections were first introduced in 1912, and prior to 2020, four incumbent presidents had been defeated after winning their party's nomination through the primary election. None of them had a primary share higher than George H. W. Bush's 72.8 percent share in 1992. In fact, Jimmy Carter (1980, 51.1 percent), Gerald Ford (1976, 53.3 percent), and Herbert Hoover (1932, 36.0 percent) had winning shares so low their general election losses should have been seen coming before the ballots were even printed. Trump, despite the COVID-19–ravaged 2020 primary campaign, polled at an incredible 94 percent in the GOP primary, the fourth-highest primary vote share of all time regardless of party. Dr. Helmut Norpoth of Stony Brook University, whose Primary Model rarely failed, gave Trump a 91 percent chance of victory based on his overwhelming win of the GOP primary.[2] Biden, on the other hand, stumbled his way through the early primaries, was blown out in Iowa and New Hampshire, and only gained his sea legs once the Democrats forced every candidate but Bernie Sanders to drop out before Super Tuesday. Notably, Biden had also attracted little interest in two previous presidential campaigns in his much younger years.

---

2   Helmut Norpoth, "Primary Model Predicts Trump Re-election," PrimaryModel.com, last updated October 17, 2020, http://primarymodel.com/2020-1.

IRREFUTABLE POINT FOUR—
INCUMBENT VOTE GAIN

The next point, number four, may be my favorite go-to point if someone asks for one single reason to doubt the 2020 presidential election results. I have a special appreciation for "incumbent vote gain" because it reaches back to the nineteenth century, making it impossible for skeptics to complain about a cherry-picked or insufficient sample size. In 1888, President Grover Cleveland, a Democrat, ran for reelection against his Republican challenger, Benjamin Harrison. Cleveland increased his 1884 vote total by over 600,000 popular votes, winning the national popular vote by almost a full percentage point, but lost the Electoral College because he lost his grip on New York (his home state) and Indiana, which he had won four years before. What is most notable about Cleveland's 1888 reelection campaign is not that he won the popular vote while losing the election (that happened twice before Cleveland and twice after), or that he lost his home state, but that he went down as the last president to gain votes from the previous election and not be reelected. This is why President Trump's 2020 pollster, John McLaughlin, believed Trump would be reelected if he received sixty-five million votes in 2020.[3] He had to have known incumbents that gain votes maintain their hold on political power. Cleveland, for 132 years, was the last person to gain votes but lose reelection until—what we are repeatedly assured to be—the safest and most secure election of all time happened. Trump didn't just gain the two million McLaughlin was looking for; he added more than eleven million to his 2016 total and *lost*.

---

3   Rev, "Donald Trump Wellington, Ohio Rally Speech Transcript: First Rally Since Leaving Office," transcript, June 26, 2021, https://www.rev.com/transcripts/donald-trump-wellington-ohio-rally-speech-transcript-first-rally-since-leaving-office.

IRREFUTABLE POINT FIVE— VOTER REGISTRATION BY PARTY

The fifth point, my guiding principle, is "voter registration by party." I have already discussed this point at length as to how it helped me perfectly predict the 2016 election and establish my picks for the ill-fated 2020 election. I will dust it back off again to demonstrate how it, along with my key research from the 2020 to 2023 timeframe, impacted the 2024 race. Trump's red state base, including Iowa, Ohio, Texas, and Georgia, appeared safe for 204 electoral votes. Florida and North Carolina, won by Trump in 2016 and again in 2020, had the Republican Party registration lean going into the latter. Florida progressed rightward, but North Carolina was stung by massive and unforeseen Biden gains that pushed the margin left from 2016. Still, both states held for Trump and gave him 44 more electoral votes. That would have been good for 248, if not for Georgia falling out of his column after several days of counting mail-in ballots. Pennsylvania's voter registration by party impact was enormous, greater than 21 to 1 in favor of the GOP for net new party registrations. The state was normally stronger for Republican reelection campaigns than the first time around and seemed like a Trump lock on all fronts, long before the election night margin came across the ticker on the bottom of TV screens across the nation. Despite the registration shift and an enormous outpouring of net new votes for Trump, a GOP record gain, Pennsylvania, and with it the 2020 election, finished left of its 2016 margin despite long-standing correlation with the registration indexes of the various battleground states. In short, to believe the outcome of Pennsylvania and similar states, one must believe that record numbers showed up to register Republican, then give Trump record vote gains, only to have the other side match and surpass those performances in the same election with no suggestive evidence through voter registration data that it was going to happen.

IRREFUTABLE POINT SIX—
US HOUSE ELECTIONS

The downballot outcomes, particularly in the US House, were noteworthy enough to provide the content for the sixth point, "US House elections." I pointed out three modern presidential landslides (both of Ronald Reagan's wins and Barack Obama's 2008 win) and the accompanying gain for the winner's party in the House. Reagan, winning in 1980 by 9.7 percent in the popular vote, also helped the GOP win thirty-four US House seats at a time when the Democrats controlled that chamber for decades. In Reagan's 18.2 percent victory for reelection, the GOP won sixteen seats from 1982's midterm losses. For the sake of parity, I pointed out Obama's 7.2 percent win from 2008 and how his party added twenty-one House seats to the majority that they already held going in. Curiously, Biden, despite having a 4.5 percent popular vote win, led the Democrats to a loss of thirteen House seats with not a single Republican incumbent defeated. One might think, with a record total of nearly 81.3 million votes when no Democrat had ever even cleared 70 million, that Biden would have tremendous coattails. Such an assumption would be dead wrong in the context of a national quasi election.

IRREFUTABLE POINT SEVEN—
TREND OF FLORIDA

Florida's coattails were what I was concerned about and looking for as the first indication of Trump's reelection. As noted previously, Florida, Pennsylvania, and Michigan had moved in the same direction in every presidential election since 1952. With seventeen elections to draw this conclusion from, I assumed that if Florida moved right from its 2016 margin that Pennsylvania and Michigan would follow. Pennsylvania's massive GOP party registration edge solidified my assessment, and Trump's leads in both states as counting progressed on election night, combined with a 3.4 percent margin in Florida and a tight race in Miami-Dade County, made it all but certain. Betting markets on the night of "Three November" moved heavily toward Trump based on the same data I had compiled for months and was watching unfold in real time.

IRREFUTABLE POINT EIGHT—HISTORIC BATTLEGROUND PERFORMANCES FOR TRUMP

For my eighth point, I referenced "historic battleground performances for Trump." Most of the time, when incumbent presidents have been unseated or when states or counties that reliably backed candidates of one party suddenly switched to the other, the party losing traction stalls out or declines in votes. For instance, Trump's 2024 performance for total votes in Alexandria, Arlington County, Fairfax, Fairfax County, Falls Church, and Manassas—six of the ten counties or cities of Northern Virginia—lags George W. Bush's performances from two decades ago. That is an example of what Richard Baris calls a "coalition shift," and one working against Republicans. Fortunately for Trump and the revitalized GOP, most coalition shifts in America have been moving in one direction—hard to the right—since MAGA politics became the way of the party. Trump's 2020 performances in battlegrounds are not consistent with Republicans losing ground. For instance, Trump's gain in Maricopa County, up 248,304 from a winning performance in 2016, is an all-time Republican record gain, topping George W. Bush's 2004 gain by almost 50,000, but not enough to win a county that always votes Republican for president. Likewise, Trump's gain statewide in Arizona was an all-time GOP record gain, but not enough to win what has been the most reliably Republican state in the union since 1952. You can find record Republican gains all over the map, like in Texas and Nevada, or near-record gains in Pennsylvania, Georgia, Wisconsin, and Michigan, which inexplicably led to left-leaning results no matter how grim the primary or registration numbers appeared for Biden's chances.

IRREFUTABLE POINT NINE— TRUMP'S RECORD MINORITY GAINS

"Trump's record minority gains" was my ninth point, referring mostly to modern Republican records, considering identity politics having set in and disproportionally warping the voting patterns of non-whites everywhere. Trump received an estimated 26 percent of the non-white vote in 2020 according to multiple studies.[4] However, they dispute if he or George W. Bush had a higher share because the Latino vote is increasingly hard to separate out, and because secret balloting makes it impossible to confirm voting preferences of any group; therefore, we are left with exit-polling data. Nevertheless, whether it is the best minority performance in generations or merely the second best, Trump's improvements with black voters should have floated his campaign in Georgia, especially with Republican strongholds bursting at the seams with massive increases in Trump votes compared to 2016; Trump gained just 10,416 votes over Romney's 2012 total and had no issue holding Georgia, but gained 372,750 in

---

4   Simone Esters, "Blunt's Wrong: Trump Did Not Get the Highest Minority Vote Percentage in 100 Years," PolitiFact, December 8, 2020, https://www.politifact.com/factchecks/2020/dec/08/roy-blunt/blunts-wrong-trump-did-not-get-highest-minority-vo/.

his reelection campaign only to drop the state for his party for the first time in twenty-eight years. Despite these improvements with Latino voters and a record gain of net new votes in Texas, his margin of victory plunged from 9 percent in 2016 to 5.6 percent in 2020, the closest presidential race in the Lone Star State since 1996.

IRREFUTABLE POINT TEN—POST-ELECTION BEHAVIOR BY POLITICIANS AND MEDIA ALLIES

The final point, "post-election behavior by politicians and media allies," is the only point to get away from history and statistics and take aim at anecdotal information and ongoing battles in the information war. Politics these days are toxic, and both sides are looking for ways to show the other up. They thrive on the utter humiliation of their rivals. When Trump won the battleground states narrowly in 2016 and the Clinton campaign sought recounts, Trump's base reveled in the opportunity to laugh at the almost-queen's futility and agony, unafraid at what further digging would reveal. Trump proceeded to become both one of the most loved and hated presidents of all time, making Bush's "Global War on Terror" and economic meltdown heyday look like a time of national unity and togetherness by comparison.

Beating Trump should have been something Democrats took great joy in, and a moment they'd love to relive as often as their Republican opponents would give them the opportunity. Instead, as the battle for righting the 2020 election burned hot, Biden traveled to Pennsylvania to discourage any audits, which were coming into view thanks to relentless fighters like Toni Shuppe of Audit the Vote PA, a hero of the election integrity grassroots, and Senator Doug Mastriano. Michigan Attorney General Dana Nessel, one-third of the state's triumvirate of top female officials who are what critics argue are the most corrupt anywhere in the nation, threatened to use state law enforcement to crack down on election integrity efforts in that state. Finally, shielded by a mix of state officials doing everything possible to prevent full disclosure of all 2020 election-related information, Colorado Secretary of State Jena Griswold announced there would be no election audits of any kind allowed in her state—one that Biden had carried by 13.5 percent in the largest Democratic presidential win since Lyndon Johnson's nationwide thrashing of Barry Goldwater fifty-six years earlier. Griswold was feeling pressure after Tina Peters, the Mesa County clerk and a Gold Star Mother, had come forward with what she believed to be forensic proof that outside actors had tampered with the results of her county's election. Sadly, Peters received a nine-year prison sentence from the state in 2024, and President Trump's early second term overtures to set her free have hit a brick wall.

I walked off the stage to applause, and checking my phone, found that I had reached a vast audience of people who now believed beyond a shadow of a doubt that the 2020 election had a stench to it that couldn't be reconciled under anything Americans had known through the country's rich history of presidential elections. Although I was in between commendations from President Trump, I couldn't have known I was on the verge of setting out to nearly every state for the next three years for one mission—"Prove it."

I received a diploma upon graduating from my very first Military Intelligence training in 2009 with the branch's creed on it. It contains the statement, "for in truth lies victory." The Cyber Symposium showed me that there were millions of Americans listening every day for the truth. Someone had to take it to them, and I'd been preparing for the mission for years.

CHAPTER 11

In the Presence of My Enemies

I spent the next four months traveling coast-to-coast preaching the newfound gospel of election integrity while still holding down a day job in the turbulent government sales sector. While I knew my time doing that was limited thanks to my increasing prominence as one of America's most notorious "election deniers," I still hadn't figured out just how the hell I was supposed to support myself or my family in the patriot economy.

In Grand Rapids, Michigan, shortly after President Donald Trump's second "shout out," a trusted mentor grabbed me and suggested I get someone I trust to handle emails and calls to book me for my events, and to control demand by charging a modest fee and travel expenses. This turned out to be wise advice, because there were more events requested than I could possibly take on while still remaining an effective (and honest) employee and still having a personal family life. Alison Williams, of the unwarranted battleground state of Georgia, stepped up to the plate and single-handedly turned me into a polished product ready to fly anywhere, with all details covered down to what kind of legroom my rental car would have. She had multiple events per week booked several weeks out, and all she asked for was a contribution of her share to be donated to her church.

Churches, convention centers, businesses, and private residences opened up to host events. Mitch Clemmons, a plumber turned election integrity fighter, got me out to Los Angeles County in front of several hundred people eager to hear the truth about the mothership of Democratic corruption, which had just repelled a statewide effort to recall Gavin Newsom with their universal mail-in voting scam. Holly Kesler hosted me in Savannah, Georgia, in front of a crowd mixed with election skeptics and old guard Georgia Republicans eager to turn the page from Trump. On one frigid night in a warehouse in Crow Wing County, Minnesota, I spoke in front of more than five hundred people and met Jason Lewis, the former congressman who had run for US Senate and finished ahead of Trump in an extremely corrupted race both men lost.

No event landed me in hotter water than the one held in Manchester, New Hampshire,[1] on November 19, my first event in any of the six New England states. The event was hosted by Marilyn Todd, and included a few local speakers, Ivan Raiklin and David Clements. As I waited my turn, I met Boston Red Sox fan favorite Rico Petrocelli, now active in New Hampshire Republican politics. Rico was an all-star and key cog in the Red Sox lineup in the 1960s and 1970s, and we spent more time talking about baseball than politics. I called him out during my speech and reminded the crowd that there should be no more "leaving your so-called blue states for Florida and Texas." New England was the birthplace of liberty in the colonies, and to see it in such dire political straits now is truly depressing. New Hampshire is the most conservative of those six states but had a few wide-open issues, such as lack of voter ID and abuse of same-day voter regis-

---

[1]   NH Voter Integrity Group, "5-Seth Keshel NH Election Integrity Seminar," video, November 19, 2021, posted November 22, 2021, 49 min., 5 sec., Rumble, https://rumble.com/vplmrd-5-seth-keshel-nh-election-integrity-seminar.html.

tration by "Massholes" to their south that often manipulated close races going back decades.

My speaking event went over well, which was the standard outcome owed to a refined presentation tailored to each individual county I visited and my increasing confidence that what I was doing was tied to a just mission. One of the attendees there, Brad Heath, didn't agree. He was there on behalf of Reuters, the global news organization, and he had his mission to take a few shots at two of the military veterans his organization was looking to take down in the public eye. On December 15, the publication ran the big exposé on me, Ivan Raiklin (a now-retired army lieutenant colonel), Colonel (Ret., US Army) Phil Waldron, and General Michael Flynn, four voices with massive reach on the issue of national election corruption who continued to press the issue far beyond the point nearly any elected office holder was willing to take it.

The piece was dubbed, "The Military-Intelligence Veterans Who Helped Lead Trump's Campaign of Disinformation."[2] As the most junior officer on the hit list, to say I was honored is an understatement—primarily because I believe the propagandists in mainstream media won't bother to take a swing unless the target is worth swinging at. The piece was released so close to Christmas, I figured it wouldn't interrupt my operations much, but I was wrong. On January 4, 2022, on a trip to South Florida, I found myself unexpectedly unemployed, with "sales revenue" as the cause for dismissal. There is no way to prove motive but getting canned at the beginning of the month with plans made the week before for future work travels doesn't exactly line up with a termination that had been brewing for long.

---

2   Aram Roston, Brad Heath, John Shiffman, and Peter Eisler, "The Military-Intelligence Veterans Who Helped Lead Trump's Campaign of Disinformation," Reuters, December 15, 2021, https://www.reuters.com/investigates/special-report/usa-election-military/.

Further complicating my life at that time was the process of divorce, which I had been dealing with for three months. In half a year, I had gone from unlimited potential to facing the very human worries of providing for children, remaining relevant on a career path that mattered, and balancing core beliefs and mission with the most basic need to make a living. I was thirty-seven years old, and with a recently magnified political profile standing for everything the people in power stood against, I didn't like my odds in stepping back into the standard job market. I had risked that to stand up for what I believed in, and folding up the flag was simply not an option. Now without a steady income and armed with a single consultant contract on the side, I took up residence in a six hundred square foot apartment in Fort Worth and committed to seeing the mission through. My personal crisis of divorce and unemployment was my first real test to see if I would stick with it when things got tough, and I suspect my father's stubbornness is what kept me on track and unwilling to step away from the issue I believed would dictate not only my own future, but that of my children and theirs.

When I encourage people to live out their convictions and take the steps of faith needed to go "all in," I reference these trying times in my life when given the opportunity to publicly recant my positions, quit, and beg for employment so I could get by. Going through depressing life changes filled me with enough defiance to keep charging ahead, and looking at my schedule, I had enough speaking events booked in January and February 2022 to stay busy. Then in February, March started booking up, and so on as the months passed. On March 14, 2022, I published my first article on Captain K's Corner, my Substack publication, which is now a best-selling newsletter worldwide and among the top right-of-center newsletters on the platform. It lands in the inboxes of some of the most important movers and shakers in the world, including prominent elected officials, key media allies, aides, business executives, and most importantly, the grassroots patriots who make action happen over all 3,143 counties and independent cities in the United States. My newsletter attracted paying subscribers by the hundreds every month throughout 2022, another key election year characterized by the American political right striving with all its might to strike back against an administration thought of as a regime fervently persecuting its political opposition with the full weight and support of the federal government. To make things even more serious, a strong majority of Republican voters had continued to believe Joe Biden had been illegitimately elected,[3] an albatross that would hang around the forty-sixth president's neck until he retired to private life on January 20, 2025.

I traveled to or through forty-eight states in 2022, drawing the ire of local journalists and GOP mainstays eager to move on from the election they had no answer for. My travels even took me to Hawaii on two separate trips, and when informed that Biden was a stronger candidate there than Barack Obama was, the attendees didn't believe it, either. I was also invited to keynote the first election integrity-themed events in Alaska, which were held in three separate cities in May. National Public Radio, which I lambasted as "National Propaganda Radio" at events, profiled me, Dr. Douglas Frank, David Clements, and Mike Lindell in a June hit piece,[4] marveling at the miles we "election deniers" covered to share research, solutions, and effective messaging points

---

3   Mark Murray, "Poll: 61% of Republicans Still Believe Biden Didn't Win Fair and Square in 2020," NBC News, September 27, 2022, https://www.nbcnews.com/meet-the-press/meetthepressblog/poll-61-republicans-still-believe-biden-didnt-win-fair-square-2020-rcna49630.

4   Miles Parks, Allison Mollenkamp, and Nick McMillan, "Election Deniers Have Taken Their Fraud Theories on Tour — to Nearly Every State," NPR, June 30, 2022, https://www.npr.org/2022/06/30/1107868327/election-deniers-have-taken-their-fraud-theories-on-tour-to-nearly-every-state.

against election corruption. I had been credited with events in the most states up to that point but was slightly behind Dr. Frank in terms of event quantity. True to intelligence officer form, I submitted an accurate map and listing of events, which they never bothered to apply.

Few Republican candidates, except for the most entrenched incumbents, were safe that year without a strong position in favor of election integrity measures. I was called upon to moderate numerous candidate forums in which the crowd most wanted to know about candidate stances on the 2020 election, especially in critical battlegrounds like Pennsylvania. Candidates would have been better off advocating for shipping factories to Mexico than they would have been by asserting confidence in Biden carrying the Keystone State fairly. One of the loudest and most impactful voices that year belonged to Kari Lake, a former news anchor who threw her hat in the ring to replace Doug Ducey as Arizona's governor.

I had met Kari briefly the previous summer, and at an event in Gila County in May 2022, I caught her on the way out the back door in a rush to get back to Maricopa County for an evening event. Because I accurately perceived her strong convictions over how corrupt Arizona's elections were (and still are), I informed her I had plenty of precinct-level research to share with her team if she had interest in reviewing it. She immediately told me to take down her cell phone number and add her to my Substack list. She craved information, read everything I wrote on elections, and showed a level of scrutiny all Republican candidates or elected officials should have. This, I thought, was what those untainted by the professional political world are capable of. With President Trump's endorsement and her grassroots appeal, no one could have imagined her November race against Democratic

Secretary of State Katie Hobbs would have been the boiling point of the 2022 midterms.

Grassroots movements are plagued by infighting, especially those existing on the political right. In one short year since the election integrity movement began in earnest, many of the key voices had lost credibility or loyal followings, particularly when their platforms became more about sparring with others than getting to the bottom of what the public demanded answers for. I had managed to avoid most of these spats, focused more on what I could prove, and as such, maintained positive rapport with grassroots patriots and credibility on increasingly mainline broadcasts. I recognized the importance of working within both factions to implement solutions and knew when to wield the rough edges effectively. Shortly before midterms, at a ReAwaken America event in Manheim, Pennsylvania, I had taken issue with local reporter Carter Walker's trash-talk article covering the event. I decided to encourage the audience to greet him when they saw him and read a few of his comments aloud as his media photo adorned my slide deck, visible to all. This is some of the feedback Dr. Mark Clatterbuck, writing for Religion Dispatches,[5] gave in review of my accountability play:

> At times during the rally, the threats of violence got frighteningly specific. After writing a straightforward news account of the rally's first day, a local Lancaster reporter was publicly called out by Seth Keshel, a nationally known personality in the election-fraud circuit.

---

5   Mark Clatterbuck, "From Shofars to Hammers: The Spiritual Warriors of MAGA are 'ReAwakening' to Political Violence," Religion Dispatches, n.d., accessed November 22, 2025, https://religiondispatches.org/from-shofars-to-hammers-the-spiritual-warriors-of-maga-are-reawakening-to-political-violence/.

> The six-foot-six former Army captain who
> worked in military intelligence, after issuing a
> lengthy attack on "the mainstream media" and
> expressing displeasure in the local reporter's
> story, projected a headshot of the writer on the
> arena's giant video screens. He wondered aloud
> if the reporter was still infiltrating their rally.
> Thunderous applause from thousands around
> me greeted this US military officer as he publicly
> threatened a member of our local press.

It irritates the hell out of me that media can conduct themselves in any way they wish, while bristling at the thought of being called out. I wasn't having it then, and I won't have it now. I didn't hear anything else from Carter Walker after he was greeted by thousands of new friends.

The 2022 midterms brought a mix of anxiety and optimism for those involved in the information war against election corruption. "Once bitten, twice shy" was a suitable phrase for those who expected the worst out of the most critical states, especially in key battlegrounds. It turns out that many of the officials who oversaw the 2020 quasi election in their respective states—such as Governor Gretchen Whitmer, Attorney General Dana Nessel, and Secretary of State Jocelyn Benson in Michigan, or Secretary of State Katie Hobbs in Arizona—had won those offices in the 2018 midterm cycle. Hobbs was preparing to administer her own gubernatorial election against Lake, which should not be allowed under any circumstances. She had also bitterly protested private citizens expressing grievances over the way she ran the 2020 race, which involved the downfall of one of the strongest Republican states of all time against the incumbent president who made a record vote gain for one cycle—save for the one in the opposite column against him, achieved in that very same election by Biden.

Ironically, Hobbs's 2018 opponent, Republican Steve Gaynor, had been called the winner on election night, only to have that lead suspiciously slip away, vaulting Hobbs to the second-highest office in the state and her moment in the sun to rip off not only Arizona's electoral votes in 2020 but its top office in the very next cycle. Even after a makeover, she was and is an uninspiring, uncharismatic, former state legislator who speaks to the people of a conservative state as if they were residents of San Francisco. Despite propagandized polling, few expected her to stand a chance against Lake, who had a solid lead in the final average of polls,[6] including one outlier from Fox 10 Phoenix/Insider Advantage with Lake up by eleven percentage points,[7] just a few points shy of Ducey's blowout reelection margin from 2018. So uninspiring is Hobbs that most Arizonans couldn't pick her out of a lineup three years after she hid from Lake at every opportunity and was installed by a corrupt coalition of subversives to govern Arizona.

Lake was inspiring, energetic, smart, had the right positions, and perhaps most satisfying for supporters, took great joy in making mincemeat of media blowhards by mocking them for wearing masks, parroting propaganda, and covering over the blatant cheating that rendered Arizona's elections a national laughingstock. My friend and colleague Mark Finchem was running on the same ticket for secretary of state, and unbeknownst to me, so was my future wife for a seat in the Arizona House.

---

6   RealClearPolling, "2022 Arizona Governor - Lake vs. Hobbs," accessed November 23, 2025, https://www.realclearpolling.com/polls/governor/general/2022/arizona/lake-vs-hobbs.

7   "FOX 10/Moneywise/Data Orbital Poll: Lake Leads Governor's Race, Senate Race Tightens," FOX 10 Phoenix, October 26, 2022, accessed November 23, 2025, https://www.fox10phoenix.com/news/2022-arizona-election-poll-lake-leads-governors-race-senate-race-tightens.

Along with all that anxiety, optimism was also justified. As long as President Trump drew breath and waited in the wings for either a breakthrough against corrupt elections or another run for the presidency, the Republican Party was his party. A midterm win putting Republicans in control of the House, in addition to holding or expanding the narrow Senate majority, would be seen as a key check against Biden's administration at a critical juncture, creating momentum for the 2024 campaign and allowing us to see what, if anything, worked in the brave new age of quasi elections tainted with mail-in balloting and ballot harvesting. The two previous midterms with a Democratic president, 2010 and 2014, saw massive Republican gains, and Biden had nowhere near the charisma or silk tongue Obama had to get out of his frequent messes. Since 1934, the president's party had gained net House seats in just three of twenty-two midterm attempts. With Democrats holding a lead of just 9 seats (as elected in 2020), a flip of the House seemed certain to me based on historical outcomes.

In the end, the Republicans took control of the House, winning 9 seats and taking a 222 to 213 lead, but inexplicably lost control of the Senate and lost three governor's mansions, while picking up only Nevada's top spot. Conservative media tried to soften the blow by focusing on the House flip, but this was no red wave. It was nothing short of an overall disaster and major disappointment owed to gerrymandered maps, bad strategy, and races now unwinnable thanks to the passage of election laws in various states guaranteeing the dominance of one party—the Democratic Party. The most shocking of all losses was the downfall of the Republican ticket in Arizona, including Lake's campaign for governor.

Because Lake had made election integrity such a crucial part of her campaign, she encouraged her Republican primary supporters to vote on primary election day, held on August 2. I attended

Lake's watch party in Arizona that day en route to a series of events, and the time spent watching the percentage of ballots tick by before Election Day votes came in was quite uncomfortable. In the end, Lake had prevailed for the nomination over Karrin Taylor Robson, but strictly because of her margins on Election Day. When the defense can't stop the running back, the offense keeps running the ball—so Election Day voting, rather than relying on the corrupt mail-in voting system promoted statewide, would be the plan for November against Hobbs.

With three months to scheme, Maricopa County officials orchestrated an election that was every bit as corrupt as the 2020 presidential race, taking nearly a week to call the election for Hobbs and leaving a trail of wrongdoing so thick even the political elite couldn't keep it out of the courtroom. Lake's legal team maintained that tabulators went down at 62 percent of the vote centers, causing lines as long as four hours at 51 percent of all Election Day vote centers.[8] Though the 17,117-vote margin between Lake and Hobbs narrowly exceeded the margin for a statewide recount, it was extremely tight considering that the state reported almost 2.6 million votes for the gubernatorial race. It is still unclear if Maricopa County properly counted the ballots that should have been inserted into the tabulators that had failed. Put another way, if one out of every 150 ballots recorded was a mail-in ballot illegally harvested and deposited in a drop box—which left-wing legal acolyte Marc Elias was guarding like a hawk and threatening anyone suggesting they be monitored by citizens around the clock once voting began—then Hobbs would have had no advantage at all and lost to Lake.

Downballot from Lake, Abraham Hamadeh dropped the attorney general race to Democrat Kris Mayes by a razor-thin margin of

---

8   Mark Sonnenklar, attorney on Kari Lake's team, email message to author, October 29, 2025.

280 ballots, with thousands of provisional ballots uncounted and county supervisors around the state threatened with major legal consequences from Hobbs, serving in her secretary of state capacity, for their reluctance to certify their county's election results.

Lake sued Maricopa County's board of supervisors, recorder, and other election officials to overturn what appeared to be a fraudulent election. When Maricopa County Superior Court Judge Peter Thompson ordered a two-day trial to hear Lake's claims against the defendants, a reluctant optimism began to spread among Lake's supporters. Her legal team presented ten causes of action in Lake's filed complaint, but Judge Thompson allowed only two of those causes of action to be argued in the election contest trial. Those were Count II—Illegal BOD Printer/Tabulator Configurations and Count IV—Chain of Custody Violations.

As I noted in my Substack article, "A Comprehensive Guide to the Lake v. Hobbs Trial,"[9] "Count II…pertains to the [E]lection [D]ay debacle related to machine malfunctions and tabulator errors. The challenge will be to prove that said debacle was deliberately incurred and given that Maricopa County apparently maintained a Republican voter 'heat map' and its magistrates have openly opposed Kari Lake, Donald Trump, and the America First agenda, this may be possible."

Maricopa County did everything but lay out spike strips on the highways to stop Republican voters from making it to voting centers on general Election Day, because they knew that Lake was encouraging her voters to vote in person that day. After all, that had been the same game plan that had vaulted Lake to victory in the GOP primary three months before. The election day tabulator malfunctions disproportionately affected Lake's voters

---

9   Seth Keshel, "A Comprehensive Guide to the Lake v. Hobbs Trial," Captain K's Corner (Substack), December 21, 2022, https://www.captaink.us/p/a-comprehensive-guide-to-the-lake.

because 70 percent of Election Day voters cast their ballot for Lake according to the Arizona secretary of state (while a majority of Hobbs's voters voted by mail, as did the overwhelming majority of her phantom voters) and the tabulators had a higher fail rate in Republican areas within Maricopa County. As a result of the tabulator malfunctions, which were widely publicized on Election Day by the mainstream media and social media, many voters stayed home, dropped out of the long lines created by the tabulator issues, and neglected to cast a ballot. Classic voter disenfranchisement.

Unfortunately, Judge Thompson required Lake to prove that Maricopa County election officials intentionally violated the election laws with respect to the tabulators and chain of custody, despite the fact that Arizona legal precedents only required that Lake prove that the violations of law affected the result of the election or at least rendered it uncertain. If Thompson had applied the correct legal standard, Lake would have likely prevailed on Counts II and IV. Instead, Judge Thompson imposed a much higher intentionality standard on Lake that was very difficult to prove with only six weeks to gather evidence and prepare for the election contest trial, and Thompson therefore was able to conclude that Lake had not satisfied her burden of proof on either legal claim. With this decision, Hobbs cemented her win against Lake.

Judge Thompson's formal opinion,[10] issued on the relative safety of Christmas Eve when few were paying enough attention to get angry, started off with letting us down easy:

"Throughout the history of Arizona, the bar to overturn an election on the grounds of misconduct in this State—or Territory—has always been a high one."

---

10   Kari Lake v. Katie Hobbs, et al., CV2022-095403 (Ariz. Super. Ct. Dec. 24, 2022), https://www.democracydocket.com/wp-content/uploads/2022/12/UA-Ruling-Lake-vs.-Hobbs.pdf.

Thompson listed off one excuse after another, acknowledged "inconvenience and confusion at voter centers," and ultimately decided Lake's team didn't present enough evidence to set aside a margin of 17,117 ballots.

After losing her first election contest, Lake appealed the decision. While the appellate court refused to overturn Judge Thompson's decisions on Counts II and IV, the court did find that Judge Thompson had made a mistake in dismissing Count III—Signature Verification, forcing Thompson to hold a second election contest trial. In that second trial, Lake's counsel, Kurt Olsen, clearly demonstrated Maricopa County's complete disregard for proper signature verification, but Lake and her legal team were once again foiled by Thompson's impossibly high bar of proving that "no signature verification" took place. Not even Superman could have validated as many signatures as fast as those who were checking off scribbles on ballot envelopes that were overwhelmingly favoring Hobbs. The court found that Lake was unable to prove that Maricopa County signature verifiers had improperly approved signatures on mail-in ballots and therefore her election contest failed once again.

Once again, the success of a key Democratic battleground campaign was made possible because of that party's iron-fisted control of the mail-in balloting apparatus, use of ballot harvesters, lawfare covering these actions, control over the slow-rolled counting process that other nations decry as clear signals of election fraud, and perhaps most importantly, the rubber-stamping of courts afraid to overturn a major election. With the disappointing results of Lake's contest, certainly not owed to the performance of her counsel or a lack of evidence, the 2022 midterm cycle disappeared in the rearview mirror and left only the 2024 presidential election as the preeminent showdown for the future of American liberty.

Trump's November 15 announcement that he would once again seek the presidency made it certain, even before Thompson's weak ruling, that election integrity would remain front and center. Still, there was significant fear of a 2020 repeat lying ahead with states run by the same villains who presided over the previous presidential race, especially with the likes of Hobbs and Pennsylvania's Josh Shapiro promoted to governorships and the unholy trio of Whitmer, Nessel, and Benson still calling the shots in Michigan.

Those of us who were knee deep in election integrity issues weren't the only ones on the fence about how to assess the 2024 landscape, especially with such a disappointing 2022 cycle about to wrap up. I visited the Mar-a-Lago Club on December 6 for a poolside event and dinner and monitored my phone for updates as Herschel Walker was denied in Georgia's runoff election for US Senate, which put a serious damper on the mood of a crowd wanting any semblance of a win. I stayed around a couple days, and on that next day, the eighty-first anniversary of Pearl Harbor, I was the guest of Cameron Moore, a friend and club member. Dinner was out on the patio, with President Trump and his guests seated at the center, under an unforgettable full moon that lit up the entire coastline. Our party was wrapping up when Cameron noticed the president greeting guests on his way out of the seating area. He motioned at me with a head nod and said, "Let's go," and a few moments later, I was having my first conversation with the man who had launched me just sixteen months earlier. I was extremely humbled as he remembered me and told me I was doing "great work." Reaching into my coat pocket, I pulled out one of my personalized challenge coins, a military souvenir exchanged as a token of respect and handed it to him. He asked me a few questions, and without hesitation, I pulled out my phone and showed him a few graphics about the 2020 election I had made. He was especially curious about some of the deep blue states, such as New Mexico, that never seem to budge despite all indications they are ready to change course. I told him I was at his service to make sure he got over the line in 2024, and he, knowing from firsthand experience, said, "I don't know if they'll let us in."

That was a wake-up call I'll never forget. We had work to do and no one else was coming to do it for us. If President Trump had no idea how things were going to pan out, then no one could let off the gas.

CHAPTER 12

Assembling the Broken Pieces

In those early days of 2023, in the wake of the midterm letdown and the disinterested, politically motivated rulings in Maricopa County, which also negatively impacted Abraham Hamadeh and Mark Finchem, I wasn't sure how to apply my focus. If anything was clear, it was that without nationwide election reform, Republicans simply weren't going to overwhelm at the polls enough to tilt the most important races as long as their Democratic opponents deepened their mastery of ballot harvesting. That is what Arizona Republicans thought they would do in the 2022 midterms, and it failed miserably. Nearly a year after returning to bachelorhood, I had transitioned out of my small Fort Worth apartment and took up residence west of town in a nice motor home, which I had expected to be a traveling headquarters.

While I had no idea what the demand for my time and travel would be, I did know I had just under two years to provide the most accurate assessment possible of President Donald Trump's path back to 1600 Pennsylvania Avenue on a map that had changed drastically in the six years since he had first been elected. For two years, I'd contended against people who insisted on proving that Trump must have won California because there were more of his campaign signs than Joe Biden's in a given area. But I had developed the ability to convince anyone who would listen that the data just didn't work out in the battleground states that would decide the winner of our next presidential election, which was widely expected to be a rematch between Trump and Biden as 2023 got started.

One of my first notable missions of the year was to present my extensive research of Arizona's electoral system, plus recommendations for improvement, on the floor of the Arizona Senate at a joint meeting of the House and Senate elections committees on February 23. With just two days' notice, I had been put up to the appearance by Liz Harris, a newly elected state representative from Chandler, representing Arizona's Thirteenth Legislative District. I had known Liz since 2021, when she headed up a widely criticized independent canvass of the 2020 election, and helped disseminate her findings over the airwaves. Her canvass came with the arduous task of interviewing potentially hostile voters, radicalized by local media calling her a threat to democracy, and compiling accurate information over one of the largest urban areas in the United States. She parlayed her grassroots rapport into a seat in the state legislature, and she knew just who to call when she needed to paint a corrupt state with a broad brush of data the press would rather ignore than investigate.

This time, it wasn't just Biden taking fire for his freak "victory" in Arizona. I concentrated a significant portion of my briefing on the new administration of Katie Hobbs that had begun its veto tour, and the local Arizona Mirror did all it could to cover for her. Caitlin Sievers wrote:[1]

> Also testifying before the committees was Seth
> Keshel, one of the originators of the Big Lie.
> Keshel, a former U.S. Army intelligence analyst,

---

1   Caitlin Sievers, "Arizona GOP Legislators Continue to Give Oxygen to Disproven Election Conspiracies," Arizona Mirror, February 24, 2023, https://azmirror.com/2023/02/24/arizona-gop-legislators-continue-to-give-oxygen-to-disproven-election-conspiracies/.

shared his theory that something was off about the 2020 presidential election in Arizona because hundreds of thousands more Democrats than he expected voted in that election.

Keshel's theory is based on voting trends in Arizona over the past 75 years, during most of which the state was solidly red. But suspicion that too many Democrats turned out in that election to be plausible ignores the fervor ahead of the election that drew large numbers of both Republicans and Democrats to the voting booths that year, with record turnouts, as well as the changing demographics of Arizona.

What Sievers failed to point out is that very little of this unanticipated turnout, which blew away any jumps present in any previous election, showed up in "voting booths." Democrats had only become competitive in Arizona because mail-in balloting had grown for three decades under the supervision of feckless Republicans who were too worried about irritating their senior citizen voting bases to rein it in, despite constant legislative power giving them ample opportunity, and just one Democratic governor preceding Hobbs for the previous thirty-two years.

It was one of my most comprehensive, bulletproof briefings. With a slight decrease in speaking events since the end of the midterms, I had perfected my templates and briefing style, turning myself into the most obnoxiously accurate intelligence officer stereotype any veteran would describe at a moment's notice. That briefing, despite its success, wasn't the most noteworthy thing that happened to me that day. February 23 was the day I met Rachel Jones, one of two state representatives of the Seventeenth Legislative District, encompassing the outskirts of Tucson.

Shortly thereafter, President Trump ran into legal troubles, and it was clear to anyone with a working brain (like those who could see the 2020 election was anything but normal) that the bureaucracy was looking to sideline him in court rather than take on his expanding base with an increasingly uninspiring and declining Biden at the helm. Prior to Trump's announcement to seek the GOP nomination and presidency in 2024, most people working closely in election integrity worked to make the case that the 2020 election must be rectified. With Trump in the race, the mission was now to make those lessons stand out for 2024 and to identify a pathway, *any* pathway, that could put him back in the White House.

Intelligence officers are trained to identify the enemy's most likely courses of action. His insight is particularly valuable and if he is accurate, the commander puts a lot of weight into what he has to say; I had learned this firsthand a dozen years before as I established trust with my commander. With so much success last time, I thought, why wouldn't they go back to the same game plan that had vaulted a candidate well past his prime to the presidency without any serious campaign carrying him? It was no accident that states were rushing to expand mail-in balloting and entrench automatic voter registration. In fact, Minnesota, Hawaii, and Delaware had adopted the latter after the 2020 election, and Pennsylvania wasn't far behind. With so many states already under the Democratic banner and appearing as if they may never vote Republican again, a few tweaks and electoral makeovers could doom the GOP forever. It was evident to me that winning campaigns in the modern era, without any legal relief, must max out every last vote and, if possible, keep an eye out for where fraudulent ballots were likely to come from. The Precinct Mapping Project was born.

I had tinkered with the concept at the tail end of 2021 to support the efforts in Maricopa County. A fifteen-year-old young man named Ben Eskew, from the key state of Georgia, created the template still in use today for precinct analysis (originally requested by Jovan Pulitzer) and helped me break down over eight hundred precincts, organize findings, and contrast with other counties. Another godsend, Cherisse Wright from Texas, contributed countless hundreds of hours researching county files to populate and organize spreadsheets for me to analyze, and once that was done, the "sizzle" would go straight to my mapper, a professional from Mississippi named Jeff Pedigo. Many indispensable figures helped make the hard work of the Biden years possible, and thanks to their efforts, every county of every 2024 battleground state except Georgia was mapped all the way down to the precinct (or precinct equivalent) level, plus hundreds of non-battleground counties. Critics of the Precinct Mapping Project say the analysis draws upon too many assumptions, but with officials and courts presiding over the most suspect counties doing everything possible to limit election disclosures, there had to be another way to get to the truth.

Remember, the 81.3 million Biden votes, or ballots, is a gaudy number few believe could have ever been possible without the changes to the 2020 election and the actions of key battleground states before and especially after "Three November." Despite the ridiculously high total, only 42,918 ballots separated the two candidates in Arizona, Georgia, and Wisconsin. The logic therefore must be that if there are too many ballots in the national count, then there must be too many easily discernible in the counts of various states, such as those in Georgia that were all but done with the count on the morning of November 4, only to count for several more days. If there are too many votes in the states, then they can be found in the counties, and if they're in the counties, then they're down at the precinct level. Here is how it worked, using Navajo County, Arizona, as an example:

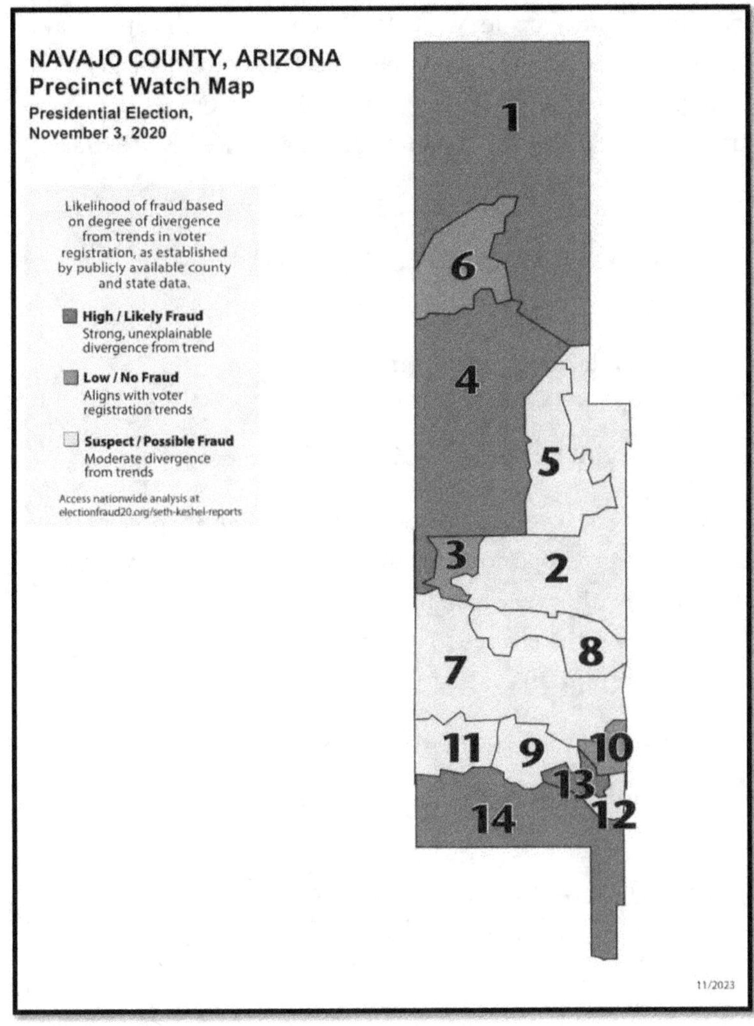

Map by Jeff Pedigo.

Prior to the 2020 election, ten of Navajo County's precincts were consolidated into a single precinct—Precinct One—Red Butte. The redrawn precinct runs flush with Utah's southern border and is squeezed between Apache County on its east and Coconino County on its west. It sits entirely within the Navajo Nation reservation and, as may be expected, is an overwhelmingly Democrat-voting precinct. In 2012, Barack Obama clobbered Mitt Romney in the ten precincts making up Red Butte today:[2]

Obama: 4,645 votes (85.8 percent)

Romney: 693 votes (12.8 percent)

Total Votes: 5,416

Presidential Turnout: 46.0 percent (11,765 registered voters)

Margin: Obama +3,952 (+73.0 percent)

Republicans running statewide campaigns in precincts like this one simply hope for low turnout, which is not an uncommon thing with overwhelmingly Native American populations. When they had the chance to choose between Hillary Clinton and Donald Trump in 2016, Red Butte voted this way:[3]

Clinton: 4,455 votes (77.8 percent)

Trump: 595 votes (10.4 percent)

---

2   Navajo County Elections Services, "Statement of Votes Cast, General Election, Navajo County, November 6, 2012, SOVC for Jurisdiction Wide, All Counters, All Races: Complete Official Results, November 20, 2012," Election Results, November 6, 2012, https://www.navajocountyaz.gov/DocumentCenter/View/1439/November-6-2012-Statement-of-Votes-Cast-PDF. The ten precincts include: Black Mesa, Chilchinbito, East Forest Lake, Whippoorwill Springs, Low Mountain, Pinon, Shonto, West Kayenta, Tachee-Blue Gap, East Kayenta.

3   Navajo County Elections Services, "SOVC by Polling Place," Election Results, November 8, 2016, https://www.navajocountyaz.gov/DocumentCenter/View/1426/SOVC-by-Polling-Place-PDF.

Total Votes: 5,726

Presidential Turnout: 46.9 percent (12,200 registered voters)

Margin: Clinton +3,860 (+67.4 percent)

While Trump still lost the consolidated precinct handily and by nearly an identical number of raw votes that Romney lost by, both candidates lagged the totals of Obama and Romney thanks to a larger-than-normal minor candidate vote share going primarily for Gary Johnson (Libertarian) or Jill Stein (Green). Total turnout was up 310 votes, or 5.7 percent. Perhaps the most shocking detail of the three-election sequence from 2012 to 2020 is that in his reelection campaign, Trump increased his vote total by 75.5 percent, moving from 595 votes in 2016 to an impressive 1,044 in 2020, a gain of 449—not far below the total gain in turnout from 2012 to 2016 considering all candidates. With Trump improving his vote total so substantially, it should have been a certainty that he would have drastically decreased his losing margin in Red Butte. Here are the certified 2020 results for the precinct:[4]

Biden: 6,500 votes (84.6 percent)

Trump: 1,044 votes (13.6 percent)

Total Votes: 7,686

Presidential Turnout: 60.1 percent (12,793 registered voters)

Margin: Biden +5,456 (+71.0 percent)

---

4   Navajo County Elections Services, "Precinct Results Report, County of Navajo, State of Arizona, November 3, 2020: Complete Official Results, General Election 2020," Election Results, November 3, 2020 General Election, https://www.navajocountyaz.gov/DocumentCenter/View/1376/Precicnt-Report---PDF.

Despite a gain of greater than 75 percent in Trump votes, Biden carried the precinct by 1,596 more votes than Clinton did four years before, which is more than 15 percent of the 10,457-vote statewide margin separating Biden and Trump in the 2020 race. When people complain only about Maricopa or Pima Counties, they're incredibly shortsighted and miss substantial indications of malfeasance in the far-flung corners of the state. To make matters more obvious, the boom in turnout wasn't preceded by a massive boom in voter registration. That was up just 593 from the 2016 election, not a big gain over the net change from 2012 to 2016. Trump lost 2020 Election Day voting 4 to 1 in Red Butte, but 8 to 1 in early voting, made up largely of mail-in balloting. The gain in Biden votes did not reconcile with such a large increase in Trump support, particularly considering the gain of 1,960 net votes cast over the 2016 election, and I consider it highly likely that the precinct and those in the immediate vicinity were targeted for ballot harvesting, which has been illegal in Arizona under Arizona Revised Statute § 16-1005 since 2016.[5]

Critics of this methodology say it is meritless because it doesn't prove fraud. That may be true, but it does identify areas in which there is little change to voter registration, but massive change in the incumbent president's vote totals that didn't help him make margins tighter. Navajo County, in keeping with decennial redistricting requirements, redrew its map boundaries, so the trail on Red Butte can no longer be followed to the most precise detail; however, Kamala Harris lagged Joe Biden by 2,629 ballots countywide, suggesting that at least some complacency on the part of ballot collectors had enabled a much wider margin of victory for Trump in Navajo County. Cherisse pulled up unofficial details on Red Butte using the Redistricter platform after

---

5   Arizona State Legislature, "16-1005, "Ballot abuse; violation; classification," Arizona Revised Statutes, https://www.azleg.gov/ars/16/01005.htm.

the 2024 election to reassemble data as if the former boundaries were still in effect, and she got these totals:

Harris: 5,120 votes (79.4 percent)

Trump: 1,263 votes (19.6 percent)

Total Votes: 6,449

Margin: Harris +3,857 (+59.8 percent)

If these numbers were verifiable in official county documents, they would show a total decline in votes of 1,237, a decrease in Democratic presidential votes of 1,380, and a decrease in the total Democratic margin of 1,599 when also factoring in Trump's modest gains over 2020. Did someone overlook this precinct in 2024, or was it not worth getting caught once I started calling it out? Election integrity activists nationwide, especially those in states like Arizona, New Mexico, and Montana, were hounded mercilessly by the media and called racists for highlighting election outcomes that made no sense.

This same methodology that makes up the foundation of the Precinct Mapping Project found no indication of 2020 ballot stuffing in Nogales, on the far southern end of the state against the border of Mexico's Sonora State. One might think—given a record single-cycle vote gain significant enough to give a Democratic presidential nominee an extremely rare win statewide in Arizona—that the candidate would blow out Democratic strongholds like Nogales by record margins. After the 2020 quasi election, that person would have been dead wrong. The effort to map out precincts and identify not only the potentially problematic ballot collection hot spots but also key areas to pick up pro-Trump votes was fruitful and sponsored by engaged citizens from state to state who contributed to sponsor every county in every battleground state, with the exception of Georgia—which couldn't be covered in full thanks to its division into 159 counties.

Numbers make sense to me; in fact, Roger Stone told me he hadn't known anyone so capable of piecing together Electoral College scenarios since he had watched President Richard Nixon do so decades before. The challenge for someone like me that understands numbers naturally is to explain them in such a way that they move the minds I would like to see moved. It does me little good to tell people who already agree with me what they already know and infinite amounts of good to get my work into professional journals, or in front of cameras that will broadcast to the masses who may not know what to think about the various claims pertaining to election integrity in the United States. This is where my sense of humor came to my aid.

From the stage at Trump National Doral Miami on May 12, 2023, speaking on the ReAwaken America tour, I described the true national pandemic as "electile dysfunction." This crass but clever play on words ignited the crowd into frenzied laughter, as I graciously expanded on the term I had been joking about for months to include characteristics and symptoms for the first time:

> Electile dysfunction is when you have difficulty maintaining an election…or when your election lasts for longer than four days.…

> There are some side effects and symptoms that are present. The first one is a sudden, severe, and noticeable loss of interest in voting. And finally, in the most severe cases like you might find in Washington, DC, or in Arizona, premature inauguration.

The crowd's reaction was unforgettable, so naturally I packed it into every event I spoke at. I turned the phrase "End Electile Dysfunction" into merchandise, like ball caps, shirts, and tumblers, which I would see at events I'd attend and even once out in the wild on someone I didn't know. I knew it would offend some who were incapable of adjusting to the new attitude of the political world, namely that modern Democrats want to run you off the road for having a different opinion, but also knew the phrase would resonate and cause people to reflect on just how dumb it is for elections to take days to decide with little to no transparency afforded to the public. Paul Fleuret, the architect of "The Captain's Battlegrounds" series on Rumble detailing 2020 election anomalies in short video clips, rushed and turned the Doral performance into a catchy video that went all over the place online.

A candidate once again, President Trump was facing the full force of "lawfare" thrown at him by the federal government, who hated his guts because he had spent most of the previous eight years perfectly executing Saul Alinsky's fifth rule, to ridicule the hell out of your opponents.[6]

"Ridicule is man's most potent weapon. There is no defense. It is almost impossible to counterattack ridicule. Also it infuriates the opposition, who then react to your advantage."

Trump had been the only Republican in modern times to turn the left's playbook against them, ripping off *Rules for Radicals* frequently. The corrupt absolutely cannot stand to be ridiculed, and in making a viral joke about the embarrassing American elections system, I forced those who run elections that would embarrass third world nations to take a position counter to mine in which

---

6   Saul D. Alinsky, *Rules for Radicals: A Pragmatic Primer for Realistic Radicals* (Random House, 1971).

they must justify measures that cause millions of Americans to scoff at them in disgust.

Even after the 2022 midterms, with the next presidential election in sight, I continued to spend a substantial amount of time on the road and even halfway across the ocean. I returned to Hawaii in March and found my way to nearly every looming battleground state, including Nevada, which hadn't backed a Republican presidential candidate since 2004. I was confident it would have backed Trump in 2020 if not for an all-mail election complete with ballot harvesting and two major metro areas full of willing and paid hands to go out and do the dirty work. While at times it felt like my life was coming back together, constant road trips and lack of legislative progress against election corruption wore on me from time to time. On a trip to western Pennsylvania that May, I texted this frustration over to General Mike Flynn. What he replied with in response, complete with a quotation from Dutch theologian Abraham Kuyper, captured my full attention:[7]

> This is for you.... Our faith tells us that with God all things are possible. But that does not mean we should sit on our hands, waiting for God to fix things. No, we must seek His direction on what He wants us to do and then do it. We must be reminded to "Stand our posts."
>
> God does not want us cowering in the trench while Satan rampages through our institutions and the world. God has tasked us with proclaiming Truth and shining His light into the darkest of places. "There is not a square inch in the whole domain of our human existence over

---

7   Mike Flynn, text message to author, May 24, 2023.

which Christ, who is Sovereign over all, does not cry, 'Mine!'"

Stand strong in your faith and your purpose my friend. You have yet to achieve what God has designed for your life. And I mean this.

Just the month before, when I had visited Dad's grave in Arlington National Cemetery, I stumbled across the headstone of Navy Lieutenant Commander Jason Michael Price, which had "Nothing great comes from comfort zones" inscribed on it. That, and the general's encouragement, served as reminders to keep pursuing the mission I had set out on nearly three years before. Price's mother later reached out to me to share personal stories of her son's heroism and how me sharing his motto touched her heart.

At the beginning of August, I did a week-long tour of Georgia with Holly Kesler, including a joint debate against a 2020 election fraud denier in Chickamauga in which forty-one of forty-four attendees sided with us. Data, properly presented and in context, is difficult to refute. I closed out August at the Trump International Hotel in Las Vegas, where the ReAwaken America speakers and team stayed while taxiing up the road to a blazing hot event center in North Las Vegas. When President Trump told me the previous December that he didn't know if they would "let us in," I had figured he meant a wholesale manipulation of the vote reoccurring. I had no idea, even on my way into Las Vegas, that Trump would be booked at the Fulton County jail and have his mugshot taken like an everyday crook. This gave me a whole new perspective on what "I don't know if they'll let us in" really meant, and at that moment, it was clearer to me than ever that Trump's political instincts are off the charts and that one of his greatest strengths lies in the clear observation that his enemies continue to underestimate them.

Along the trail, I had met a woman named Kathleen Winn, whose husband Al was one of the lead architects bringing the Apache attack helicopter to the battlefield decades ago. Kathleen had held minor office before in Arizona and hosts a radio show in Tucson, which I have appeared on regularly since the push for election integrity began. Kathleen also ran for Congress in 2022, but lost the primary to Juan Ciscomani, who won the seat to represent Arizona's Sixth Congressional District in that year's otherwise disappointing 2022 midterm cycle. As fall approached, Kathleen knew State Representative Rachel Jones and I were growing quite close; with a few months until her mother was set to move in, Kathleen asked if I would like to occupy her casita. My personal circumstances made sense for me to emphatically accept her offer, and from that point forward, my relationship with Rachel only deepened. For the first time in my life, I found myself living in a battleground state complete with its massive egos, conflicts of personalities, and enough corruption to keep a man busy around the clock.

Rachel was elected to the Arizona House, which allots two seats in each of the state's thirty legislative districts, in that dismal 2022 cycle, along with two Republican running mates who won the other House seat and the single Senate seat for the newly redrawn Seventeenth Legislative District. The Arizona Republican majority in the state legislature had redistricted after the 2020 election and carved the district out of the outskirts of Tucson, looking to salvage something out of the redder areas of an otherwise blue Pima County. The county hadn't backed a GOP presidential nominee since 1988 but had only begun to provide notably large Democratic margins once that party learned to perfect mail-in ballot collection. Had the district not been redrawn, Rachel wouldn't have won inside the old boundaries, which heavily favored the Democrats. I wouldn't have met her that day in the Arizona Senate, and it is very unlikely we would have crossed paths again given my fast-paced lifestyle and hectic schedule.

She was drawn to the political battlefield in the same way I had been. Her fury over the 2020 election, combined with the emergence of a medically driven dystopia over COVID-19 paranoia, gave her the motivation to part with complacency and use her voice for something bigger than herself. In the years leading up to her candidacy, she had worked as a business executive at UPS, taught preschool and elementary school, and selflessly raised five children. Three of those children were adopted out of foster care, and each came from a background that practically guaranteed a life of severe hardship if not interdicted by their placements in her home. One of those adopted kids, plus her two biological children, Carter and Cayla, were either already adults or nearing adulthood when I moved to Arizona.

Representative Jones, as she was then known, took no time in becoming labeled as a flamethrower on the House floor. Her clapbacks, cutdowns, and detailed explanations of critical votes punched right through the rotten veneer of the establishment political decorum that so many had come to find unbearable. Rachel focused on the voice of the people. She favored common-sense election reforms, pulled no punches on medical freedom, and spent time getting to know constituents in a personal way, giving them her phone number and an invitation to reach out directly when the need arose. Rachel rejected the political brown-nosing. While it has cost her lobbyist donations and political favors, it has gained her a reputation as one of the most authentic voices in any state house in America.

We immediately began speaking at events together, frequenting Tucson and Phoenix, and hitting Las Vegas, Atlanta, Denver, and just before Christmas time, Fredericksburg, Texas, where I was introduced by the legendary journalist, Lara Logan:

> I don't know how many of you realize that in the wake of the 2020 election, there are a number of people in this country who gave up everything and devoted the rest of their lives, every minute since that happened, to trying to fix the problem…. Seth Keshel is one of those people. He is a former officer from the Army who brings with him the discipline and the strategic eye and the analytical skills of a real warfighter.
>
> He had an exemplary service in the military…. If you know Seth as I do, you know that he's continuing the oath that he swore, that he took, when he joined the military to uphold the Constitution. That's what this is really about at its core. I cannot stress to you the amount of time that he puts into this, the amount of effort, the attacks that he takes publicly…
>
> If you think, if you think that this is an issue for Dallas or this is an issue for Washington, you are absolutely, one hundred percent deceived and wrong. And this man has spent every single minute since he saw the travesty of justice that happened in 2020 and knew it was a lie—I've learned some of my most significant things about election fraud from this man, Seth Keshel.

I had followed Lara since long before I imagined being deeply intertwined into such a hot-button issue of national survival, and to hear an introduction like that was surreal. She had been cancelled for challenging narratives, and yet here I was sharing a hall in central Texas with her with Rachel watching it all unfold. Rachel and I were an immediate power couple, and our shared mission in life was undeniable even in those early months. Rachel's faith was evident in everything she did and, unlike so many I've known over the years who wanted me to fit the mold they had in mind, she accepted me fully and believed God made me with a unique purpose in mind. She also loved my three children, who spent Christmas with me. After meeting Rachel, Pennsylvanian election integrity hero Toni Shuppe came up to me and said, "Don't screw it up." Toni had been fighting the fight for as long as I had, establishing Audit the Vote Pennsylvania in the immediate aftermath of that state's disastrous 2020 election, and rode with me side by side as I was going through such disruptive life change just two years earlier. I took her words to heart and didn't let her down. Rachel became "Mrs. K" the next year.

CHAPTER 13

Registration is the Foundation

Just weeks after I arrived and set up shop in Tucson, Pennsylvania Governor Josh Shapiro, using his executive powers, enacted automatic voter registration[1] in a state that was setting up to be the most important one on the entire 2024 map, and one in which mail-in ballots would already be distributed within a year. This seemingly harmless action by one of 2020's key players smacked me upside the head and put me into overdrive in piecing together the national election corruption equation at an advanced level.

My simplified view on "election fraud by a thousand cuts" puts me at odds with others working on election integrity solutions, whether those solutions consist of poll watching, records investigations, theorizing about electronic manipulation, or something else. Since my days as an intelligence officer, I have always favored Occam's razor, the theory that the simplest explanation is the most likely to be accurate, over more complex scenarios that require more variables to work in unison. In my mind, election administrators and primarily Democratic office holders didn't push for widespread mail-in voting in 2020 so they could have a hobby to survive all the COVID-19 paranoia, especially when so many nations have banned the concept entirely because it is per-

---

1 Amy Worden, "Pa. to Register Voters Automatically, Gov. Shapiro Announces," PennLive, September 19, 2023, https://www.pennlive.com/news/2023/09/gov-shapiro-announces-pa-to-begin-automatic-voter-registration.html.

haps the most significant vector of fraud available to those looking to manipulate outcomes and seat the wrong office holders.

With a year to go until mail-in ballots would be sent to voters, Shapiro decided to bypass the state legislature and entrench what I have come to discover as the most surefire way to create a permanent blue state—automatic voter registration. Shapiro knew exactly what I knew: Pennsylvania was rapidly turning red, and in almost every county. Sixty-two of sixty-seven counties shifted Republican by registration from 2016, when Donald Trump first won his state, to 2020, when Joe Biden mysteriously eclipsed Barack Obama's 2008 landslide vote total. Trump did the same, on his attempt at an electoral vote majority that ran right through the Keystone State. Once the 2024 election arrived a year later, sixty-four of sixty-seven Pennsylvania counties shifted toward Republicans by registration.

These shifts, especially with Democrats hemorrhaging registrations throughout the state, implied lower quadrennial Democratic vote totals and increasing GOP totals, especially since the shift in Pennsylvania was prompted by two-time Obama voters switching allegiances and becoming Trump backers. Very few of the counties have notable population growth, and much of the state, thanks to the trade issues that contributed to the plight of the white working class, has stagnant or declining population totals. There is simply no flood of new residents registering to vote and giving both parties the opportunity to pile up gains in each election, as you may find in Florida, Texas, Georgia, or North Carolina, to name a few.

It was all-hands-on-deck in 2020, and with all the media backing and excuses over COVID-19 at their disposal, Biden squeaked out Pennsylvania by barely more than a point. This time, Biden's record was dismal; the state showed as much by its decreasing

Democratic registration advantage, and without further intervention, it was set to deliver nineteen electoral votes (one fewer than 2020 thanks to US census changes) to Trump without so much as a whimper. I knew in my gut this move toward automatic voter registration was no accident, so I, after collaborating with registrations expert Kris Jurski, researched the topic.

Automatic voter registration, according to the National Conference of State Legislatures, "is a process in which eligible individuals are automatically registered to vote when interacting with certain government agencies, such as a department of motor vehicles."[2] Other states extend this through Health and Human Services Departments, or in the case of Alaska, applicants to the state's oil money, the Permanent Fund Dividend, are automatically registered to vote.

California, to the surprise of few, was the first state to adopt automatic voter registration. They did so in 2015 and implemented it fully by 2018. Oregon, the state that pioneered universal mail-in voting in the United States, followed shortly thereafter. Notably, Georgia adopted automatic voter registration just months before the 2016 election, with little time afforded to disrupt Trump's fairly comfortable win over Hillary Clinton that year, in which neither candidate seriously contested the state.

The 2020 election proved that modern campaigns are victorious when they have the superior ballot count, not so much the superior vote count. Extensive research in the aftermath of that election showed massive corruption of voter rolls, which has been effectively proven with so many Democratic states refusing to comply with the current Trump administration's requests to turn them over. I found and published evidence of substantial

---

2   National Conference of State Legislatures, "Automatic Voter Registration," last updated July 21, 2025, https://www.ncsl.org/elections-and-campaigns/automatic-voter-registration.

corruption in the voter rolls of many key Pennsylvania counties, including Montgomery County, where the Keshel family has long-standing roots. I wrote this in the aftermath of Shapiro's executive actions to adopt automatic voter registration:

"Sure, Trump will have access to a few thousand more voters in York County, but Biden will have access to tens of thousands more in Philadelphia, with gangs of ballot harvesters, operating exclusively where population density favors Democrats (the projects), collecting mail-in ballots that are sent to fictitious, ineligible, duplicated, or otherwise fraudulent registrations, over a lengthy early voting period. Lawsuits should have been flying before close of business yesterday to stop this disaster."[3]

At the time of the 2020 election, twenty states and Washington, DC, had adopted automatic voter registration and were at various stages of implementing it, ranging from barely off the ground to fully complete. The states were Alaska, California, Colorado, Connecticut, Georgia, Illinois, Maine, Maryland, Massachusetts, Michigan, Nevada, New Jersey, New Mexico, New York, Oregon, Rhode Island, Vermont, Virginia, Washington, and West Virginia. Once I had amassed that list and verified the adoption dates, it made complete sense why Delaware, Hawaii, Minnesota, and now Pennsylvania had moved to operate automatic voter registration ahead of the 2024 election. The twenty states and Washington, DC, had certified their elections overwhelmingly in favor of Biden in 2020.

Biden won eighteen of twenty states, plus Washington, DC, falling into this category by an astonishing electoral vote count of 243 to 9. Trump's 9 electoral votes under automatic voter registration came from Alaska, which took several days to call for

---

3   Seth Keshel, "Why Pennsylvania's Push for Automatic Voter Registration is Standard Democrat Playbook," Captain K's Corner, September 20, 2023, https://www.captaink. us/p/why-pennsylvanias-push-for-automatic?utm_source=publication-search.

Trump thanks to the glut of mail-in ballots, West Virginia, and the Second Congressional District of Maine, worth a single electoral vote. In other words, Biden won 96.4 percent of all electoral votes under automatic voter registration; Trump, in losing the 2020 quasi election 306 to 232 in the Electoral College, therefore won 223 of the remaining 286 electoral votes, or 78.0 percent of what was left. And that's before we consider what should have been his obvious wins of Arizona, Pennsylvania, and Wisconsin, and a race that looked like it was anyone's game in Minnesota, confirmed by the boneheaded plea for Election Day turnout from Democratic Attorney General Keith Ellison.

The chasm couldn't have been more obvious, and while reviewing all states for registration laws, I noticed another piece of analytical gold. North Dakota is the only state in the nation that doesn't bother with voter registration of any type. While they have solid security measures in place for legitimate absentee balloting, voters in North Dakota show up with an ID card at their precinct, receive a ballot, vote, and go home. I've had arguments with allies in election integrity, like Cleta Mitchell, about the validity of my assumptions about North Dakota, and get some rebuttals about demographics, population size, or an uncompetitive political landscape, but its three-cycle electoral trends vary substantially from its southern cousin, South Dakota.

Both Dakotas have become substantially more Republican by outcomes in the past two decades. Neither state is winnable any longer for Democrats in federal races, whereas both have had Democratic US senators in the twenty-first century. There is population growth present in both, but only in select areas like the Sioux Falls metro, the Black Hills, or Fargo; however, only one of those states experienced a significant boom in turnout in the 2020 election, while the other had fewer net new votes cast in

2020 than it did in 2016. The only explanation for the supposed lack of voter interest in North Dakota's 2020 election, as far as I am concerned, must lie in the fact that there is no voter registration at all to pluck names from. We saw this in the case of the election fraud investigations in New Jersey and Connecticut I mentioned earlier, and this is seemingly corroborated by how the overwhelmingly Democrat-favoring states with automatic voter registration allot their electoral votes.

Which of Biden's miraculously won battleground states once had easily predictable elections that were suddenly influenced by automatic voter registration? That would be Brad Raffensperger's Georgia, which showed an all-but-done result on the morning of November 4, which Raffensperger blurted out to the nation. Their move to automatic voter registration in late 2016 didn't come with enough time to drastically bloat the voter rolls across the Peach State's vast spread of 159 counties; however, after four years, the rolls were unrecognizable and filled with quantities of new registrations that would make the 2008 Obama enthusiasm bubble as exciting as a golf clap.

Fulton and DeKalb Counties make up core Atlanta. The two original suburban counties of the Atlanta metro are Cobb and Gwinnett, both once strongly Republican but now comfortably blue thanks to intercounty migration, increased urbanization, and electorates that are far less white than they once were. There are two GOP strongholds in the north end of the metro, Forsyth and Cherokee Counties, and two Democratic counterparts, Clayton and Henry Counties, in the southern end. The Atlanta sprawl continues on in every direction, but I refer to those eight counties as the "Atlanta Gang of Eight." By the time Trump became the Republican standard-bearer, they had drifted so far left they jeopardized the chances of Republicans carrying Georgia at all. Fulton and DeKalb Counties, with Biden margins of over 240,000 each, pack by far the most Democratic punch of any two counties statewide.

Relying on Georgia's own certified statistics, the quadrennial growth of Fulton and DeKalb Counties for net change to voter registration is as follows for the three presidential cycles preceding the 2020 race:

Fulton County
- **2004:** 447,522 registered voters[4]
- **2008:** 552,559 registered voters (+105,037)[5]
- **2012:** 567,174 registered voters (+14,615)[6]
- **2016:** 590,362 registered voters (+23,188)[7]
- **Average Net Increase over Three Cycles:** +47,613

Fulton County, thanks to the density of metro Atlanta, is now more than 40 percent black.[8] The biggest surge in voter registration since 2004 was, unsurprisingly, in advance of Obama's run

---

4   Fulton County Department of Registration and Elections, "Election Summary Report, Fulton County, Georgia, November 2, 2004, General Election, Nonpartisan and Special Elections, Official and Complete Results" Election Results Search, https://www.fultoncountyga.gov/-/media/Project/FultonCountyGa/remos/elections/Nov_2_2004_General-Election.pdf.

5   Fulton County Department of Registration and Elections, "Statement of Votes Cast: Fulton County, Georgia, General Election, November 4, 2008, Official and Complete," Election Results Search, https://www.fultoncountyga.gov/-/media/Project/FultonCountyGa/remos/elections/General-Election-Nov_4_2008.pdf.

6   Fulton County Department of Registration and Elections, "Election Summary Report: Fulton County, Georgia, General Election, November 6, 2012, Official and Complete," Election Results Search, https://www.fultoncountyga.gov/-/media/Project/FultonCountyGa/remos/elections/Nov-2012-ELECTION-SUMMARY-REPORT-Official.pdf.

7   Fulton County Department of Registration and Elections, "Election Summary Report: Fulton County, General Election, November 8, 2016, Official and Complete," Election Results Search, https://www.fultoncountyga.gov/-/media/Project/FultonCountyGa/remos/elections/NOV-2016-GENERAL-ELECTION-SUMMARY-REPORT---Official.pdf.

8   United States Census Bureau, "Hispanic or Latino, and Not Hispanic or Latino by Race," Table P2, Fulton County, Georgia, Decennial Census, 2020: DEC Redistricting Data (PL 94-171), accessed November 24, 2025, https://data.census.gov/table/DECENNIALPL2020.P2?g=050XX00US13121&q=p2.

as Democratic nominee. Georgia doesn't register voters by party, but if it did, this county would show a massive drift to the left that cycle. Registrations flatlined after the initial Obama sugar high.

DeKalb County

- **2004:** 345,423 registered voters[9]
- **2008:** 414,507 registered voters (+69,085)[10]
- **2012:** 418,611 registered voters (+4,104)[11]
- **2016:** 419,871 registered voters (+1,260)[12]
- **Average Net Increase over Three Cycles:** +24,816

DeKalb County, which is majority black, showed the same voter registration surge for Obama's initial run, then went into a lull much deeper than Fulton County did over the next two cycles. The net change to the voter roll between Obama's first election win and Trump's 2016 win was just 5,364, representing just over 1 percent total increase in voter registration.

A realistic attempt to predict voter registration in 2020 for either county may carry forward the high number (2008 for both counties), the low number (2012 for Fulton, 2016 for DeKalb), or the average for both. Here is how those would project, carrying

---

9   DeKalb County Voter Registration and Elections, "DeKalb County General Election, Official Election Summary, November 2, 2004," 2004 Election Results, https://www.dekalbcountyga.gov/sites/default/files/user306/2004%20GE%20Summary%20110204.pdf.

10   DeKalb County Voter Registration and Elections, "DeKalb County, General and Special Election, Official Election Summary, November 4, 2008," 2008 Election Results, https://www.dekalbcountyga.gov/sites/default/files/user306/2008%20GE%20Summary%20110408.pdf.

11   DeKalb County Voter Registration and Elections, "Election Summary Report: Dekalb County, State of Georgia General Election, November 6, 2012, Summary For Jurisdiction Wide, All Counter, All Races, Official and Complete," 2012 Election Results, https://www.dekalbcountyga.gov/sites/default/files/Result_11062012.pdf.

12   DeKalb Voter Registration and Elections, "Election Summary Report: DeKalb County, State of Georgia General Election, November 8, 2016, Summary For Jurisdiction Wide, All Counter, All Races, Official and Complete," 2016 Election Results, https://www.dekalbcountyga.gov/sites/default/files/user306/2016%20GE%20Summary%20110616.pdf.

forward the low, average, and high gains over the previous cycles into 2020, and how voter registration turned out at book closing for the 2020 quasi election:

Fulton County

2020 Projection: Low 604,977; Average 637,975; High 695,399

2020 Certified Voter Registration: 806,451[13]

DeKalb County

2020 Projection: Low 421,131; Average 444,687; High 488,956

2020 Certified Voter Registration: 546,711[14]

Fulton County came in 111,052 over the high voter registration projection that would have matched the Obama 2008 surge, and DeKalb surpassed the same high growth projection by 57,755, for a total of 168,807 between the pair. All other counties in the Atlanta Gang of Eight had shockingly high changes to voter registration growth between the 2016 and 2020 elections, a four-year stretch in which automatic voter registration ran wild and generated voter registrations in wildly high quantities without Obama on the ticket.

If you were wondering where all of those ballots above and beyond Raffensperger's November 4, 2020, forecast on *The Today*

---

13 Fulton County Department of Registration and Elections, "Election Summary Report: Fulton County, Georgia, General Primary-Nonpartisan General Election, November 03, 2020, Official and Complete," Election Results Search, https://www.fultoncountyga.gov/-/media/Project/FultonCountyGa/remos/elections/Nov-2020-Election-Summary-Report---5-Column---Official.pdf.

14 DeKalb County Voter Registration and Elections, "Election Summary Report: General Election, DEKALB, November 03, 2020, Summary for: All Contest, All Districts, All Tabulators, All Counting Groups, Official and Complete," 2020 Election Results, https://www.dekalbcountyga.gov/sites/default/files/ElectionSummaryReportRPT-Official%20and%20Complete%2011.03.2020.pdf.

Show came from, now you know. They came from a nearly limitless tap of registrations from which the 2020 election's massive mail-in ballot count could be assigned to and subsequently gathered up over a voting period lasting for several weeks. Factor in random pipe bursts that seem to only happen on election night, the lapdog mainstream media, fake polling, and excuses made in the name of a virus that seemingly is at its worst during times of peak political tension—and you have a recipe for the first Democratic win in a southern red state in twenty-eight years when the Republican is busy putting up one of the strongest gains in net new votes from one election to the next the state has ever seen. I found it particularly interesting that Trump had a commanding lead in Georgia at the end of election night, plus Raffensperger's apparent affirmation the following morning, but only lost the handle on the state once it was clear Biden wouldn't pull in North Carolina, which was more widely accepted as a potential battleground state. VoterGA documented many of the blatant incidents of election fraud in the 2020 election, including irreconcilable vote totals that do not match the count of available ballot images, tens of thousands of false registration dates, and other illegalities that align closely with the corruption of voter registration and all that follows it.[15]

There are many ways elections are manipulated, and this is not in dispute. There is clearly mail-in ballot fraud, which is why it is so heavily promoted in blue states; there is ballot harvesting, which is illegal in some states but not in others; and then there are theories about the electronic elections environment that vary in quality and depth, but all point to the same lack of transparency essential for public trust in elections. No matter which the-

---

15   Garland Favorito, "Who Says There Was No 2020 Election Fraud?," VoterGA, September 27, 2022, https://voterga.org/wp-content/uploads/2022/09/WHO-SAYS-THERE-WAS-NO-2020-ELECTION-FRAUD.pdf.

ory you believe the most, it is my most sincerely held belief that all forms of modern election manipulation originate with voter registration. The more corrupt the registration, the worse the potential for election manipulation.

Voter registration is the starting point for all of my assessments, including potential for cheating—even if it has been legalized as it has been in Oregon, Washington, Nevada, and California, to name a handful. With all of those voter registration records created by automatic voter registration, mail-in ballots create an easy attachment for amping up the ballot count. The only issue remaining pertains to how to get those mail-in ballots into the ballot box (or drop box, depending on where the election is held); for that, there is the California-pioneered scam of ballot harvesting, which far too many Republicans still believe they can use to keep pace with Democrats who control the cities, dense population centers, projects, and universities in which undeliverable or would-be unvoted ballots pile up.

My reputation has been forged by a willingness to forecast what people don't want to hear. That is how it was when I was in Afghanistan and had the responsibility to speak truth to aircrews and senior officers about how the enemy gets a vote, too. And it was my 2023 findings about the type and criticality of voter registration in a particular state that gave me the clearest idea of what pathways to victory existed in 2024, and exactly how they must be navigated if President Trump were to win.

CHAPTER 14

To The Starting Line

When people ask me how I am so successful at predicting presidential outcomes, I don't go right into trend analysis, voter registration by party, or demographic sentiments. I jump right into the history books and am quick to say that if someone can't correctly call three-quarters of all races for electoral votes, they have no business predicting elections at all. Far too many people scrutinize polling data and are especially lost when bothering with analyzing the national popular vote, which matters for nothing except for a tiny boost in the narrative surrounding presidential mandates. Remember, Joe Biden supposedly vanquished Donald Trump by 4.5 percent nationally, yet only 42,918 votes (or ballots) separated Biden's 306 to Trump's 232 Electoral College margin from a dead tie at 269 apiece.

American presidential elections are not made up of a single chunk of votes in which we should care a bit what a national poll, even if it were largely correct, says. The quadrennial national blood sport for the highest office in the world is made up of fifty-six separate races for electoral votes. We have fifty statewide races, the race in Washington, DC, and the races for a single vote each in the five collective split congressional districts belonging to Maine (two) and Nebraska (three), which are the only two states splitting electoral votes in such a manner. In the Trump era, Maine's solidly blue four electoral votes split when Trump commanded enough support of the white working class to win the Second Congressional District in the north, and the Second Congressional District of Nebraska (NE-2), centered around metro Omaha, slipped to the left after a narrow Trump win in 2016, flipping in the 2020 quasi election.

Barring catastrophe for either side, it was clear to me that any Republican would carry a minimum of twenty-four states, including four of Nebraska's five electoral votes and the split northern electoral vote of Maine, and any Democrat a minimum of fourteen states, including the southern electoral vote of Maine, plus Washington, DC. Many of the permanently red states, such as Oklahoma, Idaho, Wyoming, or Utah, hadn't backed a Democrat in a presidential race since siding with Lyndon B. Johnson in his 1964 national landslide win against Barry Goldwater. Others, such as Texas or South Carolina, came into the fold later and had occasionally dipped inside ten points, but were reliable and not going anywhere in a race everyone expected to be down to the "Industrial Midwest" and a few Sunbelt states. I had my suspicions about the trajectory of the Lone Star State given the ridiculous 2020 outcome, but it was clear Trump was headed for a surprisingly impressive performance with Latino voters and wouldn't allow Texas to get "Georgia'd." Eight of the fourteen solid Democratic states, like Connecticut, New Jersey, and most significantly, California, had become part of the vaunted "blue wall" in the 1992 election between Bill Clinton and George H. W. Bush and never looked back even once.

That left twelve states, plus the Second Congressional District in Omaha, up for grabs with any GOP candidate starting out with a 219 to 191 edge in the Electoral College thanks to a 2020 census that gave a slight edge to the GOP from the previous decade, despite substantial corner-cutting and botches made possible by blaming COVID-19 that ensured blue states retained as much political power as possible. My own analysis estimated Republican states were twelve to sixteen electoral votes (and US representatives) shy of where they would be if the census were conducted properly and accurately.[1] Few have bothered to challenge my assertions on the census inaccuracies since the Census Bureau itself admitted it botched the count.[2]

I separated the remaining twelve states and NE-2 into two separate piles—"decisive states" and "leaners." The leaners were races I had expected to finish within eight points and had a high degree of certainty which candidate would emerge victorious. With Trump expected to punch through the legal hurdles and win the GOP primary, I evaluated the leaners like this:

- Maine statewide—expected for Biden (two electoral votes)
- Minnesota—expected for Biden (ten electoral votes)
- NE-2—expected for Biden (one electoral vote)
- New Mexico—expected for Biden (five electoral votes)
- North Carolina—expected for Trump, and only decisive if Trump were to lose it (sixteen electoral votes)
- Virginia—expected for Biden (thirteen electoral votes)

Those six races, in my estimation, were only likely to flip to the underdog in a national landslide. Almost everyone considered North Carolina a battleground, but in my system of analyzing all fifty-six races relative to one another, it was simply a key stepping stone for Trump's path to 270 electoral votes, not a decisive state.

---

1 Seth Keshel, "The U.S. Census Bureau Stole At Least 16 Electoral Votes and 15 U.S. House Seats," Captain K's Corner (Substack), November 16, 2024, https://www. captaink.us/p/the-us-census-bureau-stole-at-least.

2 America Counts Staff, "2020 Census Undercounts in Six States, Overcounts in Eight," US Census Bureau, May 19, 2022, https://www.census.gov/library/ stories/2022/05/2020-census-undercount-overcount-rates-by-state.html.

It was the only battleground state Trump had won in 2020's certified results, and I expected it to stay with him based on what I was reading in party registration trends.

These six picks, if accurate, would move the running Electoral College scoreboard to 235 to 222 in favor of Trump, leaving eighty-one electoral votes to decide it all. The Trump wins predicted up to this point were the same that were certified for him in 2020, but worth three more electoral votes after the population-based adjustments to the census.

The following states, which were all critical to the 2020 outcome, ranked in the top seven grouping of what I called decisive states:

- Arizona—Biden +0.3 percent in 2020 (eleven electoral votes)
- Georgia—Biden +0.2 percent in 2020 (sixteen electoral votes)
- Michigan—Biden +2.8 percent in 2020 (fifteen electoral votes)
- Nevada—Biden +2.4 percent in 2020 (six electoral votes)
- New Hampshire—Biden +7.4 percent in 2020 (four electoral votes)
- Pennsylvania—Biden +1.2 percent in 2020 (nineteen electoral votes)
- Wisconsin—Biden +0.6 percent in 2020 (ten electoral votes)

With the seven states considered decisive, forty-three of fifty-six races were incredibly easy to call, and then once considering the dynamics of the six leaners, forty-nine of the fifty-six could be called, which left only seven difficult calls to make. Readers may wonder what made forty-three races slam dunks, and that is a fair question. The presidential winner can be predicted, or close states may be identified, based on past results, trend, voter registration data, and most importantly, the laws on the books.

Biden had won eighteen of the twenty automatic voter registration states, plus Washington, DC, in 2020 by a collective electoral vote count of 243 to 9. All fourteen safe-Biden states, plus Washington, DC, had already fully implemented or, like Delaware and Hawaii, were busy implementing automatic voter registration, and four of six leaners I found to favor Biden in the leaners category were under automatic voter registration, which Minnesota adopted after the 2020 race. Pennsylvania, pursuant to Governor Josh Shapiro's executive action, loomed largest as the most important battleground state under automatic voter registration, nudging out Georgia.

Four of the seven states most likely to decide the 2024 presidential winner, the decisive states, were under automatic voter registration and therefore caused the most concern for me as to which states were most capable of replicating a quasi election like the one the nation endured four years earlier. By default, I considered Arizona and Wisconsin the most likely to back Trump considering only the election integrity equation. Given the way the 2020 presidential race played out in those two states, that wasn't saying much. I took a lot of heat for considering New Hampshire one of the seven decisive states, but the logic was simple. Had Trump wound up losing Pennsylvania and Michigan (or having them stolen), but winning Georgia and Arizona or Wisconsin, the combination of Nevada and New Hampshire would have put him over the top. In that scenario, Michigan and Georgia could be swapped out, but given the leans of those two states, I could not foresee an election in which Michigan went for Trump, but not

Pennsylvania or Georgia. New Hampshire was indeed decisive, but only if won by Trump, just as North Carolina only loomed as decisive if won by Biden, who everyone had expected to be the Democratic nominee until his disastrous June debate.

I considered Michigan and Georgia, thanks to their foundations of corrupted voter registration, to be the dirtiest of all decisive states. Georgia's voter registration explosion in the Atlanta metro area presented its own unique challenge. But Michigan's situation heading into the 2024 election, spearheaded by Secretary of State Jocelyn Benson, was damning to all who had spent four years trashing everyone who had issues with election outcomes being reversed in the dark of night and damning to all efforts to scrutinize election processes, such as suspected corrupt voter registration practices, that were hammered with threats of police intervention by Attorney General Dana Nessel. Further corroborating my belief that registration corruption is at the core of electoral manipulation was a deeper dive into a voter registration fraud ring operating in Muskegon County, Michigan, particularly within the city of Muskegon itself. Greater detail emerged in August 2023, with Muskegon City Clerk Ann Meisch reporting a flood of thousands of voter registrations being dropped off at once by a company from Tennessee known as GBI Strategies, which focused on voter registration efforts. As reported by Bridge Michigan:[3]

"Muskegon Clerk Ann Meisch, who had alerted authorities, said at the time that her office had received an estimated 6,000 applications from a single organization. Most of the applications were valid, she told WZZM-13, but she estimated that 'several

---

3   Jonathan Oosting, "Muskegon Fake Voter Applications Probed in 2020, Referred to FBI, Nessel Says," Bridge Michigan, August 14, 2023, https://bridgemi.com/michigan-government/muskegon-fake-voter-applications-probed-2020-referred-fbi-nessel-says/.

hundred' had 'irregularities,' including wrong birthdays, addresses and signatures that did not match versions on file."

Investigations into the matter, which were almost certainly slow rolled out to the public to distance it from the 2020 election fallout, revealed a plan in place to expand these efforts throughout the county, which was nearly won by Trump in 2016 in what was the first Republican presidential win of Michigan since 1988. In 2020, Trump surpassed Obama's winning 2012 total in the county, which gave the incumbent president a nearly eighteen-point margin of victory over Mitt Romney, only to be beaten by Biden in the county and state by an election that relied heavily on mail-in ballots and almost certainly identical registration corruption operations throughout Michigan's eighty-three counties that remained veiled in secrecy.

Shortly after Kamala Harris became the Democratic nominee, I ripped through Michigan's voter registration data. On August 16, less than three months before the Trump-Harris winner would be known, the state's registration dashboard on the Michigan Voter Information Center website reported 8,384,910 registered voters, not distinguished between active and inactive registrations.[4] The most recently available population numbers at the time for Michigan, based on the 2023 US Census estimate, showed a total of 10,037,261 residents, not excluding illegal aliens or unnaturalized noncitizens ineligible to vote.[5] I've had people like Marc Elias and his buddies at Democracy Docket trash me for a very simple mathematical conclusion—that 8,384,910 (registered voters) divided by 10,037,261 (population) equals .835, which when

---

4   Seth Keshel, "Urgent Action Required if You Want Trump to Win Michigan," Captain K's Corner (Substack), August 17, 2024, https://www.captaink.us/p/urgent-action-required-if-you-want.

5   US Census Bureau, "Michigan," Annual Estimates of the Resident Population for Counties: April 1, 2020 to July 1, 2024 (CO-EST2024-POP), County Population Totals and Components of Change: 2020-2024, last revised May 28, 2025, https://www.census.gov/data/tables/time-series/demo/popest/2020s-counties-total.html.

converted to a percentage informs us that on August 16, 2024, a number equaling 83.5 percent of Michigan's total population was registered to vote. The latest US Census estimate, published in late 2025, shows an estimated population of 10,140,459, an increase of just one percent from 2023. Such little growth should not coincide with such explosive growth in voter registration.

Some have explained Michigan's bloated voter list away as a simple problem of voter roll maintenance, but when using the same math to compare Michigan to Wisconsin and Pennsylvania, the numbers told a much different story. I broke it down in my Substack article outlining the unacceptable circumstance uncovered in Michigan:[6]

> Pennsylvania claims 8,826,265 registered voters with a population of 12,961,683 per the same estimate used above.
>
> That means a paltry 68.1% of Pennsylvania's population is registered to vote, and that Automatic Voter Registration was needed there to boost the rolls and the follow-on phantom votes.
>
> Finally, Wisconsin claims 3,456,732 registered voters with a population of 5,910,955.
>
> Only 58.5% of Wisconsin's population is registered to vote, a number that fits within the trend line of states not operating Automatic Voter Registration, and also highlighting why I think Wisconsin will be the easiest of this trio for Trump to carry.

---

6   Keshel, "Urgent Action."

Another important thing to keep in mind when highlighting this sort of corruption is that 22.1% of the population is under 18, and therefore not eligible to cast a vote. The Census Bureau also counts illegal aliens and non-citizens in the totals, and in many states, felons can't vote ever again or at least not right away. It is safe to say that at least a quarter of the population isn't eligible to vote, meaning anything over 75% of the total population being registered should make eyeballs bulge and lawsuits fly.

According to the US Census Bureau, 78.5 percent of Michigan's population is over the age of eighteen, and therefore old enough to vote. Using the 2023 population estimate of 10,037,261, only 7,879,250 Michiganders were old enough to vote, which means voter registration in Michigan at the time of my discovery was, at minimum, 505,660 too high. That is the estimate before considering the incarcerated or unnaturalized, which also factor into Michigan's total population.[7]

Trump's pathway to an electoral majority was simple, but not easy. The solid red states, plus Maine's Second Congressional District and North Carolina, gave him 235 electoral votes, which I referred to as the "Core 235." He needed just 43.2 percent of the remaining electoral votes, or 35 out of 81, to get the needed majority. I saw no scenario in which Trump could lose North Carolina but win the election, so my models had two workable scenarios including the Midwest:

---

7   U.S. Census Bureau, "The U.S. Adult and Under-Age-18 Populations: 2020 Census," August 12, 2021, https://www.census.gov/library/visualizations/interactive/adult-and-under-the-age-of-18-populations-2020-census.html.

- Core 235 + Pennsylvania + Georgia = win (an even 270 and the most direct path)
- Core 235 + Pennsylvania + Michigan + any state = win

I had two more scenarios in case the key industrial Midwestern states of Pennsylvania and Michigan were unwinnable due to election manipulation:

- Core 235 + Georgia + Arizona + Wisconsin = win
- Core 235 + Georgia + Arizona or Wisconsin + Nevada + New Hampshire = win

Out of fifty-six races, only one-eighth of them stood to play a role in returning President Trump to 1600 Pennsylvania Avenue. Sadly, considering the state of elections throughout much of the rest of the country, another cycle would have to pass to take a shot at real election reform that might free up more of Ronald Reagan's electoral map. I had my work cut out for me, and we needed to get President Trump back to Washington in the worst way.

CHAPTER 15

Wikipedia Before There Was Wikipedia

Part of my personal resilience has been forged by being out of work. I was laid off from the oil and gas and healthcare industries, once quit a job I took in haste after a layoff in which I needed to ask permission to go to the bathroom and served as a glorified receptionist, and was canned for being too noisy on a critical topic of national survival and winding up on the wrong side of Reuters, a fate otherwise known as a badge of honor.

After my layoff from the healthcare industry, I made it deep into the interview process for a Houston-based think tank that partnered with larger corporations on a variety of problems and potential solutions. As part of the process, I took a proprietary competencies test that evaluated my writing, mathematical, social, and analytical skills, among a few other things. My scores came back mostly standard. So-so here, good there, and average throughout, except for one test in which I blew the doors off.

That test required me to take fifty basic vocabulary words and organize them into not more than four "buckets," or general categories. These were words like "tomato" or "pencil." My brain can simplify complex topics into easily understandable content, which has made my work on elections go all over the world and into countless interviews, journals, and white papers. Looking back, my work in Afghanistan required me to understand enemy activity throughout an area the size of Georgia (the US state with corrupt elections, not the nation state in the Caucasus).

Accuracy has always been more important to me than being the first person to make a comment, prediction, or assessment of a problem. I hate being forced to retract so much as a typo in an article, let alone an entire study in which I was attempting to solve a problem. Those problems first resembled "How the hell do we hit this lights-out pitcher in this Southeastern Conference game that will determine our postseason standing?" and continued over eight thousand miles across the world just four years later with questions more along the lines of "Where do we locate these guys carrying rocket-propelled grenades?" The case of predicting the 2024 election, the first presidential race to come after the rotten quasi election that had brought so much guesswork into political analysis, was a complex one but one that would require use of historical comps, solid and consistent analysis, and confidence in my assessments for which laws on whose books allowed for maximum electoral disruption.

I considered it part of my greater mission in the heat of the 2024 campaign to serve as a source of fact in pushing back against the standard media playbook of fraudulent polling, anecdotal stories spun as gospel truth, and anything and everything under the sun that could enhance Kamala Harris's chances of winding up in the world's most important office. She had been parachuted in as Democratic nominee after Joe Biden collapsed in grand fashion in the only Trump–Biden debate at the end of June, which ended with Jill Biden talking to Joe like he was a toddler—"Joe, you did so good, you answered *every* question." America knew it was time, but they didn't want his vice president any more than they wanted another four years of America in decline. In fact, she entered the campaign barely a week after President Trump had been grazed by a sniper's bullet in Butler, Pennsylvania, with very little corresponding interest in what she had to offer despite the constant pleas by left-wing commenters to notice how much "joy" she supposedly injected into the national discourse. The government's legal persecution of Trump, followed by that serious assassination attempt that barely missed kicking off major public unrest, gave rise to a mood that permeated throughout the electorate signifying that worthless platitudes and divisive political tactics were no longer tolerable or acceptable.

Harris's emergence took place over a matter of days, and in a great stroke of irony, concluded with her being named Democratic nominee in quite literally the most undemocratic way possible. She had become the party's standard-bearer without receiving any primary votes in 2024, eerily resembling how she had failed to stay in the race long enough to make it to the Iowa caucus four years earlier. As an unapologetic left-winger from California, she left little to the imagination about her policy goals and made me question if she had ever held a wrench or hammer in her entire existence. If the goal was to lure Barack Obama's Midwestern coalition back into the fold, she seemed like the worst possible pick among any mainstream Democrat. This, I thought, could only be good news for Trump.

One of the media's big narratives from 2020 was the creation of "Scranton Joe," an Irish Catholic from northeastern Pennsylvania who knew the pulse of America's working class. These sorts of media plays may range from mostly untrue to utterly fictitious, but they are used to sell the results of elections. Even before Biden pulled in over eighty-one million ballots without sincerely campaigning, the "red mirage" narrative had already been planted by the media. They needed his personal story to explain a *possible* outcome in Pennsylvania in which Biden could ostensibly outperform Trump when the latter surpassed the vote total of the candidate (Obama) who won the biggest landslide in Pennsylvania in over four decades in the same race. Harris wouldn't have this narrative advantage, and the "first woman president" angle had been tried unsuccessfully eight years earlier in Pennsylvania and in every 2024 decisive state except for Nevada and New Hampshire, which were both close calls for Clinton in 2016.

Harris's move to the top spot didn't shift my calculations much. The four major pathways for Trump remained the same and, if anything, were more plausible than before given Harris's weakness with working-class voters in the Industrial and Upper Midwest and her knack for hectoring and nagging speech habits that shifted minority men in Trump's direction every day the campaign wore on. If anything, her emergence after Biden's debate disaster put an end to any serious talk of some real white whales, like Colorado or New York, going to Trump in a national landslide brought about by voter apathy and the inability to support Biden in his condition. It also made it less likely for Trump to pull any of the five leaners I had tentatively slated for Biden but possible for Trump, such as Minnesota or New Mexico.

The media immediately poured it on thick, with polling so embarrassingly biased against Trump that the Harris campaign had to manage expectations in a race they never led for a single day. *The New York Times*, through Siena College, had her up by four points in Michigan, Pennsylvania, and Wisconsin in early August.[1] The same duo had Harris up by five points in mid-Au-

---

1   Lisa Lerer and Ruth Igielnik, "Harris Leads Trump in Three Key States, Times/Siena Polls Find," *The New York Times*, August 10, 2024, updated November 6, 2024, https://www.nytimes.com/2024/08/10/us/politics/harris-trump-battleground-polls.html.

gust in Arizona,[2] which turned out to be Trump's strongest state of the *decisive* slate, and threw in with many others, like Fox News, showing Harris leading in various battlegrounds. The distant *decisive* state almost no one other than me identified, New Hampshire, had only two major polls run in September,[3] and they showed Harris with leads of eight (Saint Anselm College[4]) and eleven (University of New Hampshire[5]) points. As aggregators spun polling averages and simulator models, President Trump's campaign seemed to have greater insight into which states were winnable this time around and which needed to be campaigned in so hard that they would become "too big to rig," a phrase Trump repeated as a way of reminding Americans of what had gone wrong four years before.

I had been passing insights through my connections that seemed to find their way into the campaign's behaviors and plan of attack. For instance, I considered Minnesota highly unlikely to be won by Trump thanks to the actions of its Democratic state leadership in entrenching the 2020 election playbook into state law. They passed laws after the 2022 midterms to allow illegal aliens to receive driver's licenses, implemented automatic voter registration, and expanded early voting to passively fulfill Attorney General Keith Ellison's wish—that the Democrats would

---

2   *The New York Times*, "Cross-Tabs: August 2024 Times/Siena Poll of the Likely Electorate in Arizona," August 17, 2024, https://www.nytimes.com/interactive/2024/08/17/us/elections/times-siena-poll-arizona-likely-electorate.html.

3   RealClearPolling, "2024 New Hampshire: Trump vs. Harris," RealClearPolling, accessed November 15, 2025, https://www.realclearpolling.com/polls/president/general/2024/new-hampshire/trump-vs-harris.

4   Saint Anselm College, "Saint Anselm College Survey Center New Poll: Partisan Intensity Drives Harris's Ballot Strength," September 13, 2024, https://www.anselm.edu/about/anselmian-hub/news/saint-anselm-college-survey-center-new-poll-partisan-intensity-drives-harriss-ballot-strength.

5   University of New Hampshire Survey Center, " Near Unanimous Support for Harris Among NH Democrats Fuels Wider Lead Over Trump," University of New Hampshire Scholars Repository, September 18, 2024, https://scholars.unh.edu/cgi/viewcontent.cgi?article=1817&context=survey_center_polls.

get all the votes they needed without having to beg a friend to go vote. I explained the mechanics of this in a May 2023 article:[6]

"This is a simple tactic. Bloat the voter rolls. Use Automatic Voter Registration to also sign registrations up to permanently receive mail-in ballots. Use the additional time, now extending into September, to collect the ballots and deposit them ahead of Election Day in the largest quantities possible. Do this like a well-oiled machine, and you have no America First wave to get leveled by."

I prefer to deal in pragmatism and actionable solutions more than wishful thinking. As much as I believed Minnesota was showing all signs of a rightward shift propelled by the America First movement in line with its neighbors, Wisconsin and Iowa, I knew the stranglehold on the Twin Cities would overwhelm any red wave found throughout the rural counties and the Iron Range in the far north of the state, where numerous Democratic officials had backed Trump in 2020. The advice I pushed toward those working in the campaign was to avoid Minnesota and focus on Wisconsin. Wisconsin was going to certainly be to the right of Minnesota, and there would be no winning the presidential election in a scenario in which Wisconsin was lost (or "lost") and Minnesota was miraculously won.

Six of the seven decisive states were in full view of both campaigns, as well as North Carolina. While New Hampshire wasn't initially on the radar of either (for Harris to think to defend or Trump to think of attacking), I first made pessimistic analytical assessments for all states. The pessimistic outlooks carried forward 2020 Democratic gains in places like Maricopa County, Arizona, or Dane County, Wisconsin, where it seemed most likely

---

6   Seth Keshel, "Minnesota's Legislature Knows I'm Right About the MAGA Wave in the State," Captain K's Corner (Substack), May 2, 2023, https://www.captaink.us/p/minnesotas-legislature-knows-im-right?utm_source=publication-search.

that ballot harvesting groups would be most active, and put limits on Harris's likely ballot counts in places like the "Trumpiest" areas of western Pennsylvania, which Biden had most likely maximized his ballot count thanks to the loosening of election rules and what I had expected to be slightly better appeal to working-class voters. My pessimistic assessments for each of the seven decisive states, plus North Carolina, came out as follows:

Arizona—Trump +1.4 percent

Georgia—Harris +0.4 percent

Michigan—Harris +0.3 percent

Nevada—Harris +1.1 percent

New Hampshire—Harris +6.9 percent

North Carolina—Trump +1.4 percent

Pennsylvania—Trump +1.0 percent

Wisconsin—Trump +1.3 percent

While New Hampshire to Harris isn't much of a surprise in any forecast, Georgia, Michigan, and Nevada were rated the most perilous for the Trump campaign in my models because of urban dominance (Atlanta, Detroit, and Las Vegas); too much mail-in voting, especially in Nevada, which practices universal mail-in voting with legal ballot harvesting; and the all-telling pox of automatic voter registration that had so heavily pushed states toward Biden in 2020. The good news for the Trump campaign is that even in my pessimistic forecast, he had 275 electoral votes on the strength of the "Core 235" plus Pennsylvania, Wisconsin, and Arizona—enough to win.

Shortly after publishing my initial pessimistic assessments in September, I was sought for more interviews than I could count.

All of a sudden, that trivial knowledge I had been ridiculed for having when I was a kid was relied upon for county- and state-level political operations, including those helping Trump's campaign, and perhaps more humorously, by gamblers looking to see through the smoke and mirrors of the polling grift. People were starving for facts, figures, and brass-tacks analysis that wasn't afraid to stand alone, like when I insisted New Hampshire was going to be close. I rattled off these numbers and figures without notes, which was noticed by viewers of various shows, like Mark Halperin's *2WAY*,[7] where I crushed the dreams of many people expecting me to corroborate polling. These daily activities, and people questioning how I retained all of what people used to call "useless knowledge," reminded me of a quote from my former Ole Miss baseball teammate, Alex Presley, who went on to have a brief Major League career:

"Keshel was Wikipedia before there was Wikipedia."

While in Halperin's virtual waiting room, I waited alongside former Republican Speaker of the House Newt Gingrich. Within days, after watching my performance on the show, Gingrich's staff reached out to me to schedule an interview on his podcast, *Newt's World*, to discuss my predictions and give room for me to explain to an entirely new audience the merits of voter registration by party analysis.[8] I didn't stop there, and made sure to baptize his audience, which included many rank-and-file Republicans hesitant to get into the 2020 fraud:

---

7   Mark Halperin, "Voter Registration Charts Like No Other," Wide World of News (Substack), December 27, 2025, https://markhalperin.substack.com/p/voter-registration-charts-like-no.

8   Newt Gingrich, host, *Newt's World*, season 7, episode 71, "Episode 771: Election Predictions with Seth Keshel," Apple Podcasts, November 5, 2024, 51 min., 23 sec., https://podcasts.apple.com/us/podcast/episode-771-election-predictions-with-seth-keshel/id1452065072?i=1000675718250&r=2605.

I don't necessarily consider myself an election denier. I would call myself more of a fraud affirmer. And Bob Dole, of course, wrote in his own farewell letter to America that he wondered if Heaven would be anything like Kansas, and… if he could vote from Chicago. So I thought it was pretty funny, and it speaks to the existence of this. Now, I can language the complaints of the 2020 election in a way that forces people who are skeptical about those sorts of things to engage and think.

I think that the 2020 election was part organic. Some of it was contrived by the media. Some of it was because of the virus that was put out there and overhyped. And then other parts of it, because the state legislatures allowed their duties to be usurped by executives and secretaries of state and created what Richard Baris called, I like to use the term, "quasi elections." And we have states where the trends are no longer discernible because the integrity of the election has been completely blown up. And I think that a lot of the numbers I'm seeing now, not only confirm Trump momentum this year, but confirm my assumptions from the 2020 election.

A lot of my analyses are built on where I believe elections to be today. Most of my stuff is elections focused. Sometimes I get into the weeds about other things, but automatic voter registration is the death wish of fair elections. Why do I believe that? Because in 2020, there were twenty states that had automatic voter registration. Biden won eighteen of them, and the count was two hundred forty-three electoral votes to nine. So once you blow up the voter rolls, then you have more entries to which you can assign mail-in ballots. And the longer period of early voting you have for these mail-in ballots to be distributed, [then] they could be filled out and then harvested and then turned back in, because ultimately, if somebody knows how to trend analyze counties like I do, they know what the possible extent of a GOP margin is in all of these different counties, so they know if they get *X* amount of ballots that they will win. I think that election rigging has taken on a new front with all the sophisticated data and technology and then the loosening of the law.

I went through my predictions as if the election would have a modicum of structural integrity connecting it to previous elections that were far more predictable, and that occurred in an age before ballot counts were inflated by what laws existed on the books in various states. By this time, I had developed a model to go with my pessimistic forecasts, which I called "the registration model." Of the seven decisive states and North Carolina, only Georgia, Michigan, and Wisconsin didn't register voters by party. I used proxies to analyze the likely shifts that would be taking place if those states did have voter registration by party, like using Pennsylvania to stand in for Michigan because they had moved in the same direction in every presidential election since 1952, and Iowa for Wisconsin, thanks primarily to the overlap between voters from eastern Iowa and western Wisconsin and their predictable variances going back decades. For Georgia, I had to dig deep into the weeds and find a proxy county to serve as a mirror.

The registration models turned out like this:

Arizona—Trump +5.8 percent

Georgia—Trump +5.6 percent

Michigan—Trump +4.1 percent

Nevada—Trump +2.8 percent

New Hampshire—Trump +0.6 percent

North Carolina—Trump +6.3 percent

Pennsylvania—Trump +4.6 percent

Wisconsin—Trump +3.3 percent

All but one of the registration models proved to be too bullish, so my final predictions were carved out of a blend of the two models, which I will explain later. I had accounted for every nook and cranny of every county and for every contingency involving 2020-level ballot fraud—or in the case of Nevada, the legalized ballot stuffing that had the potential to alter statewide races by focusing on just two counties. The only polling I cared about was the type that confirmed my suspicions on states outside the battlegrounds, such as New York and its widely noted rightward shift, which correlated for decades with rightward shifts in every state Trump needed to overcome the narrowly decided battleground margins of 2020 and become president again. Newt called me the day before the election and said, "I think you're going to be right."

Plenty of people had a personal stake in dancing on my proverbial grave in case of me having my predictions blown to hell by Democratic "election fortification" like they had been four years before. None of these voices praying for my imminent irrelevance were louder than the Gray Lady's—meaning *The New York Times*. As I was rolling out models on Substack in early fall, their reporter Stuart Thompson emailed me to request an interview to go over my assessments and predictions. I realized this wasn't likely to be a friendly piece, or even a neutral one like Polymarket did around the same time[9] when I told them and their eagle-eyed audience of gamblers looking for a hot tip that Trump should carry Pennsylvania and Michigan, would not have a margin of more than one hundred electoral votes in victory, had a one-in-three chance to win New Hampshire, and would blow out Florida by more than eight points; all contributions to some of that platform's most lucrative markets. My intelligence officer's instincts gave a bold assessment of why I felt Trump would win Michigan and Pennsylvania, even though they were among the most corrupt states in 2020 and had every capability at their disposal to do it all over again:

"My gut is that Trump has both states easily. I do not think that Josh Shapiro or Gretchen Whitmer are going to go balls to the wall to try to win their states for Harris, because I think that they want to run in 2028 and I think they want to run as the middle America working class Democrat. And they could say 'hey, Kamala is from California and lost our state.'"

In the spirit of fortune favoring the bold, I decided to take Thompson up on his offer. We did two or three video calls and, without giving too much away, I walked through my analysis of the race—the only notable analysis out there blending historical trend analysis of publicly available data with my own research into what I've insisted is election manipulation and how much manipulation, or electile dysfunction, was possible in each state, broken down by county. It was a big enough feature piece that

---

9   The Oracle, "Electile Dysfunction," Polymarket, October 10, 2024, https://news.polymarket.com/p/electile-dysfunction?utm_source=publication-search.

the *Times* asked me to drive up to the Arizona Capitol complex in Phoenix for professional photos. "Meet the Election Denier Forecasting the 2024 Race" ran online on October 15.[10]

Thompson's article contained a section covering my predictions and even noted my reluctance to call Georgia and Michigan because I believed they, running automatic voter registration, were more capable of repeating the outcomes of the 2020 election than Arizona or Pennsylvania, to give two examples. Pennsylvania had waited until late 2023 to unveil automatic voter registration, giving it insufficient time to dramatically bloat voter rolls at the rate Georgia's had grown from 2016 until the 2020 election. I had held off on calling Georgia and Michigan for Trump until less than a week before the election and figured, in keeping with my pessimistic predictions, that they would be the first to get ripped off if the same playbook was in effect.

"Pennsylvania? It's going to Mr. Trump, Mr. Keshel predicts, partly because Democrats failed to pass election laws that he says could 'rig' the race in favor of Vice President Kamala Harris. Michigan? Mr. Trump could lose there, he said, partly because the Democrats control all three levels of government, giving them the ability to enable widespread fraud."

The rest of the article dug my burial plot before the ballots were even tabulated. Many of the quotes were textbook bulletin board material, like when some college linebacker spouts off about a clearly superior football team and gives that team the motivation to show no mercy on the field once Saturday finally rolls around.

One of my favorites:

---

10   Stuart A. Thompson, "Meet the Election Denier Forecasting the 2024 Race," *The New York Times*, October 15, 2024, https://www.nytimes.com/2024/10/15/technology/seth-keshel-2024-election-trump.html.

"Sure, sometimes voter registrations do point to a real change in the state," said Lakshya Jain, an election modeler behind the analytics website Split Ticket. "But also, if that were the case, it should be reflected in public opinion polling."

The ultimate motivator:

"If he ends up getting some things right, I think it's going to be out of luck," said Logan Phillips, an election forecaster from Race to the WH, a site that predicts elections and tracks polling.

Thompson, citing my pessimistic models, noted I predicted Trump would have at least 281 electoral votes to Harris's 226, with Georgia and Michigan still up in the air. The *Times*'s online readership cackled and harrumphed about my assessments and criticized the paper for giving me, an "election denier," any airtime whatsoever to "mislead" Americans as to the state of our elections, which a majority of their countrymen didn't trust anyway. One thing was for certain—I had put my predictions on the record in a way I had not had the capacity to do in 2016 or 2020. It was win or go home, and I was about to see if my luck, as Phillips put it, was going to come up big or run out forever.

Not long after *The New York Times* pushed me out on the stage to be roasted by their audience of snooty intellectuals, the piece ran in print on the cover of the business section. The *Times* had handed me a shovel with instructions to start digging my own grave. My plan was to use that shovel to bury my critics instead.

CHAPTER 16

The New Intelligence Preparation of the Battlefield

My predictions, even the most pessimistic ones, informed me that Donald Trump should win the election. They were corroborated by other clues, such as the behaviors, patterns, and daily choices of both campaigns. Texas, thanks to a surge in Latino support for Trump, was no longer on the wish list as the ultimate Democratic fantasy, as it had been in most elections starting in 2016, and the media conveniently explained away why it was of no great importance that Florida, once a premier national bellwether state, was headed for its biggest presidential blowout since 1988.

Trump's success in Florida, which was rapidly turning into a red state rivaling the stature of Texas, was one key tell that he was on his way to victory barring anything resembling 2020's election. I published "Ten Clear Signs Trump Should Win the 2024 Election" on October 31:[1]

POINT ONE: PARTY AFFILIATION

Entering the 2024 election, twenty-nine of thirty states registering voters by party had moved toward Republicans, becoming redder or less blue, since the 2020 election. Colorado, with a shift

---

1   Seth Keshel, "Ten Clear Signs Trump Should Win the 2024 Election," Captain K's Corner (Substack), October 31, 2024, https://www.captaink.us/p/ten-clear-signs-trump-should-win.

of just 0.05 percent toward Democrats, was the lone holdout in the national shift the other way toward the GOP. In fair elections, this is a telltale sign there should be substantial rightward movement, and as you may recall, the bucking of these registration patterns all across the nation in 2020 was one of the key tells that the election was rotten to the core.

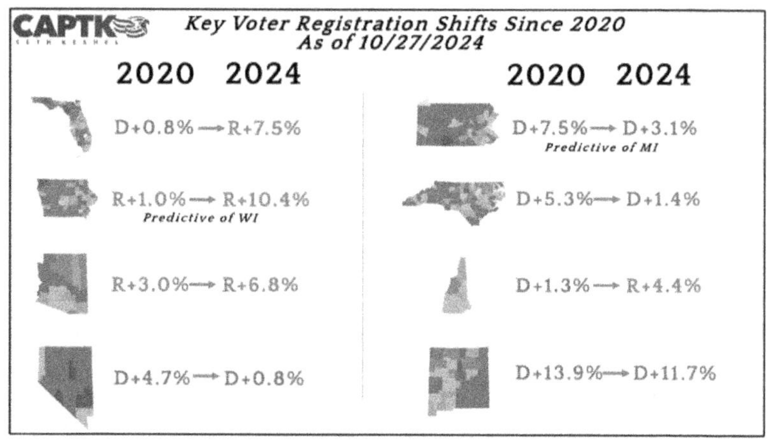

Chart by Seth Keshel.

POINT TWO: STAGGERING EARLY VOTING DATA

Democrats crushed Republicans in 2020 in early voting, especially in states that combined mail-in voting with early voting into one calculation. Pennsylvania, with its seven-week mail balloting window, was known for its now infamous, arbitrarily determined Democratic firewall, which, if met, offered little chance for Republicans like Trump, or Doug Mastriano in 2022's gubernatorial contest, to compete. In 2024, Republicans were performing substantially better across the board, preventing Kamala Harris from reaching her firewall in Pennsylvania, and outright leading all pre-Election Day voting in battlegrounds like Arizona and North Carolina.

Trump's rallies included obsessive requests for supporters to vote early and, if desired, get mail-in ballots requested and turned in. This caused a number of election integrity gurus to scratch their heads and gnash their teeth in bewilderment since we believed that early voting is used to read results ahead of time and adjust accordingly and that mail-in balloting is the most obvious vector of fraud there is. Chris Paul, a podcaster and commentator I've known since 2021, got through my thick skull a few weeks before the election that Trump was making it impossible for the media to sell any narrative that Harris was winning *anything* in the early voting period and should therefore, like Joe Biden, be expected to emerge victorious. It was a brilliant seizure of the narrative.

POINT THREE: THE DUVAL BELLWETHER

I had told *The New York Times* if two states were going to be stolen before any others, they would be Georgia and Michigan. I used Pennsylvania's party registration data to infer what Michigan's internals must look like, but I didn't find a comp for Georgia until October, when I discovered that Duval County, Florida, had mirrored the Peach State for the past two decades. When Duval went right, so did Georgia, and when it went left, you could count on the same motion in Georgia. Duval, home to metro Jacksonville and similar in demographics to Georgia, was four points to the right by registration from where it was in 2020, and with early voting looking good for a Trump win there, I had a clear indicator on where Georgia was headed. I considered Georgia essential for a Trump win, and for it to be unlikely for Trump's campaign to lose it but still expect to win the vital states in the Midwest.

	2004	2008	2012	2016	2020	2024
DUVAL COUNTY, FLORIDA						
REGISTRATION	D+9.3%	D+9.3%	D+6.0%	D+3.5%	D+5.9%	D+1.9%
PRES. MARGIN	R+16.2%	R+1.9%	R+3.6%	R+1.4%	D+3.8%	?
GEORGIA						
REGISTRATION	N/A	N/A	N/A	N/A	N/A	N/A
PRES. MARGIN	R+16.6%	R+5.2%	R+7.8%	R+5.1%	D+0.2%	?
SWING COMPARISON						
DUVAL, FL	N/A	14.3%	1.7%	2.2%	5.2%	?
GEORGIA	N/A	11.4%	2.6%	2.7%	5.3%	?

Table by Seth Keshel.

POINT FOUR: THE MIAMI-DADE BELLWETHER

Trump was close to flipping Miami-Dade County in 2020, and with a massive registration shift and good early voting data to back it up, it was clear he would pull off an outright win of the county. No Republican candidate in seven prior cases had won the county and failed to win or retain the presidency.

POINT FIVE: NEW YORK'S CANARY IN THE COAL MINE

Trump was never likely to win New York, but a series of polls showing a much tighter race than they had shown in 2020,[2] plus registration data and an expected rightward shift in the minority working-class demographic, made it inevitable that Trump would perform much better in his original home state. Beginning with the 1952 presidential election, New York had swung right from the previous election nine times. On all nine such occasions, Pennsylvania, Michigan, and New Jersey always made the same move. There was precious little room for Harris to give up any margin and expect to hold Pennsylvania or Michigan, fraudulent elections be damned. Wisconsin had shifted right on eight of the nine occasions, and Minnesota on seven.

---

2   Keshel, "Ten Clear Signs."

POINT SIX: WHERE THE VOTES AREN'T

Many pro-Trump pundits panicked during early voting at an electorate that was more female than usual. My read, based on where the male vote was weakest, was that minority men weren't turning out like they did for Obama or Biden, leaving more women than normal in the overall electorate. The men that were voting would be whiter, and therefore skew men more Republican than if all men voted. I got frustrated with Charlie Kirk over pushing these concerns, although he was probably trying to motivate people to get to the polls more than anything else.

POINT SEVEN: THE POLLS

RealClearPolitics, at the time I published the article, had Trump slightly up in the popular vote. While I don't care much for polling, Trump was undoubtedly stronger in polling this time around and had a well-known penchant for outrunning his polls, especially in the 2020 election that the political establishment tried to take without having to stoop to such lows that warrant the writing of books like this one years after the fact.

POINT EIGHT: WHERE THE ENDORSEMENTS AREN'T

The Washington Post and the *Los Angeles Times* were two papers with a knack for endorsing Democrats that sat out the 2024 race. I took these rejections as subtle signs Harris wasn't living up to the hype their media partners in crime dished out in their puff pieces about "joy" and how it was no big deal that the Democrats were trotting out one of the least popular vice presidents ever in a last-ditch effort to hold onto power.

POINT NINE: PERIPHERAL MEASUREMENTS

I watch for signs that aren't easily quantifiable, like when candidates never campaign in a state that is supposedly competitive. That campaign knows if they have it in the bag or not. In this sense, the betting markets heavily favored Trump, and GOP internal data showed a substantial movement of young voters away from Democrats, particularly at the top of the ticket. Soon after, an attempt on manipulating the betting markets would begin, and I would shoot it out of the sky as soon as it launched.

POINT TEN: TRUMP IS WINNING THE NARRATIVE

Having learned from playing defense in 2020, Trump took the bull by the horns throughout the campaign. I punctuated my column effectively:

> This time around, Trump has survived one assassination attempt, dodged a second potential attempt, evaded Democrat lawfare like the Roadrunner dodging Wile E. Coyote's antics, and become quite possibly one of the most famous and noteworthy men not just in American history, but world history. He has sat for Joe Rogan, donned trashman gear at a rally, shoveled fries at McDonalds, crisscrossed the country for rallies in deep blue New York City and Southern California, posed for a viral mugshot in Atlanta, and as if he were made of Teflon, has bounced back every grenade thrown at him straight back to the enemy camp.

As confident as I felt in my data, the sour feeling of 2020 still lingered in my gut. I didn't expect the media or the political elite who wanted to be in charge of the world's affairs to just lie down and die. There *had* to be something up their sleeves, especially with Harris being mocked for repeating the same canned phrases night after night in "girl boss" fashion, further alienating her from the minority men she would need to stand a chance against Trump. On November 2, the first big play in the information war was made to collapse the betting markets that were bordering on 70 to 30 in favor of Trump.

Ann Selzer, long considered Iowa's "gold standard" pollster known for accurately assessing the state's presidential elections, including primaries, rolled out a poll for the *Des Moines Register* showing Harris leading Trump by three points, forty-seven to forty-four.[3] Emerson College Polling had caught wind of the plan for her to release what I consider to be a poll far more devious than Biden's seventeen-point lead in Wisconsin from 2020 and beat her to the punch by dropping their own poll showing Trump leading by more than ten.[4] I had heard from Richard Baris beforehand what Selzer was up to.

In all honesty, Selzer would have been better off showing Trump up by four or five points, suggesting enough leftward drift in Iowa to take him out of competition in neighboring Wisconsin, with enough drag to keep him from flipping Michigan or Pennsylvania. She went way overboard, ignoring the fact that all ninety-nine counties in Iowa had shifted toward Republicans since 2020 and covering over her own poorly constructed poll and the fact that she had Trump over Biden by eighteen points earlier in the year. She expected readers to believe that Harris had

---

3   Brianne Pfannenstiel, "Iowa Poll: Kamala Harris Leapfrogs Donald Trump to Take Lead Near Election Day. Here's How," *Des Moines Register*, November 2, 2024, https://www.desmoinesregister.com/story/news/politics/iowa-poll/2024/11/02/iowa-poll-kamala-harris-leads-donald-trump-2024-presidential-race/75354033007/.

4   Emerson College Polling, "November 2024 Iowa Poll: Trump 53%, Harris 43%," November 2, 2024, https://emersoncollegepolling.com/november-2024-iowa-poll-trump-53-harris-43/.

weakened Trump by twenty-one points overall while everyone watching the election knew exactly which states would determine the winner. Forever losing the intellectual poker match, Harris never once visited Iowa; had she won it, she would have prevented Trump from winning his most direct path to victory and required winning another tough state, such as Wisconsin, which would have been unwinnable at that point.

Within hours, I had an email from my new friend, the former Speaker of the House of Representatives, who I remembered watching as a kid as the evening news played in the background. Newt Gingrich asked me what I had thought of the Iowa poll, which was already getting torched online for its faulty sample and a reversal from earlier in the year, when Selzer maintained that Trump was beating Biden by eighteen points[5]—a margin big enough to pull not just Wisconsin with ease, but also Minnesota, the longest-standing blue state. I spun him up on my numbers showing a landslide in the making for Trump in the Hawkeye State, along with some other colorful commentary describing possible motives, which I wasn't asked for. Gingrich squared off with Selzer the very next day on Halperin's show,[6] and went right to the well:

> You introduced me on your show to Seth Keshel,
> who focuses on registration patterns, and I was
> sufficiently perturbed by the Iowa results—and
> I went to him among seven or eight other people. And it was fascinating because he essentially

---

5   "Trump Leads Biden by 18 Points in Iowa, a Bad Sign for President in 2024 Swing States," *New York Post*, June 17, 2024, https://nypost.com/2024/06/17/us-news/trump-leads-biden-by-18-points-in-iowa-a-bad-sign-for-president-in-2024-swing-states/.

6   2WAY, "Trump vs Harris | J Ann Selzer on New Iowa Poll | 2WAY EXCLUSIVE | Sunday, 11/03/24," posted November 3, 2024, YouTube video, 57 min., 41 sec., https://www.youtube.com/watch?v=ZtFjJXftf2I.

thinks it is extraordinarily improbable, just given patterns that have been building.

Of course you did have an alternative poll that came out at about the same time that has Trump winning, I think, by ten.... I checked in with the former Speaker of the House and she said they had no indications anywhere in any of their counties of the kind of erosion.... I think Keshel's work, if you believe it, in terms of the registration patterns, would imply that we are much closer to a Reagan–Carter result than we are to 2016 or 2020.... If you look at the early voting patterns in virtually every one of the swing states—they're staggering....

If I had to bet, my bet is that Trump will carry Iowa by six to ten points.

He who laughs last laughs best, and it just so turns out the Harris poll showing her leading by three points would be Selzer's very last poll. The Iowa results, no matter how lopsided I expected them to get, paled in comparison to how North Carolina and the seven decisive states would turn out. I waited until the eleventh hour to post my final predictions of those eight states, primarily so I could have the full picture of what early voting looked like and the final changes to voter registration by party where it was available and then get as far as I could without having my predictions impacted by a late surprise.

The first of those eight states I put a bow on was North Carolina, which carried a risk for Trump with his Appalachian stronghold in the state's far west submerged by a thousand-year flood courtesy of Hurricane Helene. I had anticipated a substantial margin pickup there, perhaps enough to cancel out a growth in the Democratic margins in Mecklenburg or Wake Counties in line with 2020s, like the pessimistic scenario would account for. Since that narrow win, North Carolina had continued shedding its ancestral southern Democratic voter registration advantage, sitting over 285,000 net registrations right of its 2020 index and with ninety-six of one hundred counties leaning right from four years earlier:

2020—D+5.3% (D+391,414)[7]

2024—D+1.3% (D+105,675)[8]

Net Shift—R+4.0% (R+285,739)

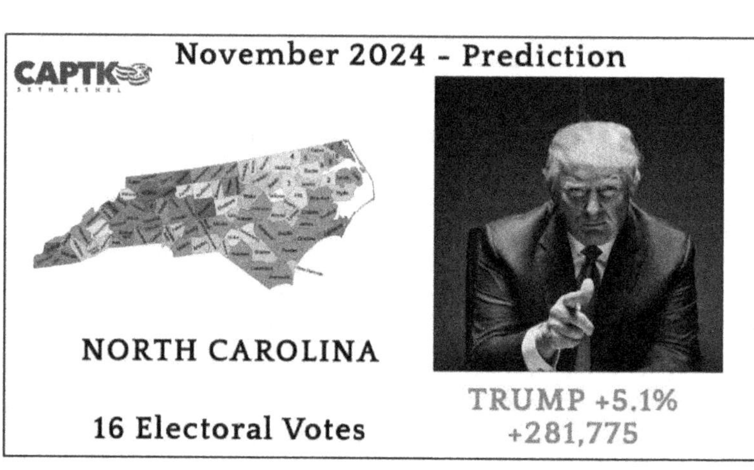

Chart by Seth Keshel.

Incredibly, Republicans held the lead for early voting. By November 1, I was ready to lock it in for Trump. My pessimistic

---

7   North Carolina State Board of Elections, "Voter Registration Statistics, Reporting Period: November 6, 2020, Statewide Total," accessed November 26, 2025, https://vt.ncsbe.gov/RegStat/Results/?date=11%2F03%2F2020.

8   North Carolina State Board of Elections, "Voter Registration Statistics: November 5, 2024," Voter Registration Statistics, accessed November 26, 2025, https://vt.ncsbe.gov/RegStat/Results/?date=11%2F05%2F2024.

model said Trump was up 1.4 percent, an almost identical margin to his win in the 2020 quasi election, and the registration model said Trump was up 6.3 percent, which seemed too bullish given the rapid urbanization of the "Research Triangle" area and metro Charlotte. Those averaged out to Trump leading by 3.9 percent. Giving more weight to the registration model due to the pro-GOP turnout numbers, I split the difference between the average and the registration model and settled on Trump leading by 5.1 percent—only 1.4 percent to the right of his 2016 margin.

North Carolina, the only real battleground Trump held onto in 2020's certified results, was in the bag, or "Too big to rig." This put Trump up to his "Core 235" and cleared the decks for the picks the market speculators were waiting for.

In a dead sprint immediately following my publication of the North Carolina prediction and extending all the way to the morning of Election Day, I released my calls for all seven decisive states, putting every one of them into Trump's column except for New Hampshire. Online know-it-alls lambasted me for not expecting Harris to carry a single battleground, although in my system, New Hampshire qualified under that banner and was going to her. Trump would get seventy-seven of the eighty-one decisive electoral votes. I read the tea leaves and held firm that while the Second Congressional District of Nebraska, Maine statewide, Minnesota, New Mexico, and Virginia would get tighter, they'd stay in the blue column for 2024.

My calls, ranked by precedence of electoral vote totals:

- Pennsylvania (nineteen)—Trump leads by 2.8 percent; the average of pessimistic and registration models

- Georgia (sixteen)—Trump leads by 4.1 percent; split the difference of the average toward the registration model, which was based on the Duval bellwether

- Michigan (fifteen)—Trump leads by 2.5 percent; over-rode the average of the models to place Michigan left of Pennsylvania based on Trump-era precedent

- Arizona (eleven)—Trump leads by 4.7 percent; split the difference of the average toward the registration model

- Wisconsin (ten)—Trump leads by 2.3 percent; the average of the pessimistic and registration models

- Nevada (six)—Trump leads by 2.5 percent; split the difference of the average toward the registration model

- New Hampshire (four)—Harris leads by 1.3 percent; split the difference of the average toward the registration model

Final prediction: Trump 312, Harris 226

CHAPTER 17

On the Screws

I got up early on Election Day, voted in person with Rachel, and zipped up the I-10 to Scottsdale, where I would be hosting the election coverage with historian Larry Schweikart and hosting guests all evening for commentary. We would be responsible for conveying accurate data and facts. It was primarily to combat what was certain to be an evening full of spin and misdirection from the mainstream media—who helped seal the corrupt 2020 bargain by holding calls for Trump, issuing the premature call of Arizona, and most importantly, providing cover for the days of non-stop counting after an unprecedented halt to the same process when Trump had what appeared to be insurmountable leads in the "Industrial Midwest" and Wisconsin.

My interview with Sean Spicer,[1] President Trump's first press secretary, a last-minute update, made the rounds that day carrying forward my assessments and pulling no punches on my belief that every head should be on a swivel looking for malfeasance in all battlegrounds. The Republican National Committee had been successful in a number of lawsuits as voting was underway, notably in Bucks County, Pennsylvania, where officials in Doylestown were kicking people out of line during the limited window in which in-person early voting was offered in the Keystone State,

---

1   Sean Spicer, "FINAL PREDICTION! Battleground States 2024," posted November 5, 2024, YouTube video, 17 min., 54 sec., https://www.youtube.com/watch?v=aPUBvCwvqXE.

even though they had joined the line in time to cast a ballot.[2] This wouldn't be the last time Bucks County made the news, either.

Just as I had with Gingrich, Polymarket, and *The New York Times*, I ripped through my predictions and explained the rationale for why I had all decisive states but New Hampshire going to Trump. After we bashed Selzer's shoddy Iowa work together, Sean asked me to give him the analysis on Georgia. The Peach State had been one of Trump's stronger battlegrounds for polling, but having lived through the 2020 race, I was having none of it. I relied on the Duval bellwether, which was shaping up for a Republican win, and the fact that the highest turnout rates in Georgia were in 2020's Trump-won counties. I doubted Harris's ability to ride days of counting to eke it out because she had failed to inspire the Democrats' minority base, and the key counties making up core Atlanta were lagging in early voting turnout, which had reached 80 percent of the total 2020 count. Sean capped off Georgia with, "Enough to win it," before moving on to Arizona.

ARIZONA - VOTER REGISTRATION INDEX TRACKER - CAPT. S. KESHEL						
ELECTION YEAR	**2004**	**2008**	**2012**	**2016**	**2020**	**2024**
REGISTERED DEM	914,264	1,022,252	952,931	1,091,323	1,378,324	1,266,536
REGISTERED REP	1,055,252	1,118,587	1,120,992	1,239,614	1,508,778	1,562,091
REGISTERED TOT	2,643,331	2,987,451	3,124,712	3,588,466	4,281,152	4,367,593
REG ADVANTAGE	140,988	96,335	168,061	148,291	130,454	295,555
REG INDEX	R+5.3%	R+3.2%	R+5.4%	R+4.1%	R+3.0%	R+6.8%
PRES MARGIN	Bush +10.5%	McCain +8.5%	Romney +9.1%	Trump +3.5%	Biden +0.3%	?

Chart by Seth Keshel.

"There's a reason why most of the betting markets and most of the pundits have Arizona as probably his most likely of what

---

2   Emma Colton, Charles Creitz, and Brooke Singman, "Trump Camp Takes Victory Lap Following Election Case Legal Win in Battleground State," Fox News, October 30, 2024, https://www.foxnews.com/politics/trump-camp-takes-victory-lap-following-election-case-legal-win-battleground-state.

I call the eight battlegrounds," I began.[3] I noted that all fifteen of Arizona's counties had a pro-Republican registration shift since the rotten 2020 election which, despite all the corruption, only produced a Biden margin of 10,457. The trend line of party registration statistics compared with the results in the twenty-first century told the tale.

Arizona voted to the right of its voter registration index in all four presidential elections from 2000 through 2012, narrowly reversing course in 2016, when Trump won by 3.5 percent with a 4.1 percent GOP registration advantage, thanks to a smaller-than-normal vote share for the two major party candidates. I have already outlined the unfathomable spike in Democratic registrations preceding the 2020 election—which sent the registration index leftward again—but either way, Arizona's presidential margins consistently run with the registration shift to the left or to the right. Not only did the registration advantage for the GOP more than double from 2020 to 2024, but it did so also with a decline of 111,788 Democratic registrations.

The state had voted an average of 88,527 left of the GOP registration advantage in the two previous Trump elections (57,057 in 2016 and 119,997 in 2020). It was a result of the soft Maricopa County vote, particularly the Latter-day Saints vote, withdrawing from Trump over John McCain loyalty and most definitely the ballot stuffing Democrats had mastered throughout the state, which lawyers like Marc Elias sought to preserve by making sure no one could monitor drop boxes.[4] Trump could run as far left of the new GOP registration advantage (295,555) as he did in 2020 and still carry the state by 175,558 or finish twice as far off

---

3   Sean Spicer, "FINAL PREDICTION!"
4   Democracy Docket, "Arizona Voter Intimidation Challenge (AZ Alliance)," last updated January 18, 2023, https://www.democracydocket.com/cases/arizona-voter-intimidation-challenge/.

that mark and still win. There would be no stealing Arizona this time, at least not for eleven electoral votes at the top of the ticket.

Sean stayed out west for my take on Nevada, where Trump's polls often showed him outrunning his own pace in Arizona. I always had Nevada left of Arizona and particularly discounted any predictions that had Trump carrying Nevada yet dropping Arizona. Since Arizona entered the union in 1912, Americans had seen both go red or blue together or Nevada blue and Arizona red, but never had they seen Arizona go blue while Nevada went red. I wasn't counting on that starting in 2024. The same thing happening in Arizona was happening in Nevada, with Democrats up to their necks in hurt based on Republicans crushing them in early voting turnout and the state nearly dead even in voter registration this time around.

NEVADA - VOTER REGISTRATION INDEX TRACKER - CAPT. S. KESHEL						
ELECTION YEAR	2004	2008	2012	2016	2020	2024
REGISTERED DEM	429,808	531,317	526,986	577,679	679,332	609,954
REGISTERED REP	434,239	430,594	436,799	488,861	591,916	600,754
REGISTERED TOT	1,071,101	1,207,761	1,257,621	1,464,819	1,821,356	2,035,166
REG ADVANTAGE	4,431	100,723	90,187	88,818	87,416	9,200
REG INDEX	R+0.4%	D+8.3%	D+7.2%	D+6.1%	D+4.8%	D+0.5%
PRES MARGIN	Bush +2.6%	Obama +12.5%	Obama +6.7%	Clinton +2.4%	Biden +2.4%	?

Chart by Seth Keshel.

Things were so bad for Harris in the Silver State that Jon Ralston, the longtime Democratic-leaning commentator, admitted as much. Democrats led voter registration by a half-point, just 9,200 registrations, in a state that had voted hard to the right of its Democratic advantages in 2016 and 2020. Trump finished an average of 57,718 right of their leads in his two previous races, losing Nevada by just 27,202 and 33,596 ballots against Clinton and Biden, respectively. As I told Sean, with the Democratic registration advantage almost completely evaporated and Latinos and

Asian Americans looking much stronger for Trump than before, Nevada was going to flip.

The real issue with Nevada, given its legalization of every election cheat imaginable, was the likelihood that Sam Brown, the Republican US Senate nominee, would get stiffed by days of counting mail-in ballots in his effort to unseat Democrat Jacky Rosen. I had met Brown, an Army veteran badly wounded by an explosion, at an event in Reno previously and shared my research on his state. After Sean documented the issues with mail-in balloting, I sounded the alarm that Brown may wind up in the "Adam Laxalt zone," referring to the Nevada political legacy who thought he had the 2022 Senate race in the bag, only to experience Nevada's legalized corruption firsthand and drop the seat narrowly to incumbent Catherine Cortez Masto.

North Carolina, which I had in the bag for Trump, was next. We reviewed the registration figures, and I went over the turnout stats from the flood zone created by Hurricane Helene. The fear was that the dampened pro-Trump turnout would negate what looked like would be a significant margin boost, allowing Democratic margin expansion in Mecklenburg or Wake Counties to tighten up the artificially close margin from 2020 that defied the party registration indicators flashing bright red all over the state.

The solid Trump electoral votes, plus North Carolina, Nevada, Arizona, and Georgia, made 268 electoral votes. If the predictions Sean was airing were correct, Trump was almost over the hump and poised to return to the White House.

The 19 electoral votes of Pennsylvania were next up for analysis. Trump's Core 235, which included North Carolina, plus wins of Georgia and Pennsylvania, remained the quickest path to victory, and for those of us focused on election integrity, it was the best bet to make sure the counting didn't drag on for days and create a moving scenario like we saw four years earlier.

The situation on the ground for Harris, about whom I had joked had likely never held a wrench or hammer in her life, reflected exactly what I expected. She was far from having her partisan firewall in place, which was estimated to be a Democratic ballot count lead of roughly 900,000. The turnout in Philadelphia was awful, and things were dire enough that Democrat-run townships were busy playing games with voters or exercising outright suppression tactics, as documented in the case of Doylestown and Bucks County, which were slapped down by a judge. I continued to rest on a couple of assessments: One, that despite all the counting and games, and not considering the massive partisan shift favoring Trump since 2020, the Irish Catholic from Scranton had only carried the Keystone State by 80,555 ballots after four days of counting in one of the worst reelection environments that could be imagined for any incumbent. Two, with the Philadelphia turnout numbers in the tank, I still had the feeling Josh Shapiro, who doubtlessly rolled out automatic voter registration as a last-ditch effort to save Biden a year earlier, wanted to keep a future presidential run up his sleeve and wouldn't be helped by a far left-wing radical from California prevailing in his blue-collar state.

PENNSYLVANIA - VOTER REGISTRATION INDEX TRACKER - CAPT. S. KESHEL					
ELECTION YEAR	2004	2008	2012	2016	2020	2024
REGISTERED DEM	3,985,486	4,479,513	4,266,317	4,217,456	4,228,888	3,998,602
REGISTERED REP	3,405,278	3,243,046	3,131,144	3,301,182	3,543,070	3,712,319
REGISTERED TOT	8,366,663	8,755,588	8,508,015	8,722,977	9,090,962	9,175,133
REG ADVANTAGE	580,208	1,236,467	1,135,173	916,274	685,818	286,283
REG INDEX	D+6.9%	D+14.1%	D+13.3%	D+10.5%	D+7.5%	D+3.1%
PRES MARGIN	Kerry +2.5%	Obama +10.3%	Obama +5.4%	Trump +0.7%	Biden +1.2%	?

Chart by Seth Keshel.

The party registration indicators strongly suggested, even with the modern Democratic fortification of elections, there should be no way for Trump to lose Pennsylvania this time.

Pennsylvania hadn't voted to the left of its Democratic registration advantage at any point in the twenty-first century, and I can't access data far enough back into the twentieth century to determine exactly how long the state has voted to the right of its party registration index. Trump had prevailed in Pennsylvania in 2016 with Democrats leading registration by 916,274, winning by 44,292—or 960,566 *right* of the Democrat advantage. As has been documented ad nauseam in analysis since then, Trump's massive vote increase in 2020, combined with a net new registered voter advantage favoring Republicans greater than 21 to 1 in the run-up to 2020, is one of the biggest tells that the 2020 election was rigged beyond belief. Still, even with the cheating, Trump ran 605,263 to the right of the 685,818-registration advantage Biden was working with. Trump's two runs in Pennsylvania averaged 782,915 to the *right* of the Democrat lead.

That lead was down to just 286,283 when Harris was on the hot seat to hold the most important battleground state against the man who had just survived an assassination attempt there not even four months earlier. She was doomed.

I pointed out that sixty-four of the state's sixty-seven counties were more Republican, or less Democrat, than they were in the 2020 election. Right before voter registration closed, even Chester County, a key Philadelphia suburban stronghold, slipped slightly rightward of its 2020 mark, suggesting Trump's improvement in a place Harris desperately needed to run up higher margins in. Sean asked me to peg which counties were the most important to watch, and I explained that Luzerne County, which had aligned with the winner of the state's electoral votes in every race from

1936 to 2016, had turned red like Ohio and was no longer predictive. We needed to be watching Erie and Northampton Counties, the two new blue-collar bellwethers in the Keystone State. I left no room for doubt that I had Trump carrying Pennsylvania, and potentially by as much as 2.8 percent even in an election destined to be tainted by the mail-in balloting flooding the state since the passage of Act 77 in 2019.

There were 287 electoral votes for Trump—enough to win, and still with room to run up the score.

We moved into Wisconsin, which the mainstream media attempted to convince Americans would go to Biden by Lyndon Johnson margins in 2020. Polling, even when conducted by those without an agenda to deceive, is difficult in the state and leads to oversampling of Milwaukee and Dane Counties. These were the two counties that the Democrats had to maximize margin in to override what was increasingly a very Trumpy hinterlands region—or the vast majority of the state's seventy outlying counties. I had little doubt Selzer's garbage poll of Iowa was intended to throw off the betting markets for Wisconsin and conceal the correlation between the two states going back nearly a century. With huge Iowa margins approaching or exceeding double digits for Trump, Wisconsin was certain to go to Trump.

It had been well to the left of Iowa in the two previous Trump races, finishing 8.7 percent left of the Hawkeye State in 2016 and 8.8 percent in 2020. It had not been more than ten points away from Iowa to either the left or right since 1936, and with Trump's progress to an overwhelming win in Iowa now shrouded in doubt thanks to Selzer, Wisconsin was a no-brainer. I split the difference between my models and called for a Trump win, leading by 2.3 percent, with nothing that Meagan Wolfe or the harshly criticized Wisconsin Elections Commission could do to stop it. They would need to settle for the downballot US Senate seat, which Republican Eric Hovde was looking to rip away from the incumbent Democrat, Tammy Baldwin. My prediction ran counter to the knowledge that four of the past six presidential elections in Wisconsin had been decided within a single point.

There were 297 electoral votes for Trump, with only Michigan left to peg among the battlegrounds I had going for Trump.

Michigan, without party registration and with way less data to go on outside of the clearly bloated voter rolls I had warned about earlier in the summer, presented more of a challenge to get right. Pennsylvania is its political cousin, and the two had moved in the same direction in every election since 1952. Pennsylvania was clearly going to lurch rightward even with a mail-ballot heavy election, so Michigan appeared set to do the same. Trump's polling numbers showed major movement in the southeastern portion of the state, particularly with Arab Americans who were sold on his message of reining in the expeditionary use of the US military. The issue for my predictions, outside of Michigan running some of the worst elections in America and being governed by some of the most heavily scrutinized Democrats to be found anywhere, is that Biden's inflated 2.8 percent margin left room for the state to move right with Pennsylvania but not flip. I expected it to be left of Pennsylvania, as it had been in every presidential election since 1992, but the question came down to a matter of "how much?"

In Trump's two races, Michigan ran 33,588 left of Pennsylvania in 2016, and 73,633 left in 2020, for an average of 53,610. I backed that raw number off my Pennsylvania forecast, kept 2020 turnout static, and came up with Trump leading by 2.5 percent in Michigan—narrowly left of Pennsylvania as history would suggest.

Now Trump: 312 electoral votes. The only puzzle piece still flapping loose was New Hampshire, which I took so much heat for identifying as a close race. My rationale was simple:

NEW HAMPSHIRE - VOTER REGISTRATION INDEX TRACKER - CAPT. S. KESHEL						
ELECTION YEAR	2004	2008	2012	2016	2020	2024
REGISTERED DEM	228,395	280,507	250,358	288,808	347,828	265,925
REGISTERED REP	267,141	282,421	273,675	308,808	333,165	304,340
REGISTERED TOT	855,861	958,528	905,957	1,007,402	1,119,232	901,784
REG ADVANTAGE	38,746	1,914	23,317	20,000	14,663	38,415
REG INDEX	R+4.5%	R+0.2%	R+2.6%	R+2.0%	D+1.3%	R+4.3%
PRES MARGIN	Kerry +1.4%	Obama +9.6%	Obama +5.6%	Clinton +0.4%	Biden +7.4%	?

Chart by Seth Keshel.

Viewing the situation from the perspective of election integrity, the state had purged its voter rolls in 2021, dumping more than 20 percent of the net voter roll count it had in the 2020 election. Shortly thereafter, the state began a massive Republican voter registration shift, ridding the Granite State of a short-lived Democratic voter registration edge. By the time the 2024 election arrived, the GOP had swung the state rightward by more than 53,000 net registrations from the 2020 quasi election.[5] The state's overwhelmingly white electorate, which became more competitive for Trump in 2016 due to his focus on the opioid epidemic, did not correlate cleanly to the other battleground states. Given that it bucked the registration indicator in 2016, I spun my own math once again.

New Hampshire, unlike Pennsylvania or Nevada, consistently votes to the left of its registration advantage. In fact, it hasn't voted to the right of it since George H. W. Bush carried the state in 1988 by 26.2 percent. With a GOP registration advantage of

---

5   New Hampshire Secretary of State, "Party Registration History 1970–2025," accessed November 26, 2025, https://www.sos.nh.gov/party-registration-history-1970-2025.

4.3 percent in 2024, precedent informed my decision-making that the margin would be tighter than that. Again, by how much?

With a larger-than-normal minor party vote in 2016, Trump lost New Hampshire by just 2,736 to Clinton in a race widely believed to have been exploited by New Hampshire's weak same-day registration standards, which allowed interference from bordering states, such as Massachusetts. It doesn't take many fraudulently cast ballots to impact a statewide election in such a small state. Trump's losing margin that year was 22,736 left of the dwindling GOP registration advantage. In the 2020 election, using a bloated voter roll and plenty of mail-in ballots to go around, Trump lagged Biden by 59,277, or 44,614 left of the brand-new Democratic voter registration advantage, the first such advantage I can verify in the history of the state. Trump's two races put him 33,675 left of registration on average. With a lead of 38,415 registrations for the GOP, he could tilt the state if he ran at 2016 strength but would suffer an extremely narrow loss if he slipped to his 2020 relative performance. My gut call was to split the average toward the registration model, which captured the latest breaks in the electorate, and put my call at Harris leading by 1.3 percent. Trump and J. D. Vance knew New Hampshire was on the radar and gave a few looks at the state earlier in the campaign, but their lack of interest in it near the end told me they thought that they didn't have it, or perhaps that they knew they didn't need it. It was the decisive call I was least certain of.

Trump 312, Harris 226. I was running with it come hell or high water. I would either nail it against the grain of a cycle's worth of polling and media narratives and in the face of all the hit pieces, or slink away into irrelevance, no matter how the official results were achieved.

Moneyball, Michael Lewis's baseball masterpiece that resonated deeply with me long before I became comfortable with myself and my own skillset, once again drifted through my mind as the seemingly endless afternoon of November 5, 2024, crept by with intermittent updates and anecdotal information about polling line sizes, turnout estimates, machine failures, precincts running out of ballots, fake reports forecasting victory or gloom for either party, and betting markets rattling off an endless stream of information. In that book, Oakland General Manager Billy Beane *hated* watching the Oakland Athletics on the field. He paced through the bowels of the stadium, hit the gym, walked through the parking lot—anything to keep his anxious mind from dwelling on every last detail in front of his eyes. Likewise, I *hate* watching elections, especially ones I'm invested in or personally feel have a massive degree of weight upon the future of a state or our country. I dread how the media will selectively withhold state calls on obvious wins or trot out all the margins from the big blue centers while slow-rolling rural results. This had never been as real of an issue as it had been in the 2020 election, when networks weren't allowed to call Ohio or Florida for Trump, but shutting down the discussion on Minnesota, Virginia, or even Arizona well ahead of what seemed reasonable was perfectly acceptable behavior.

The fear of looking like the fool with my own "Gray Lady" hit piece was a possibility, especially when I clicked through my phone and would see various Republican personalities hedging over the possibility of something that my numbers screamed was implausible.

With golden hour painting the desert, which is 7 p.m. that time of year on Eastern Standard Time, polls closed in six states. There are three layups that get called right away every year—Indiana and Kentucky for Trump and Vermont for Harris this time around. While these states seem unimportant to many, Indiana provided a smorgasbord of valuable data I used to fine-tune my messaging for the evening. Aside from our broadcast, which required me to take to the newsroom and face the camera here and there to provide map updates, I found it difficult to manage too much social media and was busy rattling most of my coverage off on X, where the world was watching.

Forget Indianapolis, I thought. Show me Vigo County, one of those crucial bellwethers that Trump won in 2020 before the media decided that they no longer had any bearing on our national elections. It had been correct in every election from 1956, when Eisenhower carried it, through 2016 when Trump did. This time around, Trump wound up carrying it by eighteen points, up from 14.7 percent in 2020's tainted race. That result, combined with others in southern Indiana that came through first, gave me hopeful anticipation that their blue-collar peers in Michigan and Pennsylvania would show the same lean.

North Carolina closed at 7:30, and a half-hour later, Florida, Michigan, Pennsylvania, and Texas. Because Florida learned its lesson from such an embarrassing 2000 election featuring the infamous "hanging chads," and because Governor Ron DeSantis had signed legislation tightening up mail-in balloting and ensuring swift counts, I learned more about the 2024 election in watching Florida zoom through its counting than I did from anything else being observed in real time. While we waited on North Carolina to creep by, Duval County was looking like an outright Trump win, which gave me hope for Georgia based on my modeling. Most importantly, he was well on his way to winning Miami-Dade County, which, as outlined in the previous chapter, had never voted for a Republican presidential nominee who would go on to lose the national race. A double-digit cakewalk in Florida, combined with a massive margin brewing in Texas, which had seen Trump win by single digits two elections in a row, showed the nation clearly which side was on defense.

At 11:18 p.m.—long after it had become obvious to me based on Trump's flips of Anson and Pasquotank Counties, plus the successful mitigation of Democratic margin advancement in Mecklenburg and Wake Counties—the Associated Press called North Carolina for Trump,[6] and with it, put him at my Core 235 electoral vote count. Trump now, even if unofficially, had won every single electoral vote that had been certified for him in 2020. His win there was even more impressive when considering that the Democrats had smoked Republicans, including Mark Robinson for governor, statewide. With North Carolina and its trail of fake polls and incessant worries about how Hurricane Helene would impact the Trumpy Appalachian region of the state in the rearview, it was time to bear down on Georgia. If he could hold his slim but steady lead there, it would be all eyes on Pennsylvania—just like I drew it up.

The core Democrat-run counties of metro Atlanta had been playing games throughout the early voting period, like when Fulton County decided to open its election offices outside of legal hours of operation to collect absentee ballots.[7] The GOP lawsuit against them was unsuccessful, so there was plenty of heartburn to go around after remembering how things shook out under Brad Raffensperger's watch in 2020. He was back again defending Fulton County, which surprised no one who had been paying attention as long as I had. Trump was gashing Harris in the overwhelmingly white counties of northern Georgia and in

---

6   Galen Bacharier. "AP: Trump Wins North Carolina," NC Newsline, November 5, 2024. https://ncnewsline.com/2024/11/05/ap-trump-wins-north-carolina/.

7   Fulton County, "Fulton Elections Offices Open November 2 and 3 for Absentee Ballot Return," November 1, 2024, https://fultoncountyga.gov/news/2024/11/01/fulton-elections-offices-open-november-2-and-3-for-absentee-ballot-return.

rural areas throughout most of the state's interior. Notably, Harris was not getting the rural black turnout that she needed to put the Atlanta Democratic strongholds in position to put her ahead and keep Trump's hopes buried. As we waited anxiously, I heard through the grapevine that Georgia was done, and put out my own premature call on X. I got roasted, but just before 1 a.m., the Associated Press confirmed my Duval County mirror by calling the Peach State and its sixteen vital electoral votes for Trump. All that mattered was what was right in front of our faces—the Keystone State.

The most positive sign available for Pennsylvania in terms of real-time information was the fact that Florida was on its way to giving Trump a margin greater than thirteen points. One of the most unmistakable signs that the 2020 election was a fraud was the fact that for the first time since 1952, when Pennsylvania and Michigan began shifting together in presidential elections without interruption, they also shifted opposite of Florida, which Trump won by a wider margin in 2020 than he did in 2016. I was counting on the massive rightward shift in Florida manifesting in Pennsylvania, which Biden took with *everything* working in his favor by only 1.2 percent. Harris didn't have the luxury of pretending to connect with working-class voters, nor the ability to act as if Scranton were any sort of second home to her.

We waited and then waited some more. I updated Larry, who manned the desk all night, by sliding him notepads filled with information. Stories were floating around, as usual when a campaign is in its death throes, that Harris was hopeful that Philadelphia would bail her out. I wasn't buying it, and neither were millions of Americans. Many thousands of them found my X account as I was putting the election on live blast. As my registration numbers out of Chester County suggested, she was running behind what she needed to get not only there, but in Delaware, Montgomery, and Bucks Counties, the collar counties of Philadelphia. Bucks, after having been reamed in court for suppressing the vote, was on its way to flipping red for Trump. I could smell the fear as Alaska was projected for Trump, a mere formality according to my modeling, but an essential cog for ensuring Pennsylvania landed Trump at 270 right on the nose.

I sifted through the county maps doing math in my head, growing increasingly confident as the East Coast turned the page into November 6, with my X account holding the proof for a growing audience:

"Trump is going to have PA. York is reporting slow and still has at least another 50k MARGIN for Trump waiting."[8]

I gave an update on the two counties I had told Sean's audience to watch in Pennsylvania:

"Trump has Erie and Northampton bellwethers."[9]

Cambria County, after equipment failures, had its voting hours extended[10] and was holding a lot more Trump margin that would push Harris back further:

"Should also have another 27k Margin minimum coming in from Cambria County, PA."[11]

My most definitive post was right around the corner, at 11:21 Mountain Standard Time:

---

8   Seth Keshel (@RealSKeshel), "Trump is going to have PA. York is reporting slow and still has at least another 50k MARGIN for Trump waiting," X, November 6, 2024, https://x.com/RealSKeshel/status/1854034531591864429.

9   Seth Keshel (@RealSKeshel), "Trump has Erie and Northampton bellwethers," X, November 6, 2024,

10   WJAC Staff, "Voting Hours Extended to 10 pm in Cambria County Due to Widespread Issues," November 5, 2024, https://wjactv.com/news/local/officials-acknowledge-cambria-co-voting-issues-file-for-voting-time-extension.

11   Seth Keshel (@RealSKeshel), "Should also have another 27k Margin minimum coming in from Cambria County, PA," X, November 6, 2024, https://x.com/RealSKeshel/status/1854036831702311391.

"PA Called We WON."[12]

Fox News had done the honors after seeing exactly what I was seeing, with the final call at 1:19 Eastern Standard Time.[13] Trump had hit the straightest path to 270 without so much as a hiccup.

I relayed the call to the audience watching our broadcast, and shortly after, Rachel joined me at the studio. One of my biggest regrets from that night is that I couldn't support her in person at her campaign watch party as she successfully ran for reelection. While I had planned for the worst a rigged election had to offer, I was surprised to find I could close up shop before midnight in Arizona. My mind would wander for hours after that, buried in the glow of my smartphone as I watched for downballot races and to monitor my other predictions in Michigan, Wisconsin, Arizona, and Nevada, which were all looking exactly as I had predicted them—on the screws.

Rachel crashed as soon as we got to our hotel, which was just down the road from the studio. I stayed up until after 3 a.m. local time, as outlets began prepping the airwaves to call Michigan and Wisconsin for Trump formally. Trump's leads in both, just like his lead in Pennsylvania, were rapidly dwindling, and as the nation slept, Democrats Elissa Slotkin and Tammy Baldwin pulled ahead of Republicans Mike Rogers and Eric Hovde, in Michigan and Wisconsin respectively. They never relinquished those leads.[14]

---

12   Seth Keshel (@RealSKeshel), "PA called WE WON," X, November 6, 2024, https://x.com/RealSKeshel/status/1854046540551057549.

13   Charles Creitz, "Fox News Projects Trump Victory Over Harris in Pennsylvania," Fox News, November 6, 2024, https://www.foxnews.com/politics/fox-news-projects-trump-victory-over-harris-pennsylvania.

14   Scott Wong, "Sen. Tammy Baldwin Wins Re-election in Wisconsin over Republican Eric Hovde," *NBC News*, November 6, 2024, https://www.nbcnews.com/politics/2024-election/tammy-baldwin-win-wisconsin-senate-election-eric-hovde-rcna173886; Alyssa Burr, "Democrat Elissa Slotkin Wins Michigan U.S. Senate Seat, Narrowly Defeating Mike Rogers," *Michigan Independent*, November 8, 2024, https://michiganindependent.com/politics/senate-2024-election-slotkin-rogers-stabenow/.

I slept for less than three hours and snuck out of the room to the lobby, where I resumed my browsing. "Red everywhere," I thought to myself, as I looked at the Rio Grande Valley of Texas and took note of counties that had never before, or not in a century, backed a GOP presidential nominee, yet were shaded for Trump. All eighteen bellwethers he carried in 2020 were in his column once again, and miraculously, this time they were predictive. The two slow-rolling battlegrounds out west, Arizona and Nevada, were going for Trump, but wouldn't be called for days because of the massive load of mail-in ballots both would produce.

My predictions were right on the mark, 312 to 226 for Trump. *He* was indeed "too big to rig" in the decisive states, but one thing was clear watching the count after the media had written off the presidential race: the downballot races were *not* "too big to rig." After another month passed, millions more agreed. Taking another good look at that bright red map and envisioning the smug grin I gave *The New York Times*, I couldn't help but think that somewhere in Manhattan, a shovel was hitting concrete.

CHAPTER 18

Too Big to Rig?

One of my first emails on November 6 was to Stuart Thompson, *The New York Times* journalist who had thrust me into the den of lions with his October feature piece. I was, naturally, crowing about my predictions all striking pay dirt. Stuart had other ideas and instantly came up with a concept for an article that would frame "election deniers" as unconcerned for election integrity as long as their own side emerged victorious. I knew where his mind was going immediately and agreed to be interviewed on my drive home without hesitation.

I had already watched Wisconsin move from a lead of several points favoring Trump, with Dane and Milwaukee Counties all but exhausted, to one inside a single point, making it five of seven presidential elections decided so narrowly. The collateral damage had been Eric Hovde's bid for US Senate, which would have fattened up Donald Trump's majority in that chamber and made it that much easier for confirmations, legislation, and other matters to get through a body compromised by dead weight Republicans like Lisa Murkowski and Mitch McConnell, and what was certain to be the vast majority of Democrats on every conceivable matter.

I gave Thompson a bunch of specifics, which wasn't what he expected given how counts were still ongoing and would be until December in places that run unacceptable elections, like

California. Rather than getting into specifics, Thompson gave me a pass:[1]

> Seth Keshel, an election denier from Arizona who spent years touring the country with voter fraud claims, found a way to thread the needle: He said he believed Mr. Trump won fairly, but suggested there may still have been some fraud in down-ballot races where Democrats were leading.
>
> "I believe the outcome is correct," Mr. Keshel said in an interview. "I don't believe that every state is right."

I had good reason for those claims. Logically, with Trump the winner through the battleground states in the east, there would be very little reason to pull out all the stops to prevent him from winning the electoral votes of Michigan, Wisconsin, Arizona, or Nevada. To do so would invite unwanted scrutiny into the elections in all four states. The follow-on mission for fraudsters in light of Trump's election, given the likelihood of the right letting its guard down out of relief, would be to find a silver lining by throwing a wet blanket on Trump's downballot success. Remember, even in the quasi election of 2020, Republicans *gained* seats in the US House, which flew in the face of any logical explanation of Joe Biden's blowout popular vote win. With Trump the popular vote and Electoral College winner, Americans were being fed a narrative that this time around, they would want Trump surrounded by Democrats to encourage responsible behavior.

---

1   Stuart A. Thompson, Jim Rutenberg, and Steven Lee Myers, "After Trump Took the Lead, Election Deniers Went Suddenly Silent," *The New York Times*, November 6, 2024, https://www.nytimes.com/2024/11/06/technology/trump-election-denial.html.

Elissa Slotkin and Tammy Baldwin had already been declared the winners in Michigan and Wisconsin, respectively, which were also officially in the Trump ledger by the end of November 6. Eric Hovde, the Republican challenger in Wisconsin who had run just behind Trump all night, was up in arms and ready to run through a brick wall to prove how Baldwin had ripped the election right out from under him. In Nevada, Sam Brown held a narrow lead over Jacky Rosen and was optimistic he would ride Trump's coattails to victory. Kari Lake, running for US Senate in Arizona, had told me her internal polling showed her running only two points behind Trump statewide, but as Arizona trickled out the ballots, early returns showed her losing to Ruben Gallego, as it was apparent Trump would win the state in a walk.

It would be several weeks until I could make an honest assessment of the 2024 election from the presidency all the way down the ballot, and even longer until I could write up California, which saw two Democrats declare victory in December for US House seats held by Republicans. The most curious thing about California is that Kamala Harris, despite it being her home state, lagged Biden's 2020 ballot count by more than 1.8 million, while Trump gained fewer than 100,000 from his own 2020 performance. Harris's plunge alone pushed the state 9 percent to the right and resulted in many county flips for Trump, including a flip of the overwhelmingly Hispanic Imperial County, which last voted for a GOP presidential candidate thirty-six years earlier. An impartial observer with a general knowledge of US politics would assume a candidate running in her own home state and underperforming the previous party nominee by 1.8 million votes would deflate any hopes of her party flipping House seats that the Republicans won in an otherwise disappointing midterm cycle two years before. John Duarte (representative for the Thirteenth Congressional District) and Michelle Steel (representative for the Forty-Fifth Congressional District)—

the Republican House members who were evicted from office by Democrats Adam Gray and Derek Tran, respectively—after weeks of counting, found out exactly why international watchdog organizations consider slow counting a telltale sign of cheating in elections, but limped away without a fight.

I thought through the most effective way to map data for the 2024 election, and with Harris lagging Biden's national ballot count by more than 6 million, it wasn't going to be by flagging states, counties, or even precincts red on a map for inconceivably high vote totals that were obvious in places like Maricopa County four years earlier. National elections operate like the dimmer on a light switch; when a candidate is hot, they're hot everywhere. When the candidate is cold, they're cold all over. When Barack Obama was a can't-miss candidate in 2008, he shifted almost every state to the left and gained votes everywhere, blowing away all previously held national popular vote figures and landing at a total that wouldn't be eclipsed for another twelve years. In 2012, forty-three states shifted back to the right, as Obama hemorrhaged much of his support from four years earlier, putting the Midwest on a collision course to flip for an ideal Republican candidate. Mitt Romney's problem was that he couldn't capitalize on Obama's losses and bring enough defectors to his side.

Harris lagged Biden's ballot count in forty-four states and Washington, DC. Her collapse helped erase a decade of Democratic inroads into Texas, sent Florida off into the Republican stratosphere, and solidified Iowa and Ohio as GOP strongholds. In Ohio, she failed to match John Kerry's vote total from twenty years earlier, yet miraculously nearly equaled Biden's ballot counts in Pennsylvania and Michigan. She probably would have surpassed Biden in Pennsylvania and made it a photo finish with Trump had she not lost considerable minority support in the eastern part of the state and left a ton of votes on the table in Philadelphia County, where she lagged Hillary Clinton's ballot count from 2016. Did Josh Shapiro call off the ballot collection network to clear the path for his own ambitions? That is something no data analysis can confirm, but considering that Harris nearly matched Biden in Michigan, only to see her margins go severely backward in Wayne County—where the monster Democratic vote resides—it makes a man wonder just how much backroom politicking was going on as Harris's Democratic peers watched her struggle to match Trump's charisma.

As I've already asserted, it shouldn't be hard for a freshman in a dorm room to pick three-quarters of the states correctly just by looking at a map of elections in the twenty-first century. The real skill comes in once the race is down to the wire in the decisive states. All it took was a continued shift of Latino voters, an influx of Republicans from failed blue states, and the tightening of mail-in balloting procedures to turn Florida into a GOP romp. I ran into Iowa Treasurer Roby Smith, an avid follower of my research who had once been a state legislator, at an event in Davenport in July 2025, and he shared with me that Iowa's election laws were tightened a little bit at a time in the years leading up to the 2020 quasi election. That would explain why Iowa, even if it suffered from an abundance of mail-in balloting, had some of the most believable and trend-aligned results of any state in that year's race. I used the 2024 data from all fifty-six races to contrast outcomes with the two previous Trump races and found that states are most easily predicted when viewed through the lens of which laws they keep on the books. Three notably bad election laws represent the unholy trinity of "electile dysfunction":

AUTOMATIC VOTER REGISTRATION

If you want to create a permanent blue state, there is nothing better for the long term than to usher in automatic voter registration. Biden carried eighteen of twenty states, plus Washington,

DC, under automatic voter registration in 2020, winning 243 electoral votes to Trump's 9. After observing that success and accurately perceiving a Republican shift present in almost every state, Delaware, Hawaii, Minnesota, and most importantly, Pennsylvania, shifted to automatic voter registration in the years following Biden's inauguration and before November 5, 2024. Trump managed to carry Pennsylvania, which was "too big to rig," and flip Georgia, Michigan, and Nevada among automatic voter registration states he had "lost" in 2020 but still lost them 18 to 6, or 221 electoral votes to 64. The most startling map is that of the states not running automatic voter registration, which Trump won by an astounding margin of 248 electoral votes to Harris's 5.

Map by Seth Keshel.

Twenty-five states not operating automatic voter registration went to Trump. Only New Hampshire and the Second Congressional District of Nebraska, which centers on metro Omaha, went to Harris in this grouping. Automatic voter registration allows for states like Michigan to bloat voter rolls to a number higher than the number of eligible voters living in a state, and when combined with universal mail-in voting, or simply states with excessive mail-in voting like Pennsylvania, it's a recipe for disastrous levels of election manipulation. This is precisely what enabled Slotkin to prevail in the Senate race downballot from Trump in Michigan and proceed to Washington to incite violence against troops and stir sedition by encouraging the military to disobey orders, which led to the tragic shooting of two West Virginia National Guard troops on November 26, 2025. That incident served as a stark reminder of the consequences of corrupt elections.

Registration, no matter if you lean more toward electronic or manual means of how elections are defrauded, is undoubtedly the foundation of election corruption. Blue states have adopted this policy in the last decade more than any other election-related policy, a telltale sign they recognize the electoral benefits of having such a policy on the books. Like a frosty beer with a plate full of spicy wings, it pairs naturally with the oldest trick in the book.

UNIVERSAL MAIL-IN VOTING

Oregon was the first state to convert to holding all-mail elections, and ran the first such presidential race in 2000, when Al Gore narrowly defeated George W. Bush. The practice had been experimented with at a more local level, like when Maricopa County Republicans allowed the practice as early as 1991, but mass mail-in voting is a new thing. Colorado, Utah, and Washington were the next three states to switch to universal mail-in voting after Oregon, and those states were joined in 2020 by California, Hawaii, Nevada, and Vermont, who used COVID-19 as an excuse to entrench the practice.

Things are so out of control in mail-in-heavy states that in the 2024 campaign, King County, Washington, resident Jami Visaya reported having sixteen ballots sent to her address in Bellevue.[2] Stunned by the carelessness of it all, she said, "In 30 years of voting, I've never had that many ballots that don't belong to me, you know?" This author finds it unsurprising that Washington hasn't had a Republican governor since John Spellman skipped out of Olympia on January 16, 1985—the day I turned two months old.

About three-quarters of the vote in Arizona is cast by mail, but what distinguishes a state with *too much* mail-in voting from a universal mail-in voting state is that in the latter, a ballot is fired off to *every* registration on the voter roll. Naturally, the universal mail-in voting states are overwhelmingly blue, going 6 to 2 for Harris, 91 electoral votes to 12, an improvement for Trump from 2020 only because he managed to flip Nevada. Nevada Democrats, however, managed to fully erode and surpass Sam Brown's lead in the 2024 US Senate race against Jacky Rosen, who has the charisma of a bullfrog, because their legislature had codified the entire 2020 cheat code into law. In that state, it is fully legal to operate what I consider to be a corrupt system automatically by registering citizens and noncitizens alike to vote, mailing that registrant—or any duplicate record listed as a registrant—a ballot, and permitting harvesters to collect those ballots over a lengthy period preceding the election. If that doesn't work, and it appears

---

2   Maddie White, "Bellevue Woman Receives 16 Ballots Addressed to Her Apartment Number with Different Names," KING 5, October 29, 2024, https://www.king5.com/article/news/politics/elections/bellevue-woman-got-16-ballots-in-mail-to-her-apartment-number/281-5e559bb3-dbab-483d-8951-bfca8247b1ab.

the state may vote in an undesirable fashion, there are always courts to provide room on the back end, as well. Brown, as I predicted both before the election and on November 6, had been put in the "Adam Laxalt zone," what I called "Laxalted," and no one could do a damn thing about it.[3]

BALLOT HARVESTING

In the old days, which weren't so long ago, a candidate with the "it" factor, who had the gravitas to lead a nation, didn't have a hard time getting people motivated to go vote *for* him, rather than against his opponent. Ronald Reagan was one of those candidates for the Republican Party, and in my lifetime, Barack Obama was the best example from the other side of the aisle. In 2008, he benefited from an eight-year shift away from the incumbent president's party, massive disapproval of that president, two unwinnable conflicts raging overseas, an economic collapse, and his own narrative of "hope and change" that hoodwinked millions. To top it off, Democrats still held the high ground with the white working class, which elected Trump eight years later, commanded the minority vote with a record share of a record turnout, and hit it big with urban and suburban moderates, who are often thought of as the key swing voters in modern elections. The 2008 version of Obama still campaigned and worked for the votes, and combined with the factors above, as well as John McCain's uninspiring campaign and the public's willingness to move in a different direction, the result was sixty-nine million votes and a massive landslide.

In baseball terms, Obama hit .350 with forty home runs that year. No one was going to beat him out in 2008, and he didn't need to game the electoral system to get his margins. Good baseball teams have a guy or two who hits .300, and maybe a couple

---

3   Seth Keshel (@RealSKeshel), "This race will almost certainly be Laxalted," X, November 6, 2024, https://x.com/RealSKeshel/status/1854194717124382913.

who hit thirty or more home runs. Elite teams have more of each, but imagine if a manager could make one tweak to his light-hitting shortstop who only makes the lineup card because of his glove work and turn him into a .300 hitter and an all-around offensive threat.

Such is the nature of ballot harvesting, which began to take root in California, now America's Democratic petri dish, during the Obama era. Ballot harvesting allows even the most uncharismatic candidates to pile up gaudy vote totals that they would have no ability to win if the voting process was like it was not even two decades ago. Elections are still won with the ballots of low-propensity voters, which left- and right-wing organizations alike chase. It makes perfect sense that base voters of both sides will get out to vote in big elections; however, it is the vote of the working man who gets home at 5:45 p.m. and says, "Hell, I like that guy and I need to go vote for him so we don't miss out," that carries the field.

Ballot harvesting, the third-party collection of ballots, goes as naturally with mail-in balloting as infantrymen go with tanks in urban combat. Corrupt administrators send out the ballots in shotgun style, to the entire roll, then the lengthy window of time from that point until Election Day permits what is no different than an adult Easter egg hunt to commence. The only difference is that one side has the data detailing which ballots are available for collection, as the Feds found out when they were investigating the local election corruption cases of Democrat-on-Democrat crime in New Jersey and Connecticut during the Biden years.

California, Nevada, Oregon, and Washington consider ballot harvesting as American as apple pie and have no laws restricting that activity. Florida and several other states, on the other hand, consider ballot harvesting a felony. Why the difference?

In 2022, Governor Ron DeSantis signed Senate Bill 524,[4] banning ballot harvesting and instituting other measures to secure Florida's elections, which were corrupt enough as late as 2018 to nearly keep him out of office altogether. The passage of this bill, naturally, required Republican dominance of state government, which is lacking in the deep blue states in which ballot harvesting is both a way of life and a pathway to one-party electoral dominance. Florida's legislature used precedent from its urban areas, particularly those in South Florida, stretching back decades to bolster public support for the measures, and at once, Florida became an overwhelmingly Republican state, first in the 2022 midterms and then again in 2024 for the presidential race.

Less obvious forms of corruption are present throughout the states. Voter turnout is traditionally calculated by taking the number of ballots cast and dividing by the number of registered voters. Wisconsin reported 3,658,236 voter registrations on November 1, 2024,[5] just before Trump's narrow win (and Hovde's narrow "loss"). There were 3,422,918 votes cast for president, which yields a turnout percentage of 93.6 percent as calculated traditionally.[6] For perspective, Arizona reported 4,367,593 registrations in its final update,[7] and with 3.4 million votes for president, has a much lower turnout percentage at just 77.6 percent.

---

4   Executive Office of the Governor Ron DeSantis, "Governor Ron DeSantis Signs Bill to Strengthen Florida's Election Integrity," April 25, 2022, https://www.flgov.com/eog/news/press/2022/governor-ron-desantis-signs-bill-strengthen-floridas-election-integrity.

5   Wisconsin Elections Commission, "Voter Counts by County," Excel spreadsheet, accessed January 19, 2026, https://elections.wi.gov/sites/default/files/documents/VoterCountsByCounty_15.xlsx.

6   Wisconsin Elections Commission, "WEC Canvass Reporting System, County by County Report, 2024 General Election, President of the United States," Election Results, 2024 General Election Results, November 29, 2024, https://elections.wi.gov/sites/default/files/documents/County%20by%20County%20Report_POTUS.pdf.

7   Arizona Secretary of State, "State of Arizona Registration Report, 2024 General Election – November 5, 2024," Voter Registration Counts, 2024 Election Cycle (2023 & 2024), accessed [MONTH] [DAY], 2025, https://apps.azsos.gov/election/VoterReg/2024/State_Voter_Registration_October_2024.pdf.

Wisconsin's workaround to lower its eye-popping turnout rate is its robust same-day voter registration capacity, which yielded 219,045 such registrations in 2020, and an alarmingly high 331,384 in 2024,[8] bloating the voter roll by nearly 10 percent in one day and artificially lowering the official turnout numbers. Iowa, Wisconsin's smaller political cousin, added just 17,635 new registrations between its October closing report[9] and its certified election turnout totals.[10] If Iowa, with 60 percent as many electoral votes as Wisconsin, would have had a proportional change in registration with Wisconsin, we should have expected 198,830 new registrations on the books. Wisconsin election apologists will point to historically high same-day voter registration totals; I am unable to understand why a Republican-dominated legislature continues to leave this gaping loophole, which stands out from Iowa's consistently unremarkable same-day voter registration totals, unaddressed.

To avoid Soviet-level turnout statistics, many states have moved to estimating turnout by taking the number of votes and dividing it by the *eligible* voting population, which naturally drives the turnout percentage total down. These efforts are nothing more than blatant attempts to make people with a nose for analysis lose the trail on statistics that are easy to trace given enough continuity. States like Wisconsin, with a hard organic trend against the Democratic establishment present for over a decade, leverage

8   Wisconsin Elections Commission, "General Election Voter Registration and Absentee Statistics 1984-2024," [NAME OF SECTION OF WEBSITE FILE IS FOUND], [DATE PUBLISHED] OR accessed on [MONTH] [DAY], 2025, https://elections.wi.gov/sites/default/files/documents/General Election Voter Registration and Absentee Statistics 1984-2024.xlsx .

9   Iowa Secretary of State Paul D. Pate, "State of Iowa Voter Registration Totals, County" Voter Registration Totals by County, November 1, 2024, https://sos.iowa.gov/elections/pdf/VRStatsArchive/2024/CoNov24.pdf.

10   Iowa Secretary of State Paul D. Pate, "2024 General Election Turnout Report," Election Results & Statistics, 2024 Election Results, accessed November 5, 2024, https://sos.iowa.gov/elections/pdf/2024/general/turnout.pdf.

same-day registration to inflate the counts in two key counties, Dane and Milwaukee, and Republicans in the state fail to learn the lesson despite dropping election after election to late-night ballot dumps in both Democratic strongholds, starting with Governor Scott Walker's failed 2018 reelection campaign.

Most blue states resist voter ID laws, but I don't think that is why they are blue. I think they, given the inherent disregard for the rule of law, naturally omit such a commonsense reform from election law. Trump won just two states, Nevada and Pennsylvania, without voter ID. Part of the 2020 steal of Wisconsin relied on the classification of certain voters, or registrations supposedly assigned to real voters, to "indefinitely confined" status and provided a workaround to voter ID requirements.

Ranked choice voting, a complicated method of voting in which votes are redistributed from losing candidates until one candidate finally takes a majority of the vote, was smacked down in numerous states on 2024 ballots, including in some of the most reliably blue states. It is the latest fad Democrats have found useful for hanging on to close seats or flipping red seats altogether. Maine's Second Congressional District, won by Trump in all three of his races, has continued to be a narrow hold for Democrats in the House thanks to ranked choice voting. Democrat Jared Golden held it by the slimmest of margins in 2024, right behind Trump's win in the district and in the state with the worst election laws in New England. Alaskan Republicans foolishly introduced ranked choice voting to the "Last Frontier," and it paid immediate dividends by making sure that one of the weakest Republicans in politics, Lisa Murkowski, held on to her Senate seat, and in the same year (2022) cost Sarah Palin the state's at-large US House seat after Don Young's death. Palin and Nick Begich, who won the seat alongside Trump in 2024, combined for nearly 60 percent of the vote in the first-choice round of balloting, only for Democrat Mary Peltola to eventually emerge the winner.

These items, combined with the prolonged counting of ballots and what I call "unique corruption" to assess features relevant to election manipulation that are notable for only a single state, make up what I consider the "Eight Cardinal Sins" of election administration:

- Automatic voter registration
- Universal mail-in voting (or excessive mail-in voting)
- Ballot harvesting
- Same-day voter registration
- Prolonged counting
- Unique corruption
- Ranked choice voting
- No voter ID

COMPREHENSIVE EXERCISE

Nevada excepted, there is no battleground state that pulls everything together quite like Pennsylvania, which is only in its infancy when it comes to the operation of automatic voter registration. Many of its counties, especially its large urban ones, start mailing out ballots in September of an election year. While Pennsylvania forbids ballot harvesting, except for the tightest restrictions for aiding certain voters like family members, drop boxes litter the landscape and offer a tailor-made vector for ballot stuffing. The most notable change to Pennsylvania's election code came with the passage of Act 77 in 2019, signed into law by Governor Tom Wolf and allowing no-excuse, mail-in balloting with inclusion on an automatic mail-ballot list.[11]

---

11 County of Berks, "Act 77 Makes Historic Changes to PA Election Code," accessed November 3, 2025, https://www.berkspa.gov/departments/election-services/act-77.

Like rain in a parched wasteland, the boom in mail-in balloting was a welcome relief for Democrats, who remained on a steady march toward political extinction in the Keystone State, made obvious through a review of voter registration by party. Bucks County Commissioner Diane Ellis-Marseglia, a Democrat, ignored the law[12] and voted to allow the counting of improperly signed provisional ballots more than a week after Election Day 2024, doing all she could to save longtime US Senator Bob Casey's seat, which was imperiled because of Trump's statewide victory and gains in eastern Pennsylvania. Republican Dave McCormick prevailed by 0.2 percent, just 15,115 votes, when it was all said and done, but without the alterations to election law, he would have coasted right behind Trump's margin, which was whittled down to 1.7 percent when it had been comfortably high on election night and much closer to my prediction of Trump leading by 2.8 percent. In contrast, Trump won Ohio by 11.2 percent, or 9.5 percent right of Pennsylvania. That is close to the 9.2 percent split in 2020, one year after no excuse, mail-in balloting hit the Keystone State. The two states were 7.4 percent apart in 2016, but prior to that, you'd have to go all the way back to 1984 to find a wider gap between the two—and only because Reagan won Ohio in such a lopsided fashion.

---

12   Liz Crawford, "Bucks County, Pennsylvania Commissioner Apologizes and Clarifies Comments About Counting Ballots," CBS News, November 21, 2024, https://www.cbsnews.com/philadelphia/news/diane-ellis-marseglia-bucks-county-pennsylvania-voting/.

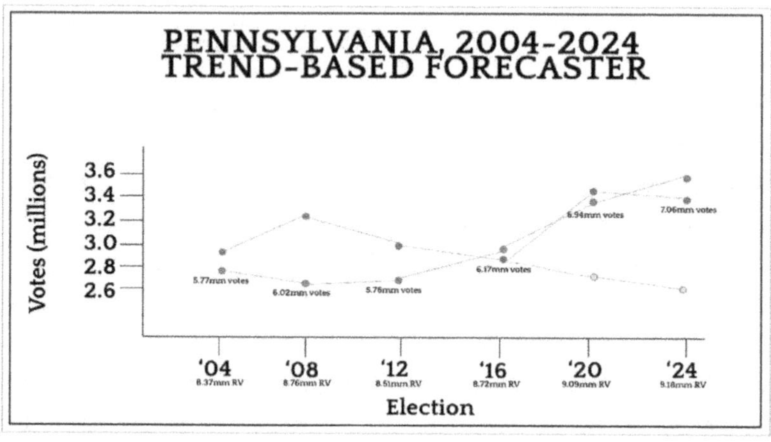

Chart by Seth Keshel.

Starting in the 2004 presidential election between George W. Bush and John Kerry, the political trend of Pennsylvania had been consistent and easily predictable for four consecutive elections:

- In 2004, with 8.4 million registered voters, Kerry beat Bush by 2.5 percent, with 5.8 million votes cast (68.9 percent turnout as traditionally measured).[13]
- In 2008, with a hard shift toward Democrats in registration, Obama beat McCain by 10.3 percent, the largest presidential landslide in the state since 1964; there were 6 million votes cast with 8.8 million registered voters, for 68.7 percent turnout.[14]

---

13 Commonwealth of Pennsylvania, Department of State, "Official Voter Registration Data, November 2004," Voting & Election Statistics, Voter Registration Statistics Archive, https://www.pa.gov/content/dam/copapwp-pagov/en/dos/resources/voting-and-elections/voting-and-election-statistics/voter-registration-statistics/2004%20election%20nov.pdf.

14 Commonwealth of Pennsylvania, Department of State, "2008 Voter Registration Statistics - Official November 4, 2008," Voting & Election Statistics, Voter Registration Statistics Archive, https://www.pa.gov/content/dam/copapwp-pagov/en/dos/resources/voting-and-elections/voting-and-election-statistics/voter-registration-statistics/2008genelectionvoterregistotals.pdf.

- In 2012, with Republicans making a slight gain in voter registration as a percentage, Romney cut five points off Obama's margin. Obama won by 5.3 percent, with 8.5 million registered voters and 5.8 million votes cast (67.6 percent turnout). Obama lost almost 300,000 votes of his 2008 total.[15]
- In 2016, Republicans surged in voter registration and cut the Democratic advantage drastically. With Trump gaining almost 300,000 votes over Romney's total and Clinton falling further from Obama's 2012 performance, the state narrowly flipped, going to Trump by 0.7 percent. There were 8.7 million registered voters (fewer than registered in 2008), and 6.2 million votes (70.8 percent turnout).[16]

The four elections spanning 2004 through 2016 all had between 5.8 and 6.2 million votes, with at least 8.4 million registered in each and no more than 8.8 million. Turnout spanned from 67.6 percent to 70.8 percent. After the passage of Act 77 in 2019, things changed drastically.

- In 2020, despite a Republican registration gain of greater than 21 to 1 in net new registrations, and Trump dwarfing his own net gains from 2016, Biden leapfrogged Trump's new vote record in the same election and won by 1.2 percent, with 9.1 million registered

---

15 Commonwealth of Pennsylvania, Department of State, "2012 Voter Registration Statistics – Official, November 6, 2012," Voting & Election Statistics, Voter Registration Statistics Archive, https://www.pa.gov/content/dam/copapwp-pagov/en/dos/resources/voting-and-elections/voting-and-election-statistics/voter-registration-statistics/2012%20election%20GenElectionVoterRegisTotals.pdf.

16 Commonwealth of Pennsylvania, Department of State, "2016 Voter Registration Statistics – Official, November 8, 2016," Voting & Election Statistics, Voter Registration Statistics Archive, https://www.pa.gov/content/dam/copapwp-pagov/en/dos/resources/voting-and-elections/voting-and-election-statistics/voter-registration-statistics/2016%20Election%20VR%20Stats.pdf.

voters and over 6.9 million votes. Turnout, or "turn-out," leaped to 76.4 percent.[17]

- In 2024, with little fresh population influx to draw from, Trump made a modest increase just shy of 170,000 net new votes, riding a voter registration gain even stronger than the gain leading into 2020. Harris finished over 45,000 votes above Trump's 2020 total, which should have been enough to win Pennsylvania in a landslide without the changes to state law. With 9.2 million registered voters and almost 7.1 million votes, "turnout" jumped to 76.9 percent.[18]

I suspect Trump's substantial gains in the eastern portion of the state, which countered stagnant or even declining margins in the incredibly pro-Trump Western counties, had the most to do with Trump carrying the most critical slate of electoral votes anywhere on the map. Harris, running behind on margin in Philadelphia and its collar counties, and with minority populations scattered throughout places like Berks County, didn't make her quota of expected votes, and therefore couldn't get over the top once all efforts to fortify her election were complete.

Trump, at least this time around, was "too big to rig" in Pennsylvania, and not by much. We can't say the same for Eric Hovde in Wisconsin, who fell to same-day voter registration, or Mike Rogers in Michigan, who walked away after the absentee counts

17   Commonwealth of Pennsylvania, Department of State, " 2020 Voter Registration Statistics - Official November 3, 2020 Election," Voting & Election Statistics, Voter Registration Statistics Archive, https://www.pa.gov/content/dam/copapwp-pagov/en/dos/resources/voting-and-elections/voting-and-election-statistics/voter-registration-statistics/2020%20Election%20VR%20Stats%20%20FINAL%20REVIEWED.pdf.

18   Commonwealth of Pennsylvania, Department of State, "2024 Voter Registration Statistics, November 5, 2024 Election," Voting & Election Statistics, Voter Registration Statistics Archive, https://www.pa.gov/content/dam/copapwp-pagov/en/dos/resources/voting-and-elections/voting-and-election-statistics/voter-registration-statistics/2024%20Election%20Nov..pdf.

piled up in Detroit. Sam Brown's lead in Nevada gradually dwindled until Jacky Rosen was called the winner late on November 8.[19] Arizona's slow count twisted the knife for Kari Lake's supporters, who were already fed up from the 2022 campaign; they were offered no choice but to put full faith in a process that is choked with dishonesty and had to accept that she ran almost eight points behind Trump. Arizonans hadn't seen a Republican win a presidential election and a Democrat win a concurrent US Senate race in thirty-six years.

Despite the first Republican popular vote victory in twenty years, and a commanding 312 to 226 Electoral College victory with wins in every widely accepted battleground (but not my own in New Hampshire), Trump would be limited to just fifty-three Republican senators and a House majority so narrow it would hardly be of any use at all. It had indeed been "too big to rig," but not in the fullest sense, and despite the monumental win, those committed to the fight for free and fair elections knew there was way too much work to do, and not enough time to do it.

The forty-fifth, and soon to be forty-seventh, president had survived Butler, outlasted the lawfare, commanded the narratives leading up to the election, and was all set to join Grover Cleveland as only the second man to win non-consecutive terms in the White House. And for that—tens of millions of Americans gave thanks and prepared to bid farewell to a president who supposedly garnered over eighty-one million lawful votes without waging a serious campaign. We were accused of being sore winners—and we didn't care one bit.

---

19   Jessica Hill, "Jacky Rosen Defeats Sam Brown in Nevada's U.S. Senate Race," *Las Vegas Review-Journal*, updated November 9, 2024, https://www.reviewjournal.com/news/politics-and-government/nevada/rosen-leads-in-nevadas-senate-race-3207152/.

CHAPTER 19

Cleveland Returns

Grover Cleveland, the first man to win non-consecutive terms in the White House, had also been the last president before Donald Trump 132 years later to gain votes from the previous election and not win reelection. As he was making way for Benjamin Harrison, his First Lady, Frances—the youngest First Lady ever—told White House staff, "I want you to take good care of all the furniture and ornaments in the house, for I want to find everything just as it is now when we come back again four years from today."[1]

Her words were prophetic. Cleveland prevailed over Harrison and Populist candidate James Weaver in 1892 and returned to the White House just as Frances had predicted. Cleveland's unconventional rotation into two terms was left unrepeated until January 20, 2025, when Trump took the presidential oath on a frigid day in Washington, DC. Rachel and I made the trip but thanks to the extreme cold weather and the cancellation of the traditional outdoor inauguration on the steps of the Capitol, we were on the outside looking in and watched the ceremony from our hotel in Alexandria.

Later in the evening, after we had already made our way to Baltimore to fly back home the next morning, the forty-seventh president spent hours celebrating with supporters and signing executive orders. Executive Order 14152, "Holding Former

---

1   "Frances Folsom Cleveland," Our White House: Looking In, Looking Out, The National Children's Book and Literacy Alliance, accessed November 28, 2025, https://ourwhitehouse.org/frances-folsom-cleveland/.

Government Officials Accountable for Election Interference and Improper Disclosure of Sensitive Governmental Information," was the first order to fly having anything to do with elections.[2] It revoked the clearances of intelligence community officials who had concealed the truth of the Hunter Biden laptop scandal from the public in order to withhold essential information that would have undoubtedly harmed the Biden campaign—which, again, "won" by just 42,918 votes spread over three decisive states.

Throughout 2025, Trump's base, particularly the new coalition of younger voters he captured in 2024, took issue with a variety of policy positions, often critiquing the administration harshly on foreign policy and, despite substantial achievement, suggesting too much focus was placed on the world's issues while not enough attention was paid to the "forgotten man and woman" and the litany of domestic troubles impacting Americans from coast-to-coast. One thing that has never been in question is Trump's unsettled grudge against the people who put the levers in motion to foist a corrupt election upon the American people in 2020. Despite the best efforts of many consultants and advisors to let it go and move on into his second term, Trump hasn't wavered on election corruption. In fact, he's used every opportunity in front of foreign heads of state and a worldwide audience to remind the world of what many of us will never forget.

President Trump wasted little time in launching a major executive order, Executive Order 14248, to address election corruption.[3] It was issued on March 25 under the title of "Preserving

---

2   "Executive Order 14152—Holding Former Government Officials Accountable for Election Interference and Improper Disclosure of Sensitive Governmental Information," The American Presidency Project, University of California, Santa Barbara, January 20, 2025, https://www.presidency.ucsb.edu/documents/executive-order-14152-holding-former-government-officials-accountable-for-election.

3   "Preserving and Protecting the Integrity of American Elections." Executive Order by President Donald J. Trump. The White House. Issued March 25, 2025. Accessed November 28, 2025. https://www.whitehouse.gov/presidential-actions/2025/03/preserving-and-protecting-the-integrity-of-american-elections/.

and Protecting the Integrity of American Elections." The order was masterfully crafted and cut right to the point by expressing the obvious injustice that, *"the United States now fails to enforce basic and necessary election protections employed by modern, developed nations, as well as those still developing."* It features many key points that address many of the grievances listed in this book:

- Enforcing citizenship requirements to vote
- Equipping federal government to assist in voter-roll cleanup
- Granting authority to US attorney general to prosecute election crimes
- Improving voting systems security
- Measures to prevent against late counting of ballots, honoring Election Day
- Protections against foreign investment in our elections

The text of the order includes, *"Free, fair, and honest elections unmarred by fraud, errors, or suspicion are fundamental to maintaining our constitutional Republic."* In any other era outside of the current one, which is tainted by "Trump derangement syndrome," such a statement would have been received with unanimous approval. In this effort to bring commonsense reform to American elections, however, lawsuits went flying immediately and have tied up provisions of this order ever since.

While meeting with Russian President Vladimir Putin in Alaska, the two leaders discussed mail-in balloting, with Trump sharing that Putin affirmed the 2020 election was decided by fraudulent mail-in balloting.[4] The press, naturally, rushed to defend the integrity of that election, but few people consider 81.3

---

4   Amy Sherman. "Fact-Checking Trump's Claim the U.S. is the 'Only Country' that Uses Mail-In Voting," PBS News, August 18, 2025, https://www.pbs.org/newshour/politics/fact-checking-trumps-claim-the-u-s-is-the-only-country-that-uses-mail-in-voting.

million votes for a candidate that failed to run a serious campaign believable five years later. Realizing that claiming that America was the "only country" using mail-in ballots would send the media on a fact-checking journey to highlight how many countries refuse to adopt the practice, he held nothing back.

Still, little went well for Republicans when it came to US elections in 2025. To no one's surprise, Republicans held Florida's First Congressional District and Sixth Congressional District seats on April 1, which had been vacated by Matt Gaetz and Michael Waltz after the 2024 election, but by drastically reduced margins of victory—which is the norm for special, midterm, and off-year elections for members of the president's party. The low point of that evening's elections, however, was the landslide defeat of Brad Schimel, the GOP candidate in what was technically a nonpartisan race for a seat on the Wisconsin Supreme Court. He was trounced by faux moderate Susan Crawford, a circuit court judge from uber-liberal Dane County, by a whopping 10.1 percent margin. Incredibly, Schimel exceeded the vote total of Janet Protasiewicz, the liberal judge elected in 2023 by 11.0 percent, by more than 40,000 votes.

With 1,062,330 votes, Schimel also blew past these recent winning vote totals for a Wisconsin Supreme Court seat:

- Jill Karofsky, 2020, 855,573 votes
  (+10.5 percent margin)
- Brian Hagedorn, 2019, 606,414 votes (+0.5 percent)
- Rebecca Dallett, 2018, 555,848 votes (+10.5 percent)
- Rebecca Bradley, 2016, 1,024,892 votes (+4.9 percent)
- Ann Walsh Bradley, 2015, 471,866 votes
  (+16.1 percent)

Crawford's vote total of 1,301,137 exceeded Rebecca Bradley's earlier all-time record for any race for such a seat by 276,245 and approached Hillary Clinton's presidential election vote tally in the Badger State from just eight years earlier. Schimel had a vote total consistent with a winning candidate—until he ran into the Democratic ballot collection buzzsaw that left him wholly uncompetitive. Just six years earlier, it was common for Wisconsin Supreme Court candidates to win races with 600,000 votes or fewer.

Trump spent considerable time throughout his first year back in the White House demanding Republicans in Congress and in the states to overhaul the voting process, especially regarding voter ID, mail-in balloting, and one-day elections. On October 26, just over a week ahead of a slate of high-profile elections in blue states, Trump took to Truth Social to write, "No mail-in or 'Early' Voting, Yes to Voter ID! Watch how totally dishonest the California Prop Vote is! Millions of Ballots being 'shipped.' GET SMART REPUBLICANS, BEFORE IT IS TOO LATE!!!"[5] As longtime critics and supporters alike were getting impatient with slow economic numbers and an intense focus on foreign policy, the White House never wavered on needed election reform.

They wouldn't need to wait long to see automatic voter registration, excessive mail-in voting, and ballot harvesting back in action. CIA veteran spook and Congresswoman Abigail Spanberger outran her average polling lead[6] by almost five points to blow out Republican Winsome Earle-Sears in the Virginia gubernatorial contest, and with that kind of margin, had long enough coattails

---

5   Alex Galbraith, "'Rigged and Stolen': Trump Calls for Ban on Mail-In, Early Voting Ahead Of Midterms," Salon, October 26, 2025. https://www.salon.com/2025/10/26/rigged-and-stolen-trump-calls-for-ban-on-mail-in-early-voting-ahead-of-midterms/.

6   RealClearPolling, "2025 Virginia Governor - Earle-Sears vs. Spanberger," accessed November 28, 2025, https://www.realclearpolling.com/polls/governor/general/2025/virginia/spanberger-vs-earle-sears.

to pull Jay Jones across the line against Republican incumbent Attorney General Jason Miyares. While this sort of downballot impact looks unsurprising on paper to a disinterested observer, it shocked millions of Americans because Jones had been exposed in a text messaging scandal in which he fantasized about murdering a political opponent and his children.[7] *The New York Times*, despite their whiff against me in 2024 and extremely biased reporting, is one of my favorite destinations for tracking election returns, and they tell this tale regarding margin breakdowns by voting method:[8]

- Election Day (56 percent of votes reported): Miyares (Republican) +2.2 percent
- Early (33 percent): Jones (Democrat) +7.9 percent
- Mail (10 percent): Jones (Democrat) +47.2 percent

What those who defend Virginia's loose election laws want you to believe, with just 0.4 percent of the vote going to candidates other than Jones or Miyares, is that Election Day voters broke 51 to 49 percent for Miyares, and early voters went 54 to 46 percent for Jones, suggesting modest competition, yet went 73 to 27 percent for Jones on over 330,000 ballots by mail. I, for one, struggle to believe such a lopsided demographic that chooses to vote exclusively by mail exists.

Jones's final margin was 219,277, or ahead by 6.4 percent.

Virginia Democrats pushed automatic voter registration in 2020, and in the same session, green-lighted no excuse, mail-in

---

7   Markus Schmidt, "'Beyond Disqualifying': Jay Jones Controversy Jolts Virginia's Pivotal 2025 Elections," Virginia Mercury, October 5, 2025, https://virginiamercury.com/2025/10/05/beyond-disqualifying-jay-jones-controversy-jolts-virginias-pivotal-2025-elections/.

8   *The New York Times*, "Virginia Attorney General Election Results," updated December 1, 2025, https://www.nytimes.com/interactive/2025/11/04/us/elections/results-virginia-attorney-general.html.

balloting.[9] With late-night ballot dumps and the turning away of poll watchers and count observers so resoundingly unpopular and reminiscent of third world strongman practices, it is only logical for ballot stuffing to shift to the front end of voting activities. Instead of monitoring the vote total of one candidate in real time, like that of Miyares in this case, the six-week-long mail balloting period is just fine for getting as many ballots into drop boxes and count centers as is needed for comfortable margins. I am confident Miyares knew the dangers of prodigious quantities of mail-in ballots when he voted against the expansion of mail-in balloting in the "Old Dominion" in 2020 as a member of the House of Delegates.[10]

Despite predictable races steeped in the off-year political dynamics of a first-year Republican presidency, the MAGA base lost its mind over the November 2025 election outcomes not just in Virginia, but in California, New York City, and New Jersey. Gavin Newsom rode an overwhelming party registration advantage, universal mail-in voting, and the scarcely needed efforts of an army of ballot collectors to shove Proposition 50 down voters' throats and further gerrymander a state in which Democrats already hold over 80 percent of US House seats.

In New York City, a century of Republican apathy finally came home to roost as Zohran Mamdani, a foreign-born radical leftist, divided the Democratic base in a three-man race no one else had a chance to win as soon as Democratic primaries ended. Next door in New Jersey, a common theme prevailed once again. Republican Jack Ciattarelli, who narrowly lost the gubernatorial race to incumbent Phil Murphy in 2021, soared past Murphy's

---

9   Virginia Department of Elections, "The Virginia Department of Elections Launches Absentee Voting Campaign," September 14, 2020, https://www.elections.virginia. gov/news-releases/archive/2020/newsfeel-free-absentee.html.

10 "Virginia HB1 | 2020 | Regular Session," LegiScan, accessed November 28, 2025, https://legiscan.com/VA/bill/HB1/2020.

winning vote total only to get squashed by US Representative Mikie Sherrill by more than fourteen points, as she cleared Murphy's winning mark by more than a half million votes.

New Jersey, which allows all registered voters to request a mail-in ballot with no excuse necessary, has a system wide open to manipulation, which was proven by none other than Biden's FBI.[11] With more than six weeks to scoop up mail ballots, Ciattarelli never stood a chance. For a more believable margin, with Sherrill polling ahead by an average of just 3.3 percent on Election Day,[12] perhaps team blue should have capped her off at 1.7 million.

Very little went well in smaller elections, like Pennsylvania's municipal and judicial races; however, Americans were treated to one silver lining, even if it requires an understanding of dark humor to fully appreciate. After a full week of counting ballots, political neophyte and open socialist Katie Wilson pulled into the lead against incumbent Seattle mayor Bruce Harrell,[13] where she would remain. Harrell, running in the largest city in King County, lost his position to the same shoddy system that sends voters like Jami Visaya[14] more than enough ballots, when consolidated, to flip election outcomes. Live by the sword, die by the sword.

Donald Trump was "too big to rig" over eight battlegrounds in 2024. Many of his downballot GOP allies were not. The next Republican presidential nominee, or any candidates for any

---

11   Seth Keshel, "The Four-Part Life Cycle of a Fraudulent Mail-In Ballot," Captain K's Corner (Substack), May 4, 2024, https://www.captaink.us/p/the-four-part-life-cycle-of-a-fraudulent?utm_source=publication-search.

12   RealClearPolling, "2025 New Jersey Governor - Ciattarelli vs. Sherrill," accessed November 28, 2025, https://www.realclearpolling.com/polls/governor/general/2025/new-jersey/sherrill-vs-ciattarelli.

13   Catharine Smith, "Katie Wilson Pulls Ahead of Seattle Mayor Bruce Harrell—by 91 Votes," KUOW, November 10, 2025, https://www.kuow.org/stories/katie-wilson-pulls-ahead-of-seattle-mayor-bruce-harrell-by-91-votes.

14   Maddie White, "Bellevue Woman Receives 16 Ballots Addressed to Her Apartment Number with Different Names." KING 5, October 29, 2024, https://www.king5.com/article/news/politics/elections/bellevue-woman-got-16-ballots-in-mail-to-her-apartment-number/281-5e559bb3-dbab-483d-8951-bfca8247b1ab.

important offices after then, will not be running as one of the most famous people in world history. Without the needed changes to our electoral system, they will have to swim upstream against what has become an increasingly legalized system of manipulation of our elections, from vote-getting contests to structured ballot collection operations. It thereby flouts the spirit of the electoral process and devalues the investment of time, energy, and critical thought that Americans spend on how to cast their votes centuries before it became easy to engineer the outcomes of an entire nation with a high degree of certainty.

Trump's first year flew by at a hectic pace, with so much of his agenda fulfilled within six months that supporters became restless by the end of the year. The positive feelings and excitement over the administration's wins were mixed with lows, like the tragic loss of Charlie Kirk in September. The election losses, though predictable, serve as a reminder of necessary bold and decisive action that must occur from the chief executive and Congress if Americans are to regain control of the electoral process. I have been honored to have briefed Trump's White House on multiple occasions on election reform concepts and key research of electoral manipulation, and have aided in identifying the most actionable paths to pursue remediation of this most critical national emergency—the loss of trust in nationwide elections.

Cutting deeply enough into the corruption may cost Trump every last ounce of political capital he has, split factions of the Republican Party, and cause members of his administration to refer to him as a "sore winner" and abandon ship altogether, but as things stand today, the game of ballot collection favors those willing to stoop to the lowest of lows, recruit hordes of ballot collectors, flood voter rolls with ineligible entries, and ensure the largest counties are pre-situated to count ballots for days to ensure close races tip just one way. As far as this author is concerned, absent an act of Congress, drastic and historically significant executive action is the only way to safeguard the future of self-government for "We the People."

Cleveland has indeed returned, but how will he go out, and how will he be remembered if Americans are forced to relive "Three November" every four years? That is perhaps the most pressing question as the 2026 midterms bear down on the nation.

The Future of Fair Elections

By now, it should be clear that unless elections change for the better, and soon, Americans run a real risk of taking part in quasi elections that are nothing more than organized ballot collection games from now until the end of the Republic. If the Trump administration, or anyone who supports it, rests on the laurels of a 2024 election victory and takes only half-hearted measures to address the systemic corruption present in our elections, we will lose freedom and liberty here and will be at the mercy of a political ruling class with no incentive to consider "the consent of the governed."

For several years, I have discussed "Ten Points to True Election Integrity." They began like any other wide-sweeping concept—in crude form and with enough breathing room to fill in the gaps pending any new developments or understanding of what causes the chronic and persistent condition of "electile dysfunction." Together, these points represent the most succinct and understandable pillars for creating order that have been long since sacrificed at the altars of convenience and the gaming of a system meant to reflect the will of the people.

POINT ONE: CLEAN UP THE VOTER ROLLS

Chapter 13, "Registration is the Foundation," makes it clear that the foundation of all election corruption is found in the voter rolls of the various states and counties. Unfortunately, few have the foggiest idea of how to go about "cleaning up" voter rolls, and I've made an additional point that trying to identify and remove bad registrations in a state operating automatic voter registration is akin to someone brushing his teeth while eating Oreos.

States like California, Washington, and Oregon will never become competitive without an end to the registration corruption, primarily through an end to automatic voter registration. While it may not be a realistic expectation to have all states run elections with no voter registration at all, like North Dakota does, I don't see why it wouldn't be possible to conduct a study to determine the most corrupted voter rolls and force the worst offenders to reregister those who wish to vote. We renew our vehicle registrations annually and file tax returns every year, so I'm not so sure why, in an age of unprecedented automation, a broken database couldn't be reconciled by having citizens present identification and reregister.

Automatic voter registration provides the credit line for fraudulent voting and must be ended. Without an end to the corruption of voter registration, all following points are pursued in vain.

POINT TWO: BAN ALL ELECTRONIC ELECTIONS EQUIPMENT

I've taken a lot of heat over the years for discussing more of the manual aspects of election manipulation, or ballot stuffing, instead of dialing in what "the machines" can or can't do. The primary reasons for this are simple. First, the type of trend analysis I do makes it easier to see discrepancies that, when pieced together on a map, suggest localized and strategic efforts to stuff ballots in certain places while ignoring others. Second, no one seems to be able to get their stories straight when it comes to exactly what the capabilities of the electronic elections infrastructure are for defrauding election results.

Even though Dominion Voting Systems sent me a cease-and-desist letter, I've been an equal opportunity opponent of all vendors, like Elections Systems and Software and Hart InterCivic. In a county-approved vulnerability assessment of Otero County, New Mexico, David and Erin Clements highlighted a wide variety of issues observed in that county's Dominion equipment that undermine the "safe and secure" narrative we've heard since the 2020 election.[1] Since that report, there haven't been many people willing to dive into these systems and bring scrutiny onto their own practices and approved procedures. When they have, they wind up with egg on their faces, like in the case of Valencia County, New Mexico, which had its rebranded Liberty Voting Systems software (formerly Dominion) send an extra 204 ballots into the count for its 2025 elections.[2] How many of these mistakes were missed in 2020 audits?

Others have given their own assessments on machine vulnerabilities, like J. Alex Halderman when he reviewed Georgia's Dominion systems in 2023 and found them severely detrimental to fostering trust in election outcomes.[3] For those who won't consider investigative reports, everyone should agree that putting faith in "black box" voting systems in which voters must trust the machine to accurately relay vote counts is a stupid idea. We held

---

1   Otero County Commission, *Audit of the Otero County November 2020 General Election and Vulnerability Assessment of the Election System Used in New Mexico,* (Otero County Commission, 2022). https://dow9ovycsk6w7.cloudfront.net/media_items/69241-Otero_County_Audit_Report.pdf?1660596423.

2   Vincent Rodriguez, "Valencia County Finds Voting Machine Error with Nonexistent Ballots," KOAT, November 21, 2025. https://www.koat.com/article/valencia-county-voting-discrepancy-2025/69511630.

3   J. Alex Halderman, "Security Analysis of the Dominion ImageCast X," CITP Blog, Center for Information Technology Policy, Princeton University, June 14, 2023, https://blog.citp.princeton.edu/2023/06/14/security-analysis-of-the-dominion-imagecast-x/.

elections by primitive means for centuries in this country, and in order to create a system the people can trust, must do so again.

POINT THREE: MANDATE VOTER ID AND PAPER BALLOTS

Next time you go to the airport, try to sneak past the TSA screen without presenting ID. I don't think you'll get far before you get tased. We have to show ID for so many things that people should be insulted so many states *don't* have requirements for voters to verify their identities to cast a ballot. Since we have already turned our elections primitive, voters presenting proper ID would be properly logged, receive a paper ballot, fill it out, and put it in a good, old-fashioned ballot box. This is how voting is done in North Dakota by the vast majority of its citizens.

POINT FOUR: SEVERELY RESTRICT MAIL-IN VOTING

I would like to use the word "ban" to describe how I feel about mail-in voting, but every time I do, someone addicted to the rare convenience of not having to venture outside, or using a disabled relative as an excuse to promote it for all, ruins it for me. Severely restricting mail-in voting turns the practice back into "absentee" voting, in which very few are putting a ballot in the mail. The only voters who should be voting absentee are those who are legitimately disabled and still have the mental capacity to cast a ballot, deployed military members, or those who meet legitimate absentee requirements.

We go to the rifle range in person, get our hair cut in person, shop for groceries in person, drive golf balls in person, and watch our kids play sports in person, but we can't expect citizens to engage in an active process of selecting representative government by getting off of their rear ends to cast a ballot once or twice every other year? It's almost like someone is trying to game the system by making elections a passive game of ballot collection. Almost. Since we know states who have gamed their systems in this manner will never act to strike the practice, Trump's Department of Justice must be heavily engaged in demonstrating the unfairness of this practice to override the states' inevitable defenses citing the "Elections Clause" of the Constitution.

POINT FIVE: SEVERELY RESTRICT EARLY VOTING

Early voting takes up the other side of the corruption coin it shares with mail-in voting. It is promoted as "access" but functions as the invaluable window of time in which mail-in ballots are harvested in major metropolitan areas and piled up as the Democratic "firewall." To put it in plain language, imagine an Easter egg hunt in your backyard with all the kids in the neighborhood. You have put fifty eggs in the yard, and if your son gets twenty-six, he wins by default. If you give all the kids twenty seconds to find as many eggs as possible, your son may lose. If you give the kids fifteen minutes and your son knows exactly where to find them, he's golden.

T-I-M-E spells success for mail-in balloting, and it is sold to the voters in terms of convenience—"You wouldn't want to find yourself unable to get to the polls on Election Day, would you?" I am confident corrupt elections officials monitor early voting splits and, if necessary, coordinate with parallel agencies to adjust any of the other sliding pieces of modern elections to ensure outcomes, like in the 2022 Arizona statewide races. Iowa Treasurer Roby Smith, when he was a legislator, was key in cutting back the time for early voting incrementally, and all GOP-run state legislatures would be wise to start exercising control over this.

Opponents will cry about long lines at polling places, which makes point six even more important.

POINT SIX: SMALLER PRECINCT SIZES

In 2024, President Trump took nearly 58 percent of the vote in Maricopa County's Precinct 0626—Pebble Creek—gathering 4,057 votes out of 7,040 cast for the top race.[4] The county's records reported 7,453 registered voters in that one precinct; more than a dozen precincts in Maricopa had more than five thousand ballots tabulated for the presidential race. Precincts of such vast size *require* workarounds to avoid long lines and claims of voter suppression, so early voting and access to countywide voting centers are the standard mitigating solutions trotted out by administrators to deal with any inconveniences.

Getting elections away from the precincts makes it impossible to implement commonsense reforms that everyone agrees would provide the confidence Americans desperately need for the electoral process to serve its purpose. Creating and enforcing precincts of manageable size, like 1,500 registered voters per precinct (requiring more precincts in counties like Maricopa), is the only way to return to primitive means of casting ballots and having them counted by hand and tabulated at the precinct. These smaller precinct sizes would also allow for a significant reduction in the early voting window and go hand in hand with cutting back on mail-in ballots since it would be easy to stroll over to the local precinct and take part in the time-honored community activity of exercising the right to vote.

---

4   Maricopa County Elections, "2024 Canvass, General Election, November 5, 2024," Election Results Archive, https://elections.maricopa.gov/asset/jcr:3618433a-5ef5-42b7-84f2-4871cf80a60b/11-05-2024-0%20CANVASS%20COMPLETE.pdf.

POINT SEVEN: BAN BALLOT HARVESTING

There is plenty of precedent here for state- and federal-level action, but ballot harvesting is difficult to detect and even more so when leftist lawyers spend millions trying to keep citizens from monitoring drop boxes, even though there is supposedly nothing to hide. Florida, as documented in this book, has strong laws on the books to control millions of mail-in ballots, criminalize ballot harvesting, and severely restrict access to drop boxes; surprisingly, many blue states have tough laws over ballot harvesting. Still, one of the biggest disparities in the national elections landscape is that while some states criminalize ballot harvesting, others fully legalize and encourage the process. Elections in California, Washington, Oregon, and Nevada are nothing more than glorified ballot collection contests.

Implementing a ban on ballot harvesting, even if mail-in balloting is brought under control to only permit legitimate absentee balloting, will restore the spirit of elections—active citizen engagement requiring some effort and intent to be part of the process. Any overhaul of ballot harvesting law should also strictly forbid the use of unsupervised drop boxes in line with point six—smaller precinct sizes, which would default voting to in-person locations.

POINT EIGHT: ELECTION DAY HOLIDAY

Our country seems to have a month or holiday for every cause imaginable, yet for some reason, no one has truly thought to extend it in such a way that would celebrate the sacred concept of self-government *and* protect elections at the same time. Promoting a federal Election Day holiday every two years would gut arguments for a massive portion of the population that workarounds are needed to make voting possible, even though almost none of the current shortcuts we have today were around forty years ago.

With most Americans enjoying a federal holiday on Election Day, in-person voting would become a cultural norm to celebrate the day, just like carving turkey on Thanksgiving Day or opening presents as a family on Christmas morning. Sufficient practices would still be in place to accommodate doctors, nurses, pilots, or others who aren't able to take the day off yet still manage to vote legally in today's elections. So much of what is required to make elections fair in the perception of the public requires fully countering narratives that tell voters that convenience and access is more important than trust so that our election outcomes are fair, legal, and reflective of the will of the people.

POINT NINE: NEW REPORTING REQUIREMENTS FOR TRANSPARENCY

Imagine that, instead of the counties making up metro Philadelphia and Atlanta, the rural counties of Pennsylvania and Georgia withheld their votes until the urban areas had fully reported, then trickled out ballots for four days until Trump overcame overwhelming Biden leads in both states. How do you think the lapdog media would have reported on that? Do you believe the American left would have accepted the results of the 2020 election?

Elections must be properly staffed for precinct-level voting, tabulation, and reporting work for counties of any size, but for the sake of fairness, I see no reason why the largest counties in a state shouldn't be required to "show their cards" first. In Arizona, Maricopa and Pima Counties account for three-quarters of the vote, which is enough to completely vanquish the outlying thirteen counties. In Nevada, Clark and Washoe Counties are even more critical for Democratic hopes, with nearly 90 percent of the statewide vote hanging on those two counties.

In addition to the largest counties reporting votes first, which is most likely a state legislative reform at this point, citizens should expect accurate ballot counts showing exactly how many will be tabulated, including a breakdown for absentee, uniformed and overseas citizens absentee voting, and provisional ballots that *does not change*. Given Georgia's miraculous discovery of roughly two hundred thousand ballots after Secretary of State Brad Raffensperger had the election all but written in stone on the morning of November 4, 2020, these new reporting requirements may be best described as "The Raffensperger Rules."

POINT TEN: SERIOUS PENALTIES FOR ELECTION FRAUD

Ecclesiastes 8:11 (NIV) tells readers, "When the sentence for a crime is not quickly carried out, people's hearts are filled with schemes to do wrong." Historians throughout the ages have pondered the theme of justice, and a universal belief throughout human history is that unless the consequences of a crime are unacceptable to would-be villains, criminal behavior should be expected.

As of 2026, there has been no significant punishment of anyone associated with the last-minute rule changes, illegal election procedures, turning away of observers, ballot stuffing, destruction of records, or other forms of outright cheating that occurred in the 2020, 2022, or 2024 election cycles. If we are a serious country committed to stopping election corruption, then we must also be a just country and create examples so strong that future generations will understand that interfering in free and fair elections is unacceptable, un-American, and comes with the risk of rotting behind bars.

THE TIME OF ACTION

Americans may never again have a president with as much of an axe to grind against election corruption as they do with President Trump. Some of the fixes above are state-level concepts, but ending the outright lawlessness of states in which it is impossible for Republicans to win against the rigging of elections through the law, densely populated urban centers, and local media juggernauts will require the intervention of the federal government—either through executive action, congressional remedy, or full-scale lawfare from the Department of Justice.

Most conservatives abhor federal overreach and support, in theory, the rights of states to exercise maximum freedom in crafting laws that work for their own citizens. My firm belief is that various states have used their freedoms and the Elections Clause to effectively "rig" elections by the laws they have on the books and, in doing so, have created a national contest between the states with legitimate election contests and those that conduct elections by holding nothing more than adult Easter egg hunts to collect ballots over a prolonged period.

This is the time for the federal government to show some teeth and get busy establishing a fair system in which the eyes of the country are upon more than the eighty-one electoral votes that decided the last election. The first president, George Washington, knew the federal government had to rightly exercise its power, or it would never survive its infancy. Today, if the federal government doesn't take serious risks in addressing glaring deficiencies in our elections, we will not survive to the midway point of the twenty-first century.

In one of his last letters to me, Dad reminded me he was extremely proud of me and my "work in defense of all we love as Americans." In those days, I felt that service in Afghanistan demonstrated love of country. Today, I believe love of country will be demonstrated by the lengths to which those who know the truth are willing to go to right the wrongs that deny Americans the right to life, liberty, and the pursuit of happiness as we prepare to celebrate 250 years of self-government. A free people purporting to be the "city on a hill" and a guiding light of freedom to the world must never tolerate their own nation holding elections that are the laughingstock of the world if they wish for their children to enjoy a bright future.

ACKNOWLEDGMENTS

To individually thank everyone involved in the essential battle for preserving America's sacred electoral system would require a separate book. Since 2021, I have traveled from one corner of the nation to another, and even across vast expanses of land and ocean to Alaska and Hawaii, presenting election reforms and data analysis in forty-five states and our national capital, Washington, DC. At every one of my presentations, I have been hosted by moms and dads, veterans, professionals, patriots young and old, and at times, candidates who believed enough in this critical topic to be publicly associated with someone who gave no quarter to those turning a blind eye to a process an alarmingly high percentage of Americans believe is no longer salvageable.

I would never have obtained any meaningful prominence without the efforts of those who have opened their homes, churches, VFW halls, and community centers against the wishes of colleagues who hoped for all discussion of the 2020 election to vanish into thin air. These are the unsung heroes of the movement to return our country's elections to a place they were not so long ago—a place of trust and confidence in outcomes. To all of you who have carried the banner, especially in the least promising times, *thank you.* Future generations will directly benefit from all the work you have put in.

I owe so many people for imparting wisdom, providing an audience, and talking sense to me when I wondered if such a battle was worth the emotional energy and public scrutiny. Many of them, from well-known public figures to media personalities to grassroots leaders, are commended within these pages, as are those who directly assisted me in making content, compiling data, or creating detailed maps, like Paul Fleuret, Cherisse Wright, and Jeff Pedigo—who have done this work for years while paid far less than they are worth. Many wielding significant online impact eagerly shared our work, like Brian Cates, Eric Wold, and countless others who could have worried only about themselves.

Along the trail of my journey, I met Rachel. She is my strongest supporter, has always had my back, and encourages me to drive ahead. Her impact in my life goes far beyond my role in shaping the conversation around election reform and has helped me become a better man, father, and friend. All my life's dreams include her, and it has been a tremendous honor to watch her serve as such a role model and defender of liberty and freedom in the Arizona legislature.

Many with much to lose trusted my insights when the fog of war crept in. From countless shows in those early days of the Biden administration to Sean Spicer, Steve Turley, Newt Gingrich, and many others as the 2024 election approached, I have eternal gratitude for those who trusted my insights and forced accountability by helping inform worldwide audiences of ways they could get involved in such an important fight.

My children have always kept me grounded in the mission, reminding me our fight is for posterity and the better future in what Lincoln, and later Reagan, called "the last best hope of man on earth." Eden, Eli, and Willow—I am proud of you and thankful to be your Dad.

I owe gratitude to those in my family who have believed in my cause for helping shape me and for believing I would find my calling one day. My mission has reconnected me with my own

Dad many years after his death. As he was dying and I was serving in Afghanistan, he wrote to remind me of the importance of maintaining a good attitude and a clear mind, allowing the enemy no advantage or upper hand. I hope I've done him proud.

My extended family from the past includes many teachers, mentors, and coaches who had high standards for me because they knew I should expect more of myself. Lifelong friends like Jimmy Davis and Preston Walker, or those like Kyle McElhaney, James Tesauro, Steve Cassell, and Greg Jantz who came along later, helped me gain important self-confidence and life skills when I needed it most. Dr. Jantz tragically died on July 4, 2025, but made a lasting impact on my life.

I have nothing but gratitude for the many baseball teammates I had over the years who never made me feel like I wasn't part of the team just because my talents were put to use outside the white lines.

Many soldiers and officers molded me from green lieutenant to capable captain in a brief time frame. Without the strategic lessons I learned in military service, I wouldn't have the discernment I have today, nor the ability to categorize so much data and still put out an actionable assessment. To our many veterans who have once again answered the call to serve out of uniform—thank you.

President Donald Trump changed my life when he touted my research in August 2021. I've had the privilege of meeting him twice and briefing key members of his White House on multiple occasions. Despite significant pressure from the political establishment, he has never conceded the 2020 election that represents one of the most shameful chapters in American history. For his leadership in this regard, an entire nation owes him a debt of gratitude. Had he moved on from the 2020 election, any election integrity movement would be but a skeleton of what it is today.

As I was authoring this book, Charlie Kirk was killed in broad daylight in Orem, Utah. I met Charlie just one time, but he was one of those guys everyone felt like they knew, either through mutual connections or through admiration in the way he took the fight to the field day in and day out. I feel it is only appropriate to thank him for his commitment to a brighter American future and carry on the banner as he would have expected all who respected him to do.

Finally, and most importantly, none of what I have accomplished or been called to stand for is possible without the divine help I have received. I committed my life to Christ as a young man and though I've failed miserably to live up to His standards, He has used me and given me the strength to withstand a relentless assault from those who seek to preserve the status quo. I am still standing today.

ABOUT THE AUTHOR

Author Photo by Christopher Smith

Seth Keshel, MBA, is a former Army Captain of Military Intelligence and Afghanistan veteran. His method of election forecasting and analytics is known worldwide, and he has been commended by President Donald J. Trump for his work in the field. He is a 2008 graduate of Ole Miss and earned his MBA from Liberty University in 2017. He lives in Tucson, Arizona, with his wife Rachel and has three children.